DOUBLOONS

DOUBLOONS
The Story of Buried Treasure

By
CHARLES B. DRISCOLL

Illustrated by
HARRY CIMINO

COACHWHIP PUBLICATIONS
GREENVILLE, OHIO

TO MY TREASURES:

GENEVIEVE, MARY, PATRICIA

Doubloons, by Charles B. Driscoll
© 2025 Coachwhip Publications edition

First published 1930
Charles B. Driscoll, 1885-1951
CoachwhipBooks.com

ISBN 1-61646-619-7
ISBN-13 978-1-61646-619-0

CONTENTS

AUTHOR'S NOTE

Let us dispose of the question: "Is it all true?" I should not like to answer an unqualified yes to that. At once we are hard aground on Pilate's reef: "What is truth?" It has sunk many a good cargo of factual narrative.

This book deals with many pirates, and the standard of truth in pirate lore is different from that obtaining in, let us say, a learned treatise on geometry. Many who have written about pirates set up Captain Charles Johnson as the very father and guardian of truth in matters piratical. Perhaps that is because Captain Johnson has been dead for at least a century and a half, and is almost as shadowy a figure as Shakespeare or the author of the Psalms. But, accepting for the moment this standard of comparison, I do not hesitate to say that this book will assay as high in pure truth as the works of Captain Johnson.

It is impossible to verify everything one writes about pirates. It is inevitable that the figures and deeds of these fascinating villains should be somewhat softened and colored by the fancy of the author. No tales of the pirates are as true as a good abstract of title to real estate, but neither is any respectable recital of piratical deeds as untrue as the best obtainable biography of a candidate for the Presidency or for Parliament.

In this book I have endeavored to warn the reader fairly when the element of fancy or romance seems to me about to creep into the text. And I have been at some pains to discover, where possible, the line of demarcation.

I have been writing on pirates and buried treasure in magazines for several years, and in some of the chapters of this book I have borrowed material from my own articles when it has seemed to me the best available matter on the subjects in hand. I thank *The American Mercury, The North American Review* and *Coun-*

try Home for permission to quote from articles I have written in those publications.

To Simon Lake and Lieutenant George Williams I owe much for generous coöperation in gathering data on which they are the leading authorities in their respective lines. I acknowledge great indebtedness to J. Frank Dobie, of the University of Texas, for assistance in tracing the legends relating to Lafitte in Texas. Dr. Philip Gosse and Captain Malcolm Campbell of London; Hubert Palmer of Eastbourne, England; Montfort Amory, Barnet B. Ruder, and Robert I. Nesmith of New York, have been helpful and gracious in forwarding my research. Daniel Ravenel, H. F. Church, Dr. W. Cyril O'Driscoll, and T. R. Waring, all of Charleston, S. C., were instrumental in putting me on the track of authentic and unpublished source material concerning Major Stede Bonnet. I am immeasurably indebted to Miss Lillian Blood for invaluable assistance in preparing the manuscript. Helpful correspondents in all parts of the world have rendered much assistance, and I regret that there is not space here to thank each of them separately.

DOUBLOONS

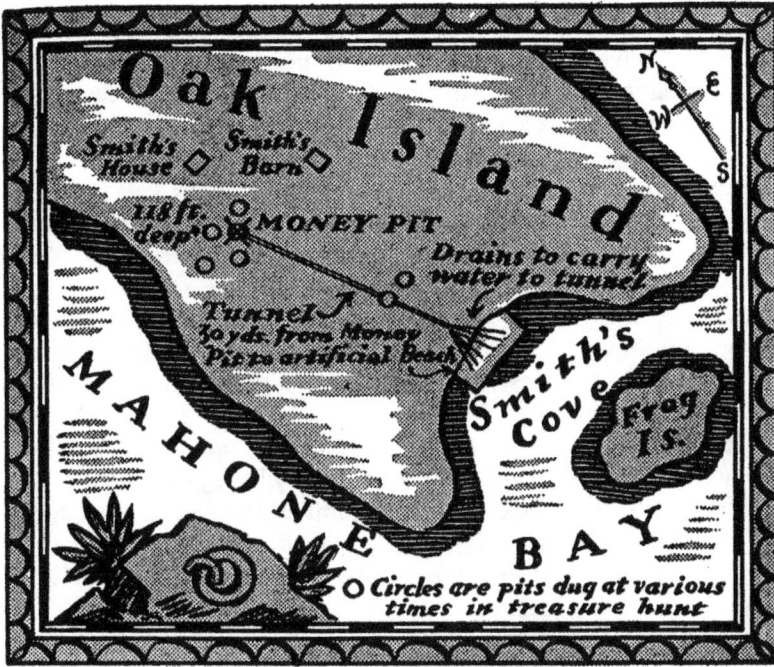

Oak Island

Smith's House ◇ Smith's Barn ◇

118 ft. deep ○ MONEY PIT

○ ○

Drains to carry water to tunnel ○

Tunnel, 50 yds. from Money Pit to artificial beach

MAHONE

Smith's Cove

Frog Is.

BAY

○ *Circles are pits dug at various times in treasure hunt*

N E W S

I. *The Treasure of Oak Island*

OAK ISLAND, in Mahone Bay on the east coast of Nova Scotia, looks like a theatrical set for some ultra-romantic melodrama. It lies only four miles off the little summer resort town of Chester, where a colony of modish Philadelphians spends quietly aristocratic summers.

I found great difficulty, none the less, in discovering anybody in Chester who knew anything about the treasure trove of Oak Island. I finally hired a boatman with a clumsy launch to take me out to the Island. He had heard of "Kidd's treasure," he said, but he had never landed on the Island, nor had any party of tourists, during his twelve years of service on the bay, ever asked to be taken to the treasure. There are three hundred islands in the bay, and Oak Island is just one of the three hundred to the average tourist.

The boatman landed me on the end of the island farthest from the treasure pits, but, as it turned out, I was not sorry for that.

After making the boat fast to a great rock on a little beach, the boatman and I wandered about, and presently came upon the Only Inhabitant. He is weather-beaten, slightly stooped, shy, but not unapproachable.

His hair and mustache are grizzled, but not unkempt. There is a patient, baffled expression in his mild blue eyes.

Long ago, that look tells you, John McInnies learned to disregard the taunts and the laughter of skeptical men. He knows the treasure is there, and he does not resent the disbelief of others.

I found him neither enthusiastic nor uncommunicative. He would answer questions that were put clearly and simply, but he would not volunteer information. It was all the same to him whether I believed in the treasure or doubted.

"How long have you lived on this island?" I asked.

"All my life. Handy on to sixty-three years. I was born in that house right there."

The house is a tight little cottage, and through the window I could see a large portrait of Queen Victoria in her young womanhood, hanging on the parlor wall.

"All your life on this island! How large is the island?"

"Two hundred and fifty acres. Maybe a mile long, and half that wide, some places. Big enough for me, and I use only a little of it."

"Where did your father come from?"

"Oh, he was born here too. James McInnies was his name. Born in the same house."

"Indeed! And now you are the only one here?"

"Yes, and I am a bachelor. I have my dog, Sailor, you see, and a horse to help me with my little farming, and one cow."

"How about your father's father?"

"Daniel McInnies, he was, and born right here."

"Well, well: a long line of McInnieses have been on Oak Island. And what of Daniel's father, your great-grandfather?"

"He was another Daniel McInnies, and everybody knows about him. He was one of the original discoverers of the treasure, you know. After he got interested in the work here, he settled down and built a house right on this spot. We've all lived here ever since, to be close to the treasure, I might say, but I'm the last of the lot."

◇ ◇

Tired, patient eyes has John McInnies, as he looks out to sea and back toward the deeply-pitted tract near the beach, where the treasure lies, and far back across the optimistic years. Four generations of a long-lived family, chained on this lonely spot by the strange spell of that buried gold! And John McInnies has no claim upon the treasure now, nor has any of his kith or kin. Many years ago the McInnieses signed away their rights to the gold that will one day be brought up from the slime and ooze of the dark earth. Signed, that is to say, with a cross-mark, for none of the tribe in these four generations has had time to learn to read or write. They have been held too close to the treasure pit, and there is no school near it.

"Send me a copy of whatever you write," said old John. "Maybe I can get somebody over at the town to read it to me some day."

It was a little more than a hundred and thirty three years ago that Great-Grandfather Daniel McInnies landed on Oak Island and became ensnared, along with his children's children, by the spell of that yellow treasure that still lies hidden near the beach.

In the fall of 1795, three young woodsmen, looking for adventure and game, beached their canoe on the sand in a lonely little inlet in the shade of towering evergreen oaks that stood a little back from the beach. Two or three live oaks still stand, but in those days there was a goodly grove of them. Book-botanists will be tempted to quit the story right here, for they say the live oak does not grow so far north, and is seldom found north of Virginia. All I can say to that is, go to Oak Island and see, as I did. It is not difficult to get there.

Anthony Vaughan and Jack Smith were the companions of young McInnies on that fateful trip on that mild October day so long ago. The three lived somewhere on the mainland, not far away, and between periods of irregular employment were wont to hunt and fish together. They were born in the woods, all three, and they were at home in the dark forests.

As a lurid poster to the city man was a sawed-off oak limb to these woodsmen, at the edge of the virgin forest of Oak Island. Surely, someone had been here before, and long ago, at that. For there, about four hundred feet from the water's edge, stood a live oak tree of giant stature, with a limb sawed off! The limb was fifteen or eighteen feet from the ground, horizontal, and its stump extended now about four feet out from the tree trunk. The limb was dead, and the bark on it was deeply scored, especially on the upper surface. The woodsmen examined it carefully, for to them it was the sign of a mystery that must be looked into. It had been supposed that none of the three hundred or more islands in Mahone Bay had been explored or inhabited, up to that time, and here was evidence to the contrary.

The story told by most of those who have been close to Oak Island lore says that there was an old ship's block dangling from the scored limb when the woodsmen made their discovery. This is a most important item if true, and I spent many weeks trying to verify this part of the tale, without success. You will see later on why it is extremely important to know whether there was a ship's block hanging to that stump of a limb in October of 1795. Some of the earliest accounts mentioned the block, but some of them said it was of iron and others said it was of wood, and none of them gave any description of it or told where it might be seen. I am forced to believe that that bit of marine tackle was just a piece of romantic gossip, added to give verisimilitude to the pirate theory that was generally held to account for the burial of the treasure.

From the moment they sighted the sawed-off limb, the woodsmen were on the track of a mystery. Well, their great-grandchildren have grown old on the track of the same mystery, and the great-great grandchildren of two of them already have children who are old enough to be optimistic about the early solution of it.

For the descendants of Smith and Vaughan still live in the neighboring mainland town of Chester and in other parts of the province of Nova Scotia, and repeat the tales their aged grandparents heard long ago from grandparents of theirs who have long been dust.

Directly under the sawed-off limb, at the foot of the giant evergreen oak, the three adventurers observed that the sod was noticeably sunken. The depression was roughly circular, and measured thirteen feet in diameter.

This observation led instantly to the inevitable conclusion. Someone, or some persons, had buried something at the foot of this tree, lowering it into the hole by means of tackle attached to the sawed-off horizontal limb.

In 1795 real deep-water pirates had not disappeared from the seas, and every young man in the western world had heard tales of treasure the pirates had buried. These three woodsmen at once thought of pirates and treasure. They paddled home in feverish excitement that night. They would return and get the treasure tomorrow. What a long tomorrow!

◇ ◇

The young men returned early the next day, bringing shovels and spades. They began to dig, and they found that they were surely working in a shaft that had once before been opened and filled, for they noticed that the earth was much less hard within the circle that had been marked by the depression in the sod than outside it. Also, careful observation noted the scoring of some pick-like implement on the sides of the shaft they were emptying.

That first day the young men did not exactly reach the treasure. But they did reach, at a depth of ten feet, a solid platform, made of rough oak planks three inches thick, put together without nails or bolts.

Next day the platform was removed, with much labor, but no treasure chest was found beneath it. How disappointment must have filled those youthful hearts when, after all this hard labor, only the yielding earth was found beneath such a portentous covering of planks! It was the first disappointment of a long and fateful series.

The young men proceeded with their digging for many days. When they reached a depth of twenty feet, they struck a wooden platform almost exactly like the first one. Removal of the planks was more difficult this time, and the diggers found it necessary to bring block and tackle and make use of the old scored limb that some other mysterious diggers had used—how long before?

The planks were hoisted out, and nothing but earth was found beneath! You may be sure that three hearts beat fast and furiously as the three boys pledged their words to one another to "keep right on at this job until it's finished."

Vaughan was then only sixteen; the others a few years older. All three lived to old age, and they kept their mutual pledge as well as they could.

Winter came on early and interrupted the work just as the diggers had struck a third platform of heavy planks, at thirty feet below the surface. Meantime a large bucket had been rigged with tackle for hoisting out the clay.

That winter the boys made plans. They realized that they must get help. They thought they should have a horse, a few more tools, and enough money to furnish them with a month away from their regular work while recovering the treasure.

They went about through the neighboring villages and countryside with their story, and could elicit no active interest. They found a more difficult barrier than any platforms of oak, and that was superstition. The impression was abroad that there was something queer about Oak Island. An old woman living on the mainland at Chester, four miles away, told tales she had heard from her mother, who had been reared on that same shore. In the time of the old dame's grandmother, it had been generally understood, she said, that the island was accursed. Strange lights had been seen there at night, and fires had gleamed, and boatmen who had gone out from the mainland to investigate had never returned. Indeed there was a persistent legend that the devil himself had selected this lonely island for his northern headquarters, and was wont to walk abroad there by nights in search of stray souls.

One after another, men who became sufficiently interested in the treasure trove to promise help heard the weird stories, and on second thought declined to be identified with the venture.

The following summer the boys were unable to do any work on the treasure pit itself, but they built a hut in the woods near the oak grove, and spent many a day and night there, showing the romantic layout to men whom they were trying to interest, and talking over plans among themselves. They were obliged to do some sort of productive labor for a living, but they devoted all their spare time to planning for the excavation of the treasure pit.

During seven years the boys grew older, and the treasure trove remained unexplored. Smith married a girl of Chester, who was vastly thrilled by the prospect of eventually sharing in the treasure in which her adventurous husband so fervently believed. The Smiths set up their home in the hut beside the treasure pit, and later built a house there and began the rearing of a family. McInnies also married a girl who was willing to live on the island and wait for the great gold strike. They had a little house some distance away from the pit itself, exactly where there was built somewhat later the house in which their remote bachelor descendant was destined to watch out the long afternoon of a quiet life. Vaughan married and settled down in the mainland area known as the Western Shore, and there George Vaughan, a descendant, lives to-day, and believes in the treasure.

When Smith's first baby was about to be born, his wife said: "He must not be born here on the Island. Of course, I don't believe in the old superstitions about the curse on the ground here. But we seem so tied down by the treasure. I think our boy ought to be born on the mainland, and then maybe he won't want to live here all his life beside the treasure pit. No, I haven't lost faith in it, but I don't want to start out a second generation depending upon it."

She had her way. She went to Truro and stayed in the home of Doctor John Lynds, the young physician who cared for her and the new baby.

The young doctor was immensely interested in the story of the treasure of Oak Island. He became acquainted with Jack Smith, and when the young mother was able to travel, he took her to her island home and went to look at the treasure pit. He was decidedly interested. He waived payment of his bill. "That'll pay for one share of stock in a company we must form to get this treasure out," he said. And so it came about that the first Oak Island Treasure Company was formed.

By this time Smith had made many observations about the island that added to the mystery of the treasure. He had cleared a small space for his farming, and in doing so had found that a good deal of the ground was covered with red clover, which was as foreign to Nova Scotia as were the live oaks. He also noted that while some of these oaks were quite old, there was all about them a growth of underbrush and trees that was much younger, as though the area had once been cleared of all but a few oak trees, and later had grown this new crop of trees and shrubs unlike the growth on the rest of the Island.

Also, Smith noted that the ground near the beach at a neighboring inlet apparently had been levelled off by the labor of man. This was a very important observation, which later was fully verified.

The little inlet near the oak grove already had become known as Smith's Cove, and is so known to-day. Digging about the beach in the cove one day at low tide, Smith came upon a great rock, solidly imbedded in the beach structure, into which was fastened an ancient hand-forged iron ring-bolt. It was plain that here had once been a place for mooring ships! How long ago? No one was able to throw any light upon this problem.

◇ ◇

Dr. Lynds went about among his acquaintances and talked up the treasure venture. He was a man of many friends and much influence. He obtained plenty of takers for the stock. Among the prominent men who went in for the highly speculative business of digging for treasure were Col. Robert Archibald, Capt. David Archibald, and Sheriff Harris. These are still good names in that part of Nova Scotia.

For two years the Treasure Company carried on the work. That means two short summers, for no work was done during the Nova Scotia winter.

The shaft went down to a depth of ninety-five feet. Every ten feet some sort of marker or obstruction was found. Most of these were platforms of oak or spruce planks, but one was a layer of putty, which sounds foolish enough when first you hear of it, but not quite so silly when you learn that a waterproof putty was formerly carried in large quantities by every well-stored ship, and its use among seafaring folk goes back to very ancient times.

Another of the ten-foot "markers" was a deep layer of charcoal, spread over a layer of a tropical fiber, resembling the fiber that grows on the outside of a cocoanut.

At about this point I think I can detect a few guffaws and a derisive sneer or two from the gallery. And someone says, "Bunk! Charcoal and putty and fiber! Who'd put stuff like that in a hole that treasure was buried in, and who'd bury treasure a hundred feet deep anyhow?"

Believe me, skeptical objectors, if I were making this story up I could do much better than this. I'd make it sound much more probable. And I wouldn't put any putty and charcoal and fiber into it at all. But I didn't put them there. Who did? In due time I shall offer you my guess, and then you may have yours, which will be just as good, I suspect.

Some of the putty was used by Smith in glazing his house, which up to this time had not been a very magnificent house, and had had no glass windows.

The fiber is more important. It becomes quite a factor later in this record. I have seen a handful of it, which has been preserved. It may not be cocoanut fiber, and it may be sisal or something quite similar. It is curly and coarse and unquestionably of tropical origin. I don't know what it is.

At ninety feet, the diggers unearthed a thin flat stone, about three feet long and sixteen inches wide. On one face it bore peculiar characters which nobody could decipher. The searchers felt, however, that the treasure hunt was getting hot.

The stone was shown to everyone who visited the island in those days. Smith, in the course of the improvements he was making in his house, built this stone into his fireplace, with the strange characters outermost, so that visitors might see and admire it. Smith by this time felt sure that he was destined to be very prosperous in the near future, and he was making his house larger and more interesting for the visitors he expected to entertain there.

The Smith house afterwards burned down, I have been told, though of this I am not certain, for there is a ruined house now standing on the site, and it may well be the one Smith improved so nobly during the life of the first treasure company. The stone was removed from the fireplace many years after the elder Smith's death, and was taken to Halifax, where the local savants were unable to translate the inscription. It was then taken to the home of J. B. McCulley in Truro, where it was exhibited to hundreds of friends of the McCulleys, who became interested in a later treasure company. Somehow the stone fell into the hands of a bookbinder, who used it as a base upon which to beat leather for many years. A generation later, with the inscription nearly worn away, the stone found its way to Creighton's book store in Halifax, and what happened to it after that I was unable to learn. It was seen there in 1896. But there are plenty of people living who have seen the stone. Nobody, however, ever seriously pretended to translate the inscription.

On a certain Saturday evening, after the mysterious stone had been taken out of the shaft and duly examined by the crowd of optimistic diggers, work was suspended over Sunday. In Nova Scotia one doesn't work on Sunday, even to unearth barrels of gold. To this day, trains do not run in or out of Halifax on Sunday.

That Saturday night, the excavation had reached a depth of ninety-five feet, and before knocking off for the night some soundings were made with an iron rod, driven straight down into the bottom of the pit. At approximately five feet below the bottom, or one hundred feet below the surface, the inevitable planking was struck again. So, with all the anxiety of a marginal buyer in a falling market, the treasure seekers went to their homes for a quiet Sabbath.

On the following Monday morning they came to the pit and found sixty feet of water in it!

Day and night, for a week, bailing crews worked. They lowered the level of the water considerably, but when they went home for the Sabbath the pit filled up again. It was decided to abandon the effort to get the treasure out that way.

Another shaft was sunk, a few yards away from the treasure excavation. The original pit, ever since the shafts began to multiply, has been known as the "money pit."

The second hole went down to a depth of 110 feet, and then a horizontal shaft was driven toward the money pit. Hindsight doesn't require much cleverness, but it seems to me that the result of this operation might have been foreseen. When the horizontal tunnel was almost under the money pit, the water burst through.

Strangely enough, it never seemed to occur to anybody that the water might be coming from the ocean. It didn't occur to anyone to taste it until about forty years later, when someone fell into one of the pits and got his mouth full of salt water.

When the second shaft was flooded, the company gave up the work and decided to think it over for a while.

The three young men who had sworn to keep on digging until they found the treasure saw the years come and go, as other ambitious men have done since the world began. All three reared families, but did not greatly prosper. After all, why break one's back working for a living, when presently one is about to lift chests of gold coins right up out of a hole in the ground?

Jack Smith grew old in his fine house beside the grove of ancient oaks, and his hopes bloomed every spring with the red clover. Daniel McInnies regretted that his children had nowhere to go to school. But never mind. Before they should grow too big for instruction the treasure would be brought up, and then they could go to Europe to school and make up for lost time. And so it went, to-morrow and to-morrow and to-morrow, until old Daniel McInnies, white-haired and feeble, died and was buried in the hard and mysterious soil of Oak Island. He left with his son Daniel explicit instructions for continuing the work to recover the treasure.

Vaughan was still living, but old and shaky, when, in 1849, another treasure-hunting company was formed. He went over to the Island, where the children of Smith and McInnies were living with their half-grown children, and, with his cane, poked about amid the wreckage until he found the exact location of the money pit. The pit had filled up and almost disappeared.

Robert Creelman, of Upper Stewiacke, was one of the investors in the 1849 venture. He had many long talks with the aged Vaughan, who repeated to him in detail the story of the discovery of the tree with the sawed-off limb and the subsequent developments of the treasure hunt that already had lasted a lifetime.

Dr. Lynds, too, was living, and joined the new company with all his old optimism. He was sure the treasure would be brought to light before he should be too old to appreciate it.

The shaft was started with much cheering, and that summer of 1849 saw it grow downward, with firmly cribbed and braced sides, to a depth of eighty-six feet. Then the water came in. Bailing with large casks was undertaken, but proved a failure.

At this time, J. B. McCulley, a neighbor of Dr. Lynds, was manager of the Treasure Company. It was he who had taken the inscribed stone home to show to his friends.

McCulley knew a coal prospector who was out of work, and got him out to Oak Island with his "pod auger," a kind of primitive boring apparatus operated by a belt running from a horse-power gin. The water level remained about thirty-five feet below the surface. Just above the water a platform was built, and the drill mounted on it, with complicated arrangements for transmitting the power from the surface.

Now began the most interesting experiment in the history of the treasure hunt. The drill was in charge of a foreman named James Pitbaldo, who had strict instructions to drive it down slowly, withdraw it slowly, and to keep the bit untouched until one of the officers of the company should be called.

Old Dr. Lynds had introduced some semblance of scientific method. He insisted that the bit be cleaned carefully after each withdrawal, and that every grain taken from it should be carefully dried before the fire in the Smith house, sifted, and examined under a glass.

Several members of the treasure company took turns occupying a place on the platform with Pitbaldo when the drill was sent down for the first time. The excitement around the pit was tremendous as the reports of progress were shouted up from below.

By listening and feeling the bit and observing its actions, it was possible to tell what kind of surfaces it was striking with its point. The platform was struck at the hundred-foot level and bored through. It was five inches thick, and the slivers brought up from it were spruce. It was easy to make exact measurements from above by noting carefully the progress of the drill.

The auger dropped twelve inches after penetrating the platform, as though it had reached an empty space. Then it slowly bit its way through four inches of solid oak.

Now came the peak of excitement. The bit was revolving in a mass of pieces of loose metal!

Chips of the oak had clung to the bit when it was brought up while boring through the wood, but several times the drill was hoisted while it was going through the loose bits of metal, and there was nothing. If the drill had finally struck a chest of gold coins, such a result was to be expected, for of course it would but jostle the coins about, and not cut into them.

Now the bit is being slowly raised again. This is done carefully, for it is realized that it would be easy to shake off any precious fragment that might cling to the auger, and it would be almost a miracle if the mud and water encountered on the way to the treasure would not wash away any item of evidence. But old John Lynds stood by and cleaned the bit carefully, and wrapped the dirt up in a cloth. Over at the Smith house every particle was being closely examined.

This time no magnifying glass is required to see the evidence. Three tiny gold links, part of an ancient chain, are caught on the bit, imbedded in the mud!

The sensation among the workers is profound. All the officers of the company rush off to the house to see the latest find examined, and to watch for other pieces of gold among the clay that is being dried and sifted.

Meantime, there is just time for Pitbaldo to drop the auger once again before quitting for the day. Only one other person is close by when the auger is drawn up. He is John Gammell, of Upper Stewiacke, a shareholder of the company. He sees Pitbaldo quickly detach something from the side of the bit with his fingers, examine it a moment, and then slip it into his pocket.

"Better give that to Mr. McCulley, hadn't you, Pitbaldo?" says Gammell.

"Oh, I guess not," replies the foreman. "The directors have a meeting to-morrow. I'll show it to them then. It's a thing the directors ought to see all at once."

That night Pitbaldo disappeared, and the suspicion at once arose that he had pocketed a valuable piece of evidence. This suspicion increased later, when Pitbaldo turned up in Cape Breton Island in the company of a miner who presently made efforts to question the validity of the Treasure Company's title to the treasure trove, and tried to acquire title for himself.

When drilling was resumed next day, the bit, after going through twenty-two inches of the loose metal, penetrated eight inches of oak, then another layer of loose metal, twenty-two inches deep, then four inches of oak. Here, according to the obvious interpretation made by the observers, were two oaken chests of treasure, one above the other, and each one made of four-inch timbers. Afterwards the bit ground through what appeared to be a six-inch platform of spruce, and then slid easily through seven feet of clay without striking anything hard.

The drill was moved a few feet, and again dropped. It struck the platform as before, went through it, dropped eighteen inches, and then began behaving oddly. There was a jerky motion, and the bit was found to be cutting irregularly into wood on one side, and striking nothing on the other side. The watchers said it was striking the curved exterior of a wooden cask. Repeated examinations of the bit disclosed small splinters, such as might have been chipped off cask staves, and also some strands of the coarse vegetable fiber heretofore mentioned.

This ended the operations for that summer of 1849. John Gammell, who had seen Pitbaldo put the article taken from the bit into his pocket, had become a directing force in the treasure company, and he was mightily curious about Pitbaldo. He spent part of the winter hunting for him, and found him all too late. Pitbaldo had gone to work in a gold mine and had been killed. No mortal will ever know what John Pitbaldo put into his pocket.

It was decided that there was nothing to gain by boring the treasure chests full of holes, so the man with the drill departed that fall and came no more. During the summer of 1850 the same company continued operations. It sunk a shaft ten feet from the money pit, to a depth of 109 feet. It had learned nothing from a previous attempt of this kind. A horizontal shaft was driven toward the money pit, and the water and mud burst through, quickly filling the new shaft to about the same level as the water constantly maintained in the main pit.

Bailing operations then started in both shafts, and an enormous amount of water was pumped out by two ingenious contrivances worked by two teams of horses. It was vain. The bailers did not realize that they were fighting the Atlantic Ocean, which the persons who buried the treasure had been at pains to enlist on their side.

A. A. Tupper, one of the foremen on this job, wrote a detailed account of the operations some years later, when he was a resident of South Framingham, Massachusetts.

Bailing was abandoned, and a serious study of the water problem was made, with amazing results. Here we have one of the most incredible parts of this treasure story, and a part that I certainly would omit if I were inventing the tale for the amusement of my readers.

Much thinking and some observation convinced the treasure hunters that ocean water was entering the money pit through an artificial channel. There were dozens of reasons for thinking so. None of the shafts showed any signs of water until they were driven right up against the money pit. The money pit itself showed no water at all until it had gone down ninety-five feet and the platform at one hundred feet had been struck by the sounding-bar. Once the water entered, it came in a flood that could not be conquered.

The water in the shafts was observed to rise and fall about eighteen inches with the rise and fall of the tides.

It seemed reasonable to presume that those who dug the pit in the first place and laid the treasure down would have been drowned out by this same flood, had it been available for drowning purposes at that time. They had succeeded in digging their pit and putting their treasure into it, but those who came after them had to face a flood of salt water. This must be looked into.

◇ ◇

Careful exploration of the beach and the intervening ground disclosed the astonishing fact that those who anciently hid the treasure had with infinite pains and remarkable engineering skill constructed a tunnel from tidewater to the treasure trove, cunningly devised so that any meddlers should be thwarted by the ocean itself!

The tunnel does not lead from the nearest shore point, but from a gently sloping and well-protected beach some thirty rods away. The beach at this point has been, at some far-off date, entirely reconstructed by the labor of man, apparently for the sole purpose of causing it to furnish a steady flow of salt water into the treasure pit.

The treasure-hiding engineers knew better than to make a tunnel through which the tide would rush in full force, for such a work would lead to nothing but ultimate destruction. The ocean, driven by storms, would tear right inland through such a leading conduit, and dislodge or displace the treasure, at the very least.

Indeed, in the course of time this kind of channel probably would cause the ocean to eat into the land and ultimately cover up the hidden property completely, so changing the contour of the Island that nobody could ever get to the treasure, even with the most accurate maps and directions.

So the beach, between low-tide and high-tide marks, was carefully dug out and rebuilt in such fashion that it would act as a gigantic sponge, holding the water from the incoming tide and steadily pouring it, by gravity pressure alone, through a long and gently-sloping tunnel, into the carefully-guarded treasure pit. The flow at no time would be violent, but as long as the ocean and the beach should last, it would be there—the vigilant ally of the mysterious absent ones who knew how to outwit the ambition and ingenuity of generations then unborn.

This is how the flood from the beach was provided for. For a distance of 145 feet along the beach and from low water to high water, the natural structure of the beach was excavated. The builders then filled in a foundation of large beach rocks, loosely placed, so that there was space between and among them for the water to run. Placed among these rocks in a fan-like pattern, five drain-lines were constructed, spreading out toward the ocean-side and converging toward the land-side. These drains were made of the flatter rocks, with sides and tops so laid that the water could trickle into them easily, much as American farmers made their drains prior to the general use of drain tile.

Over the heavy beach-rock structure was laid a thatch of eel-grass, which may have been two feet thick when laid down. Over this was spread a compact mass of the tropical vegetable fiber heretofore mentioned. There was a great deal of this, carefully packed down. It served as the chief sponge-like agent, to gather the water and hold it for slow and steady delivery between tides as well as during the tide-run.

Over the sisal (or whatever it is) the sand and gravel of the natural beach was carefully replaced, leaving a sloping surface that would not arouse suspicion.

The effect of all this was exactly what was wanted by the engineers who put away the treasure. The water from the tide infiltrated slowly through the beach-sand, and filled the giant sponge of fibrous hair to repletion. Here, then, was a permanent reservoir, always having its supply of water renewed and never in any danger of running dry. The fibrous plant and the eel grass resist the action of water, particularly when kept from the air, so that no decay had taken place when the beach was uncovered by the searchers, and I recently held some of the fiber in my hands and can testify that it is still as fresh and serviceable as when it came from the tropics.

The converging drains, which collected the water, led into a tunnel similarly constructed of flat rocks, and leading directly from the beach to the treasure pit.

The obvious question arising here is: How did the hiders of the treasure expect to get it out? Would not the ocean work against them as it has worked against their opponents in this extraordinary game of treasure-hunting?

There are two possible answers. One is that it is within the bounds of imagination to assume that those who hid the treasure expected to leave it there forever.

The other, and to me more probable solution, is that the treasure-hiders kept a complete map and plan of the works, with exact location of a secret water-gate which the searchers have never discovered. That this gate, once closed, would hold back the sea-water. It even seems probable to me that such skillful engineers may have closed the gate before they put their treasure, all dry and safe, into its lasting home, and that the searchers sprung the gate when they struck the last platform with the sounding-rod. The rock with the strange inscription may have been the warning to the initiates that the water-trap was just ahead. Those in the secret may have had exact instructions as to how to disconnect the trap or raise the last platform without springing the flood-gate. But outsiders would certainly blunder upon the platform, disturb it without locking fast the secret gate, and thus call in Old Ocean, the ultimate guardian of the precious treasure.

This, I admit, is speculation. It is my own theory, and I have not heard anything like it from anyone connected with the treasure search. But to me it seems reasonable and explanatory.

The tunnel leading from the beach to the treasure pit has never been traced from source to exit. Only fragments and sections of it have been found here and there.

When the existence of such a water-tunnel was first suspected, engineers who were consulted said that if there were such a bore, doubtless there was somewhere, between the beach and the treasure pit, a vertical shaft which had furnished air to the builders of the tunnel. Desultory search for such a shaft proved fruitless. But by accident it seems to have been found.

One of the later Smiths was plowing in his little field, between the pit and the reservoir beach, when his oxen suddenly began to flounder and sink into the ground. The plowman jumped aside, but both oxen went down and wedged themselves into a pit, fifteen feet deep and of irregular diameter. This probably was the mouth of the shaft leading down to the tunnel. But by the time this incident occurred the captains and the planners had departed, during a lull in operations, and nothing was done for many years about following the lead thus accidentally uncovered.

At this point it is well to remember that in all the history of Oak Island, since the discovery of the sawed-off oak limb, there has never been a real engineer associated with the treasure-hunt. All of the engineering has been amateurish, and the labors of the diggers have suffered the handicaps of amateurism.

◇ ◇

The 1849 company constructed a makeshift cofferdam of clay to hold back the tide while the artificial beach structure was being examined. The work was only fairly under way when the weak cofferdam collapsed under the assault of the tide. Since there was not enough money available to build a real cofferdam, this part of the work was given over, and the company proceeded to spend the rest of its money in the futile business of sinking another shaft.

This one went down 118 feet, about twenty feet south of the

money pit. As usual a horizontal tunnel was then started in the direction of the money pit. I cannot imagine what these amateur engineers expected to gain by this method of disturbing the treasure, but apparently their imagination was good, for they put their cash into it. The horizontal shaft was driven to a point directly under the money pit.

The workmen were at lunch in the Smith house when the treasure pit collapsed with a tearing, roaring noise, into the horizontal shaft the men had just left. When the workers came running to the works they found the subsidiary shaft rapidly filling with water and mud that were being forced into it from the place where the disturbed treasure had been lying.

That was the last of the so-called 1849 company. The funds were all gone.

The next treasure company went to work in 1863. Good old Dr. Lynds and Old Man Vaughan had gone to join the other pioneers of the treasure hunt.

It was now sixty-eight years since the three young men had started out to get the treasure which was to make their lives so much easier to live. All of the early associates of the three discoverers had gone in search of more lasting treasure. The sons of the first seekers after the secret of Oak Island were approaching middle life. But they believed in the treasure. How could they do otherwise?

Now there was a new force to reckon with—on the side of the searchers. The steam engine had become a common servant of ambitious man. A powerful steam engine was purchased with the first funds of the new company. One of the chief owners of this organization was A. A. Tupper, who had been a foreman in the 1849 company. He was a skilled miner, and directed the underground work.

The steam engine was hitched to a powerful pump, which was set to work in the 118-foot shaft, the last one sunk by the last previous company. It was planned to pump the shaft dry, and to bring out the treasure through the horizontal tunnel connecting with the money pit. The workers argued that the treasure probably was lying in the horizontal shaft, forced over toward the

118-foot hole by the rush of mud and water that marked the collapse of the money pit.

The pump did its work well, although it had much thick mud to contend with. The vertical well was pumped nearly dry. The water was kept below the 100-foot level all the time, and below that was so much mud that it was felt the workers could be supported upon the plastic mass while they dug and fished for the treasure.

The work of strengthening the cribbing and shoring up the horizontal tunnel was started, but Tupper came up one day with this dictum:

"I won't let my men work down there any longer, unless experts say it's safe. To me it looks mighty dangerous. Those walls are only soft mud, and I think they're about to collapse."

Contractors were brought in for "expert" opinion, and they agreed with Tupper. No way could be devised to make the walls safe while the men were working on them to make them safe. Another impasse. The ocean and the ancient treasure-hiders won again. Work was abandoned, just when many thought the treasure was almost within reach.

◇ ◇

Now came the Halifax Treasure Company, with more capital behind it than had been at the command of any of the working organizations that had gone before. Some of the best business men in Halifax took stock, and an arrangement was made with the stockholders of the company that had brought out the steam pumping engine to go ahead with the work in coöperation with the newly formed Halifax Company.

This new capital made the dirt fly. Oak Island became a scene of feverish activity. Shafts were sunk here and there and elsewhere. One project was to drain off the ocean, or such part of it as flowed toward the money pit, by intercepting the intake tunnel and diverting the flow before it reached the pit. For this purpose many shafts were sunk between the money pit and Smith's Cove, as well as farther afield, and horizontal shafts were driven out in every direction.

But the intake tunnel was not tapped. The Halifax Company dissipated its funds. Its stockholders became discouraged, and at length the workers were drawn off. The steam engine was laboriously shipped back to Halifax, and the ancient enemies of the treasure-seekers scored one more knockout.

◇ ◇

For thirty years the treasure trove again lay unmolested. For another long period the men who had sought the secret gold stood by and watched the grass and brush heal over the scars they and their forefathers had made in the kindly earth that had seemed so cruel in its refusal to give up its hidden gold.

The next treasure-hunting company was incorporated in 1893. It included among its leaders and investors the sons of many of the men who had worked in the 1863 company, and some whose remoter forebears had participated in the earlier diggings. In fact, by this time the province of Nova Scotia was beginning to be rather well dotted with the homes of descendants of Oak Island treasure hunters.

With the advent of the 1893 company, however, there comes into the drama of the treasure a new character of first-rate importance. When this company began operations, Frederick L. Blair was a young insurance salesman. At the age of seventeen he first invested his savings in the projected company. Friends of his in the insurance organization by which he was employed were interested in the treasure, and to young Blair the thing looked romantic and promising.

If only he could have seen a motion picture of young Vaughan at sixteen, swearing to dig until he got the treasure, and then another picture, showing Old Man Vaughan, poking with his cane among the débris of his youthful hope!

Young Blair put more and more of his savings into the treasure company of the day. When he came into money of his own, all of the cash and credit he could muster went to the purchase of stock from stockholders who were becoming discouraged.

A. M. Bridgman was president of the 1893 company, which did not get to the digging stage until 1895. Bridgman made some extensive historical researches before going into the venture. One of his investigators was A. S. Lowden, who became foreman on the job.

Lowden made extensive notes on conversations with James McInnies, father of the present inhabitant of Oak Island, and grandson of McInnies the Discoverer.

(I use the spelling of the name as it was given me by the lonely guardian of the treasure himself. None of the records I have examined uses this form of the name, however, and many who have known the family from of old tell me the name is McGinnis, or Maginnis. They contend that the last survivor of the family is so ignorant of the alphabet that he doesn't know how to spell his name.)

James McInnies was a very old man and this was his last opportunity to contribute to the written record of the treasure. He told the story in detail, as he had heard it from his father and grandfather.

Lowden also talked to Robert Creelman, who had been interested in the 1849 company and had had the treasure story directly from Discoverer Vaughan. Creelman was eighty years old at this time, and Lowden thought it worth while to include in his report of his conversations the fact that this veteran of the treasure hunt was "well preserved, vigorous, with strong religious tendencies of the Old Presbyterian school. He is not a man to make any kind of a statement to deceive."

The 1893 company, having a capital of $60,000, spent one summer excavating the pit into which the oxen of Farmer Smith had fallen. At fifty-five feet the hole went into salt water. The winter was spent digesting the assurance that this was indeed the air shaft leading to the intake tunnel. But nothing more was done about it. Nobody thought of the idea of a possible secret water gate.

After the company had spent most of its funds without going

near the money pit, its affairs were placed in the hands of a committee of shareholders, partly upon the motion of young Blair, who was beginning to be active in the affairs pertaining to the treasure search.

This committee, at the beginning of another season, directed operations against the old money pit itself. The pit was cleared of wrecked cribbing and débris to a depth of thirty-five feet. Here was found the platform upon which the 1849 company had erected its drilling machinery, and below the platform the pit was found to be open, but its cribbing was so badly twisted that not even a small pipe could be driven straight down to the bottom.

Operations were shifted to one of the neighboring shafts, and through a communicating tunnel the workers managed to clear the money pit to a depth of 111 feet. At this level an opening of the intake tunnel was found and exposed to examination. It was an opening about two and a half feet wide, partly filled with well-rounded, smooth stones from the beach. The sea water poured steadily between these stones.

The operators admitted that they would never be able to pump out the ocean as fast as it was flowing in through the tunnel. Therefore, they would endeavor to stop the flow near its source.

Five holes were bored, more or less at random, near the reservoir beach, in the hope of finding the intake. Into each of the five-inch holes dynamite was lowered and exploded. It was thought that in this way the intake tunnel might be collapsed and closed, or at least obstructed so that the flow at the money pit would be considerably reduced.

One of the five-inch holes evidently hit the tunnel. When 127 pounds of dynamite was exploded in it at a depth of 180 feet, ocean water rose in it to tide level, and the water in the distant money pit boiled and became turgid from the force of the explosion.

Having proved another point, the treasure hunters charac- teristically abandoned further efforts to stop up the conduit from tide-water. The amateur "experts" disagreed about the next step, and so took no more steps in that direction.

Meantime, further operations were going on at the money pit. Through a two-and-one-half-inch pipe a bit was sent down, and boring operations, for the purpose of reassuring the discouraged investors, were undertaken. The results obtained this time were almost as astonishing as those that rewarded the pioneer efforts of the first boring adventure.

This time the drilling was done with improved machinery, and extended much deeper than anyone had ever before thought of going. At 126 feet the drill struck oak wood, and then iron. The pipe could not be driven beyond this obstruction, but the drill went on.

At the interesting depth of 153 feet the point struck stone. Samples brought up looked decidedly like man-made cement to the drillers, so specimens were sent to an analytical laboratory in London for analysis. The laboratory forwarded its report, with the carefully guarded statement that the analysis was the same as that commonly reported on cement, and that it was the well-considered opinion of the chemists that this was not a natural stone, but one that had been mixed and made by man.

Here was another amazing discovery. It seemed to indicate that the careful treasure-hiders had cemented the floor of the cell into which they had lowered their gold, and that the entire structure of the subterranean treasure house must have been approximately forty feet from floor to ceiling!

The cement floor was found to be seven inches thick, and lay upon solid oak flooring five inches thick.

Well, it would seem that somebody had buried something, all right! The drill finally ran through the last of the artificial construction at 154 feet and three inches below the surface.

Further drilling confirmed the earlier observations of this company. Cement walls, floor and roof, reinforced by iron and heavy oak timbers, were struck again and again. Also, loose metal pieces in great masses, closely packed.

It was during this prospecting in the drowned treasure house that a handful of clay, scraped from the point of the drill, yielded one of the most sensational items appearing in the entire history of the heart-breaking search for the treasure.

Careful screening of the clay disclosed only a tiny ball of soft material, about the size of a pea, but when it was dried out before the fire it proved to be a piece of parchment. This scrap of parchment I examined myself under a glass a short time ago. It is a small fragment, torn from a sheet on which something was written in what appears to be India ink. The portion of the writing remaining looks like our script letters w and i, joined, but of course may be almost anything in almost any language, since it is simply a succession of angular vertical strokes, joined as in handwriting.

This was a powerful stimulant to the imaginations of those who had sought so long for some sign to renew their faith that the treasure was really down there beneath the mud and water and wreckage of machines and hopes and fortunes.

A bit of parchment! A mere scrap, torn from some document by the revolving drill. But it had been written upon in some remote time by a human hand.

The boring of so many holes through the treasure chests doubtless had let the avenging sea-water in and had spoiled all the records, if records there were, within the chests of the treasure house. But let them go! Here was enough! Here was evidence of the existence of the hidden hoard. Here was a document to inspire the workers to greater efforts than could have been compelled by any complete and detailed inventory of the treasure. For here was mystery—and promise!

Excitement once more reached fever pitch among the treasure-seekers. Everybody was confident that the greatest treasure in all history would soon be brought up for distribution among the faithful stockholders. More money was needed to prosecute the work, and was forthcoming. It was furnished by stockholders, and stock couldn't be had by outsiders.

The existence of a treasure of fabulous aspect had been fairly well established. Now to get it out!

Frederick L. Blair was one of those who came forward with more money at this time. He had come into a fortune, and knew of no better way of augmenting it than by investing in this sure thing.

In two years the company sank six shafts near the money pit, ranging in depth from ninety-five feet to 160 feet. The theory was that it would be possible to sink deep holes enough to take off the water from the pit in which the treasure lay and get the goods out while the deep holes were filling up.

It was now October, 1897, and Blair had assumed much of the responsibility for the operations, and was more heavily interested financially than any other stockholder. He had put aside an opportunity to stand for election to parliament, and a friend of his in the insurance business had taken it up. Blair decided to devote the next few months to getting out the treasure.

The draining of the treasure pit was partly successful. When the deepest shaft reached 160 feet, the water began to rush in, and the water in the money pit began to fall. It fell fourteen feet in an hour, and then began to rise again, slowly. As soon as the 160-foot pit filled up to a level with the water in the money pit, both levels rose slowly together, until the money pit was again flooded to the old level.

Once more the event had proved that the workers were both industrious and clever, but not quite up to the Atlantic Ocean and the ancient ones who had hidden their treasure so well.

After further expensive borings and the establishment of interesting facts concerning the possible existence of a second intake tunnel, the treasure company ceased work. When accounts were settled up, the control of the treasure site was vested in Blair.

◇ ◇

Again the silent grass and the encroaching rust took charge of the sadly-pitted area beside the sentinel oaks. Years were passing, and Frederick Blair was rearing a family while he laid plans for getting at the treasure.

In 1905 he obtained from the Crown and the Canadian Parliament a grant of treasure trove rights touching any treasure that might be exhumed at Oak Island. A portion goes to the Crown, but the terms are liberal as they affect Blair. The one-time insurance salesman, who had refused a chance to run for parliament, had a friend in the legislative body, and all was well. Blair would make one supreme effort, get the great casks and chests to the surface with the aid of improved modern machinery, and the hoodoo of Oak Island would be vanquished.

He obtained a lease on the treasure farm for a period of forty years.

In 1922 Frederick L. Blair launched his major offensive. He had heavy machinery for drilling, digging and carting away. A New York contractor was sent to Oak Island with a big gang, and the work began to hum.

The summer residents of the charming old town of Chester, on the mainland, awoke to the fact that something was going on at Oak Island, and boatmen did a thriving business, taking tourists close enough to the Island to view the works.

Night and day the gas engines chugged and the donkey engines puffed. Much dirt was moved.

Detail here is useless, and the headache is still too new to be probed. Suffice it to say that the Ocean and the ancient buriers of treasure were again victorious.

Superstition has not died out in Nova Scotia. In that respect, perhaps, Nova Scotia does not greatly differ from the United States.

I met several persons in and about Chester who referred darkly to "the Big Dog" in connection with the latest failure at Oak Island. I had a hard time getting anyone to tell me anything about the Big Dog, but there were plenty who would say: "Well, if you don't know about it, you wouldn't believe it. No, maybe there's nothing in it. I know nothing about it anyway."

Finally someone who doesn't believe in the Big Dog told me that the superstition has persisted, among the more ignorant inhabitants, that Aziel, the demon who guards treasure in the name of Satan, has always had the treasure of Oak Island in his care, and has appeared in the form of a dog, somewhat resembling a Great Dane, whenever the treasure was in danger of being disturbed.

You couldn't pay one of those superstitious folk enough money to induce him to set foot on Oak Island. "I'll have nothing to do with The Dog," say many of the villagers. "Has any luck come to them that have tried to get his treasure away from him?"

I suspect that someone connected with the latest working at the treasure pit must have owned a mastiff or Great Dane, so often is this story of Aziel and his faithful watching repeated in the vicinity of Chester. Of course those who repeat it refer to similar stories told long ago by the old folk who from the first were anxious to believe that the treasure was buried under a curse or a compact with the devil.

◇ ◇

Now, how *did* the treasure get to Oak Island? Who could have buried it there, and why should anyone bury it so deeply and so securely, and then leave it there, forever guarded by the Ocean—a more formidable guardian, perhaps, than the Great Dog himself?

Of course, it is inevitable that the hoard should be referred to as "Captain Kidd's Treasure." The boatmen who consent to take you out to Oak Island from the Chester landing refer to it as Captain Kidd's. The old printed prospectuses, put out by the successive companies that were organized to seek the treasure, invariably referred to it as "probably hidden there by the redoubtable pirate, Captain Kidd."

This heresy is easily disposed of. Captain Kidd, whose name has become a synonym for pirate all over the world, was never a pirate, and never buried any treasure anywhere, if we except a chest or two he hid on Gardiner's Island, when he sailed in to meet accusations of piracy before the Governor of New York. Furthermore, he probably was never within many miles of Oak Island. He was an honest sea captain who had the bad fortune to get in the way of several crooked politicians, one of whom chanced to be Governor of the Colony of New York, and another of whom happened to be King of England. Several others were members of the House of Lords of the British Empire, and all together they had poor Kidd done to death to save their own skins—and reputations.

So Captain Kidd didn't bury the treasure on Oak Island.

Did any pirate or company of pirates do it?

I doubt that any of the several thousand pirates of whom we have record had anything to do with this treasure. The most lucrative pirating was done in the Caribbean and in the Atlantic Ocean, south of the Virginia Capes. Why should any pirate or any piratical organization that we know anything about waste time sailing so far north as Oak Island to deposit treasure? There were plenty of uninhabited islands in the Caribbean and there was plenty of wild ground along the Spanish Main and farther north, within the cruising radius ordinarily used by pirates.

Furthermore, why should pirates expend the time and energy that must have been lavished upon this unique undertaking at Oak Island? It would take a ship's crew years, probably, to dig the great shaft, build the vault as it evidently was built, and construct the tunnels through which the water flow was assured for all time. I believe pirate crews were generally much more profitably employed.

Pirates who buried treasure usually intended to come back and get it soon. Whoever buried the treasure at Oak Island apparently had no thought of returning to claim his gold during his own lifetime. The protective and secretive work was planned to last for generations at least.

It is fairly important that one have some notion of the probable and approximate date of the laying down of the treasure, if one is to make any plausible speculation upon the probable identity of those who put away the gold so carefully.

How I wish I knew whether there was a ship's block, or pulley, hanging on that oak limb when Vaughan and Smith and McInnies first sighted the treasure place in 1795! That would tell something.

It is my belief that the treasure is of much more ancient origin than any of the treasure-seekers has ever supposed. We know only that it was there in 1795, and apparently had been there for a great many years.

Put forward as a possible clue to the age of the treasure works are the circumstances that persons working or idling in the vicinity of the treasure pit have picked up a stone whistle, such as was used by boatswains in the days of Queen Elizabeth, and a coin of uncertain origin and nationality, bearing the date 1301.

These might indicate something concerning the persons who hid the treasure, and again they might have been dropped by much later visitors to the island, for it is not improbable that a boatswain's crew may have been sent ashore there for wood and water without any reference whatever to the treasure.

Having, it seems to me, eliminated the pirates, as we know them, from the equation, I put forward as a tentative and fairly plausible theory the supposition that the treasure may have been hidden thus by a Norse colony, somewhere between, let us say, the birth of Christ and the year 1400. These would be extreme dates, and my best guess, based upon extensive study of the Norse and Icelandic sagas and other records of Scandinavian exploration and settlement, would place the date close to 1200 A.D., or between that date and 1300.

If there was a ship's block, or any kind of wheel pulley, hanging on the limb when the three young men arrived upon the scene, my theory is not so very strong. It is barely possible that the Norsemen may have known about the block and tackle system of hoisting as early as 1200 or 1300, but it is only a remote possibility. The principle of a revolving wheel within a shell, for making a rope run more easily in the hoisting of sails, was not generally known in Europe until after the First Crusade. Of course, we do not know what isolated American colonists might have developed.

But, anyway, I discard the block as improbable, partly because it doesn't fit in very well with my theory, and partly because the evidence that it ever hung on the oak limb is extremely thin.

The story of the Icelandic and Norse settlements along the coast of North America is a long one, and I can't go into it here. But I feel reasonably certain, along with many men who are much more reliable authorities than I, that there was a very early settlement somewhere on the western coast of Nova Scotia. It seems probable and even likely that there may have been one on Mahone Bay.

Such a colony may have flourished, isolated from the entire northern and eastern world, for four or five hundred years. It might have become a wealthy and somewhat cultured state in that time.

For some reason the Scandinavian colonies disappeared, leaving hardly any traces of their existence. I think the causes of their disappearance were usually two: influenza epidemic and attacks by the savage natives of the continent, called Skrellings in the Norse records.

I picture an old and flourishing Norse colony, grown older than the United States now is, but not very populous, due to recurrent epidemics and the circumstance that there was only a shipload or two of white settlers in the beginning.

The colony is wiped out at last by sickness. The last survivors retreat to Oak Island, and, while holding off the Skrellings, plan to take to the sea in their only ship when their number has been sufficiently reduced to make such a move necessary and possible.

They busy themselves during the last days—perhaps years—in the construction of a safe and everlasting repository for the state treasure and the things they all have loved and cherished, since they cannot take much besides food and clothing with them on their ship, which is pretty sure to be overcrowded.

The Norse were always engineers. They always liked to build ditches and shafts and tunnels and underground works. To this day the Scandinavians are among the world's best engineers.

What happened? Well, the work was completed, and the last survivors finally sailed away—and, let us say, their ship perished in a storm.

A far-fetched theory?

I admit it. See if you can do better and fetch the theory less far.

And don't neglect to account for the isolated grove of live oaks, so far from the native habitat of that tree, the growth of red clover, and the presence of the tropical fibrous material! I haven't done that, you see. But I could, by setting my first settlement far enough back and making my colonists voyagers into tropical seas.

◇ ◇

I found Frederick L. Blair in his home on Beacon Street, in Boston. He talked about the treasure, and I asked many questions. My host raised a deprecatory hand:

"Would you please speak a little lower?" he said. "My wife is nervous. She doesn't like to hear people talking about the treasure. She thinks I could have spent my life more profitably and more usefully. Well, maybe she is partly right. I do not blame her for feeling that way. It is true that I have put my life and all my earnings into it, and I did not get the treasure."

There was a sad look in the very bright eyes of the treasure-seeker as he showed me a letter from his boyhood friend, written on stationery of the Canadian Parliament.

"Well, my friends have done better than I, in a way. But I could not help it. The treasure is there, and I just missed it."

He showed me all the evidence, all the correspondence and old records, the bit of parchment under glass, and samples of the tropical fiber taken from the mysterious beach whence I had just come.

"I'm getting all these things in order," he said. "I am not young any more, and I will be passing on one of these days. I have spent most of my money, and I am thinking of going back to Nova Scotia to raise chickens.

"But the evidence and the lease, which has a good while yet to run, I will pass on."

He leaned forward and spoke lower still, but there was a note of final triumph in his voice and a strange light in his eyes—

"For, you see, I have two young sons, *and they both believe in the treasure of Oak Island!*"

Marks the spot where the treasure lies

II. *The Treasure in Tobermory Bay*

TOBERMORY BAY is quiet, landlocked water. It is a small indentation on the east side of the north end of the Island of Mull, on the Sound of Mull, about the middle of the western coast of Scotland. Mull is a part of Argyllshire, and Tobermory, where fewer than a thousand people live, is the only town on the Island. In summer discriminating vacationists come here from Glasgow and London. American tourists have not yet discovered this remote summer haven.

The town of Tobermory consists of a long row of buildings facing one wide street that skirts the bay. A pier projects into the bay at about the center of the town. Eighty-four yards from the end of the pier, at a depth of sixty feet, lies one of the most tempting treasures of the sea.

There is scarcely room for doubt that this treasure can be recovered entire with machinery and methods already well known to marine engineers. Yet it has lain there since 1588.

◇ ◇

That was the year of the Invincible Armada. You have heard the story, with many variations, of the vanishing of the sea-power of mighty Spain and the rise of Great Britain as the ruler of the oceans, growing out of the failure of one of the most grandiose naval expeditions in all history. The treasure came to Tobermory in one of the galleons of the Armada.

The purpose of the expedition was to land an army in England and take possession of the British Isles for Philip II of Spain. There was never the slightest chance of success for this ambitious project.

The Spanish fleet consisted of about 130 vessels, but probably not more than half of these, or about sixty-five, were fighting ships. The others were transports and auxiliary vessels of various kinds. The ships had been supplied by various provinces and cities of Spain, and one grand galleon, the *Florencia*, was furnished by the Italian state of Tuscany, as a grand gesture of friendship for Spain.

There were about 7,000 sailors and 17,000 soldiers in the Armada, and the expedition was instructed to stop at the Netherlands and pick up the army of the Prince of Parma, which was to give over its conquest of the Dutch for the moment in order to finish up the English job promptly.

It chanced that the Prince of Parma and his army were nicely blockaded in Dunkirk by a Dutch fleet, but the King of Spain did not know that when he sent the Invincible Armada on its fateful mission.

There are many popular fallacies concerning the Armada's adventures in general circulation among English-speaking peoples. There is the story that Sir Francis Drake was bowling with his men on the green when news was brought that the Armada was bearing down upon England, and that he finished the game before going aboard ship and preparing to put to sea. There is a general belief that Drake was the "conqueror of the Armada," and that he did the job with a few tiny vessels, miserably armed and equipped. These stories, of course, are of the usual historical hero-tale pattern.

Drake was not in command of the English fleets that went after the Armada as it sailed up the Channel, but was one of seven commanders constituting the fleet council of the supreme commander, Charles Lord Howard of Effingham, Lord High Admiral of England. While the total number of Spanish ships was either 128 or 130, and not more than half of these fighting ships, the English fleet that chased the Armada numbered in all at least 190 fighting vessels. Some of these were armed merchantmen, but they were well armed and well manned, and they were light, fast sailers, while the galleons were tall, unwieldy, slow, badly armed, and crowded with soldiers and other landsmen. William Wood, in his *Elizabethan Sea-Dogs,* estimates that the English were at least five times as strong as the Spaniards in armament and seamen-gunners. So, even if there had been no storm, the Spanish Armada never had a chance of winning anything but disaster for Spanish arms.

As a matter of fact, there was not much fighting. The total English loss was not more than one hundred men killed. The swift English vessels out-maneuvered the clumsy floating castles of Spain, ran in close, but not close enough for boarding, and poured shot into the hulls of the big ships. The Spaniards were unable to depress their guns enough to hit the English ships at short range, since the guns were so high up in the air and the English targets were low and close.

But the Armada reached Calais in fairly good order, each vessel putting down two anchors. During the night the English sent seven fire-ships, all ablaze, toward the galleons. While none of these fire-ships actually touched a Spanish vessel, the Spaniards became so excited that they cut their cables, leaving an-

GOLD MADNESS

chors behind, and had several bad collisions in their efforts to get
out to sea.

Now a characteristic piece of bad management in preparing
the great Armada for the conquest of England was the failure to
provide a supply of spare anchors. Most of the Spanish vessels had
no anchors left after they cut their cables at Calais, and this
lack was their undoing, far more than any English ammunition,
for the men under Lord Howard were but scantily supplied with
powder and shot.

Next day there was fighting, wherein two Spanish ships were
driven ashore and one was sunk. Both sides ran out of gunpowder
before the end of the day.

That night a storm blew up from the north-west, and when it
was about to cast most of the Armada upon the rocks, changed to
the south-southwest, increasing to gale force. The Armada continued on through the Channel and into the North Sea, running
before the wind. The English fleet followed the damaged enemy
past the Firth of Forth, and then turned to take shelter from the
storm.

The Spaniards found no shelter. They thought to make the
voyage around the Orkney Islands, veering south around Scotland
and Ireland, and so back to home ports. But the weather in the
North Sea was terrible, and provisions ran short. The lack of
anchors made it impossible, after reaching the latitude of the
Shetland Islands, for many of the vessels to keep off a lee shore,
and so they were wrecked, one after another. Some went ashore
on the Shetlands, and between thirty and forty were wrecked on
the Irish coast. Thousands of the Spaniards who came ashore
alive were killed on Irish soil, while others (nobody knows how
many) were sheltered in the castles of Irish chiefs, and the descendants of many of these Spaniards are Irishmen with Spanish complexions and features to-day.

Several galleons made port in Galway Bay, their crews nearly
dead of famine and exposure. These men were fed and sheltered
by the Irish inhabitants, but two thousand of them were shot
and hanged by the English occupation forces. The English his-

torian Froude comments, "Dreadful! Yes, but war itself is dreadful and has its own necessities."

On July 29 the Invincible Armada, entering the English Channel on its way to fetch the Prince of Parma and his army for the great invasion, had sighted the Lizard Head. All through September and October the surviving vessels, with sadly diminished crews, in many cases unable to work their ships, drifted into Spanish and Portuguese ports.

But the *Florencia* did not return. She was the pride of the Armada, known in the records as a battleship of 980 tons, carrying 52 guns and a complement of 486 men, mostly soldiers. She had been fitted out in most luxurious style by the people of Tuscany, who spared no money or labor in making their galleon worthy of the name of their capital and of the part she was designed to play in the conquest they felt sure the King of Spain would find so easy.

The *Florencia* stopped at Vigo for formal transfer from Italian to Spanish ownership, and to take on Captain Pereira, (also given as Pareira and Fareija) a Portuguese, who was to command her throughout the impending battle. At Vigo a crew, mostly Portuguese, was taken aboard, and some special armament was added to that which had been supplied in Italy.

Perhaps it was at Vigo that a great cannon, eleven and one-half feet long, designed and decorated by Benvenuto Cellini, was mounted on the great galleon. This cannon, recovered from the wreck of the *Florencia* in 1670, stands to-day, mounted upon stones, in the garden beside the castle of Inverary, seat of the Duke of Argyll, in Argyllshire, Scotland. It is of bronze, seven and one-half inch bore, and was designed for Francis the First, King of France, when that gay monarch had Cellini working for him at Fontainebleau. It bears in relief the F for Francis, the fleur-de-lys of France, and the salamander in flames. The cascable, or large ball at the breech end of the cannon, is fashioned as a pomegranate, and is bored through so that a rope might be run through the hole to assist in handling the gun.

There are some shrewd conjectures on record as to how this French gun happened to be part of the armament of the *Flor-*

encia. One of them is that it was one of the French guns captured by the Italians at the Battle of Pavia, during a French invasion of Italy. The Italians may have included the Cellini item in their equipment of the great ship they were contributing to the expected Spanish triumph.

There is much mention in the records of a precious crown, gleaming with jewels of great price, which was taken aboard the *Florencia* at a Spanish port. This crown was to adorn the head of the ruler whom the Spaniards should crown sovereign of England.

Tradition says that this crown was designed for the head of a certain beautiful Spanish princess who went aboard the *Florencia* at Vigo with much ceremony, and occupied royal quarters in the castle of the ship during the fateful voyage up the channel, around the Shetlands, and down to Tobermory.

The *Florencia* shipped a great load of gold and silver coin either at Vigo or at Corunna, to pay the personnel of the Armada and to provide whatever might have to be bought after the landing in England. The amount of this treasure has been a matter of dispute ever since the hunt for it began, but fairly conservative estimates, based upon figures that seem to have historical justification, place the figure somewhere between a million and a half and two million dollars.

◇ ◇

It was in November, 1588, that the *Florencia,* with tattered sails and starving crew, limped into the peaceful Bay of Tobermory.

Captain Pereira was not afraid of encountering hostility on the part of the Scotch. He knew that they were taking little or no interest in the troubles of the English at this time, and that they had troubles of their own. Besides, he had gold to pay for what he needed—food and water enough to carry him and his crew and passengers back to Spain, and a respite from the storm to enable him to patch up his battered vessel.

But it chanced that the Scotchmen ashore were indeed very deeply engrossed in troubles of their own, and these speedily became the troubles of the Spaniards as well.

There was a war on between the Macleans and the Macdonalds. With the latter clan was allied the Clan MacIan. The war had been more or less a going enterprise for several generations, with fortune favoring one side and then the other. The history of this clan fighting is in itself a very interesting story, but only one phase of it concerns the *Florencia* and her treasure.

Sir Lauchlan Maclean was chief of the clan that held mastery of the Bay when the galleon came in, seeking succor. When a messenger from Captain Fareija (to use the form of the name recorded by the Scots) came ashore and stated the object of the ship's visit, Maclean did not fall over himself in eagerness to accept the gold offered for supplies. He inquired about the ship's crew and armament, and was happy when he heard that there were many well-armed soldiers aboard.

The canny Scotsman scratched his head and devised a bargain.

He sent this message back to the Spanish Captain: "I will sell you all the food and water you need, at prices to be agreed upon. But only on condition that you lend me one hundred of your soldiers for a short assault upon the castle of my enemy, the MacIan."

The Spanish Captain was not loath to give his soldiers a little exercise, and he did not think it possible that any of them would come to harm in a brief battle with these half-wild clansmen of the hills.

So the bargain was made, and the hundred well-armed Spanish soldiers were sent ashore.

Sir Lauchlan was elated. Now he would show those Macdonalds and MacIans, and also all his other enemies, the Clanranald and the Clan Tan and all the islanders who had been cutting the heads off respectable Macleans for centuries! He would make good use of these warriors before he sent them back to their galleon.

But here is a simple recital of the affair, taken from "The History of the Clan Maclean," by J. P. Maclean. You will note that the galleon is here called the *Florida*. She is also referred to in some of the records as the *Admiral of Florence:*

The "Florida," commanded by Captain Don Fareija, was forced by weather and want of provisions into Tobermory Bay. Sir Lauchlan Maclean entered into an agreement with the Spanish Commander by which he was to have the assistance of 100 armed mariners from the "Florida," to aid him to fight the Macdonalds, the Clanranald and the Clan Tan in the Isles of Rum, Eig, Canna and Muck, and to besiege Mingarry Castle.

When he was still investing the castle a message came from Captain Fareija requesting that the Spanish soldiers should be sent back at once as the "Florida" was preparing for sea. At the same time Maclean of Treshnish sent him word that the provisions supplied to the Spaniard had not been paid for. Sir Lauchlan remonstrated with the Don for his contemplated injustice, and full satisfaction was promised. On the faith of this the men were sent back, but Maclean, not relying entirely upon Captain Fareija's promise, detained three Spanish officers as hostages till the debt should be paid. At the same time he sent Donald Glas Maclean, son of John Dubh Maclean of Morvern, on board the "Florida" to receive an adjustment of the demands of his people. The Spaniard at once disarmed the emissary and made him prisoner, and cautioned him at the peril of his life to hold no communication with his friends. Finding that the ship was making preparations to put to sea, Donald Glas conceived a plan which, though it meant certain destruction to himself, promised a speedy and terrible retribution to his captors. Finding that the cabin in which he was confined was in close proximity to the magazine, he found an opportunity in the night time to force his way into it, and laying a train in as concealed a position as possible, he awaited the final decision of Don Fareija to carry his plan into effect.

There are other versions of the incident, and details vary in the accounts that have come down to us. But it seems clear that there was a dispute between the Captain of the galleon and the Chief of the Macleans. Some accounts say the provisions were delivered by the Scots but not paid for by the Spaniard. Others say that the matter in dispute was the price to be paid for the food, and that the supplies never were delivered, because Maclean demanded an exorbitant price in addition to the services of the soldiers.

Some accounts tell us that none of the one hundred foot-soldiers ever got back to the ship, but that they continued to live in Scotland for years after the disaster, eventually making their way back to Spain. Certainly the three officers held as hostages by the clansmen remained long in Scotland, and it is probable that the best accounts of the amount of treasure aboard the ship were derived from tales told by these survivors.

The most dramatic and generally accepted version of the sinking of the galleon has young Donald Glas Maclean setting fire to his train of powder when the galleon began to make weigh, and perishing with the ship and most of her officers, men and soldiers.

Whatever the cause, the *Florencia* blew up in the Bay and went down in sixty feet of water, and there she lies to-day.

If there was a Spanish princess aboard, with her ladies-in-waiting, she went down with the others, and the searchers of 340 years have failed to identify her bones or locate her crown.

◇ ◇

The galleon seems to have been in Tobermory Bay for several weeks before the explosion. William Asheby, of the English Embassy to the Court of Scotland, reported to Sir Francis Walsingham concerning her, and the report, damaged so that some of it is illegible, is still preserved in the State Papers of Scotland, thus:

. . . this six weeks on the . . . Scotland a great ship of Spain . . . about . . . the Isle of Mull, in Maclean's countrie, which, they here reporte cannot go from thence; those Yrishe people releave them with victuelles, but are not able to possess her, for she is well furnished both with shott and men; if there be any shippes of warr in Ireland they might have a great praie of this ship, for she is thought to be verie riche.

Another letter from Asheby, written to Lord Burghley from Edinburgh, says:

The Spanish ship I mentioned in my last, which was driven by tempest to the west part of Scotland, to the Isle called Mull, in Maclean's countries, is burnt, as it is here reported by treachery of the Yrishes, and almost all the men within is consumed by fire; it is thought to be one of the principalle shippes, and someone of great account within, for he was always—as they say—served in silver.

The three officers who had been held hostages on shore eventually made their way to Edinburgh, where they made formal complaint against Lauchlan Maclean before the King and Council. It seems quite probable that somewhere in the course of the proceedings the officers must have given the true name of their ship and the amount of treasure she contained, although no such disclosure on their part is now extant in the archives of Scotland.

In March, 1589, King James of Scotland and his privy council handed down a decision regarding the misdeeds of Lauchlan Maclean. The laird of Tobermory had been brought in to answer the charges of the Spanish officers, not only concerning his getting the galleon blown up, but also a detailed charge that he, in company with a large band of thieves and roustabouts, "besides the number of one hundred Spaniards, came to the properties of His Majesty, Canna, Rum, Eigg and the Isle of Elenole, and after they had wracked and spoiled the said islands, they treasonably raised fire, and in maist barbarous, shameful and cruel manner, burnt the same island, with the men, women and children there, not sparing the youths and infants; and at the same time past came to the Castle of Ardnamurchan, besieged the same, and lay about the said castle three days, using in the meantime all kinds of hostilities and force, both by fire and sword."

The decision of the King and Council was, in effect, that Maclean was guilty of almost every crime and offense against the peace except making a left turn against the red light. But the punishment due to these crimes was remitted, except only that due for "plotting of the felonious burning and flaming up, by sulphurious powder, of a Spanish ship, and of the men and provisions in her, near the Island of Mull."

The unfortunate incompleteness of the records leaves us in ignorance of the nature of the punishment meted out to the chief of the Macleans, and, further and more regrettably, of such information concerning the contents of the *Florencia* as may have been given by the Spanish officers in their charges and testimony.

The story of the heroic act of young Donald Glas Maclean in blowing up the *Florencia* is clouded somewhat by the claim of the Smollett family that the explosion was brought about by John Smollett, of Cameron House, Dumbarton. The Smollett family tradition says that this John Smollett was commissioned by Queen Elizabeth to take measures for preventing the departure of the galleon from Tobermory, because of rich treasure she was believed to be carrying. Whether the commission was carried out through the agency of the Clan Maclean or by the direct action of Smollett himself, the family history doesn't say.

This John Smollett was the great-uncle of Sir James Smollett, Laird of Bonhill, who was the grandfather of Tobias George Smollett, the novelist, adventurer, editor, doctor, and historian. Tobias wrote, after a long visit with his distinguished grandfather:

> Mull affords several bays where there is safe anchorage, in one of which the "Florida," a ship of the Spanish Armada, was blown up by one of Mr. Smollett's ancestors. About 40 years ago (about 1726) John, Duke of Argyll, is said to have consulted the Spanish registers, by which it appeared that this ship had the Military chest on board.

The galleon lying in such shallow water close to shore, must have interested the islanders of Mull from the very day of her sinking. But the Spaniards were careful to set afloat false information as to the identity of the ship lost at Tobermory. Their navy was not yet wholly disabled, although the Armada had suffered disastrous losses that were the beginning of the undoing of Spanish sea power. After the return of the Armada ships that survived the storms, the Spaniards sent out several offensive expeditions of minor character, and did some creditable fighting. There is every reason to believe that they hoped to recover the treasure lost in the *Florencia* when they should come into possession of Scotland. Therefore they broadcast reports that the ship lost at Tobermory was a small trading vessel, of no consequence at all. This story was published over the signature of one Marolin de Juan, Chief Pilot of the Armada, and was widely circulated in Argyllshire.

The Earl of Argyll was Admiral of the Western Isles, and the wreck in Tobermory Bay was his by reason of his vested rights. This ownership has been confirmed in numerous documents of sale, gift and grant, of which subsequent Earls and Dukes of Argyll have been the beneficiaries, and the ownership of the galleon and its treasure is still vested in the family, which still occupies the feudal castle of Inverary, and keeps bright the hope that the Spanish gold will soon see daylight again.

But two Earls of Argyll have lost their heads on account of that treasure at the bottom of Tobermory Bay, and many a romantic speculator has lost all his funds in the efforts that have been made to bring up the cargo of the *Florencia*. Thus it is with treasures.

The story of the Argylls and the treasure begins with Archibald, seventh Earl of Argyll, who was a boy of thirteen when the galleon sank. As he grew older, he appears to have accepted as true the Spanish pilot's story that the wrecked ship was of no value. As Admiral of the Western Isles he was interested in other projects, especially in winning the hand of the daughter of William Douglas, eighth Earl of Morton. There was an early marriage and, while still a young man, the Earl of Argyll was left a widower. He then married Anne, daughter of Sir John Cornwallis, ancestor of the Lord Cornwallis who lived to hand his sword of command to George Washington at Yorktown.

The Earl's second wife was a Catholic, and soon Argyll secretly joined her church, sold their extensive Kensington property, and departed with his wife for Spain, where he lived for several years at the Spanish court. So he was proclaimed a traitor in his homeland, as the official record shows:

On 16th February, 1619, the Earle of Argile was, with sound of trumpets, and two or three heraults of armes, openlie declared traitour and rebell, at the Mercat Cross of Edinburgh, for not compeering before the Lords of Secreit Counsell.

All this was very important to the Seventh Earl of Argyll, and to the story of the treasure in Tobermory Bay, for while he was at the Spanish court the converted Scotsman dug into the archives relating to the Armada. Particularly, he learned that the treasure-ship of the Armada had never returned to Spain, as the Spanish propaganda in Argyllshire had represented it to have done.

When Argyll had thoroughly digested the contents of the Spanish records relating to the galleon that lay in Tobermory Bay, he faced about, returned to England, and "offered himself in all dutiful obeisance to His Majesty." The Earl was fishing for that galleon, but King James died before a formal claim could be entered.

This Earl of Argyll died shortly after King Charles the First ascended the throne of England. But the knowledge he had obtained at the Spanish court was passed on to the Eighth Earl of Argyll, who made his position fairly secure by carrying the sceptre of Scotland before King Charles the First at Holyrood Palace, Edinburgh, in 1641. Politics were beginning to revolve around the wreck of the *Florencia* as a buzzard wheels above the carrion he is about to claim.

The Eighth Earl, having rendered the King many valuable political services, and having made himself the leading political personality of Scotland, begged the King to make him a legal grant of the Tobermory galleon which his father had lost by reason of his defection.

But King Charles the First was not to be deprived of anything that had value without exacting all the payment he could command. No Scotch nobleman could out-bargain the King. The Earl was required to pay a high price for the sunken galleon, which was, after payment of the cash, transferred to him and his heirs by a "Deed of Gifte."

The galleon had then been down fifty-three years, and nothing of value, so far as known, had been taken from the wreck.

The instrument conveying the wreck to the Earl (who had just been created a Marquis) specifically excepted the Spanish crown that was supposed to be in the vessel. This was to be the property of the King of England, when and if recovered. Poor

King Charles! He was destined to lose his head along with his crown, long before anybody could lay hands upon the crown at the bottom of Tobermory Bay.

While the clause excepting the crown from the grant of the galleon's cargo to the Argyll family no longer holds good, every Earl of Argyll and all the salvors who have worked upon the wreck up to the present day have let it be known that they would voluntarily present the crown to the ruling monarch of England, when and if the famous symbol of sovereignty is recovered.

The grant of the galleon to Argyll, under direction of Charles the First, recites that:

In the year 1588, when the great Spanish Armada was sent from Spain towards England and Scotland, and was dispersed by the mercie of God, there were divers ships and other vessels of the armada, with ornaments, munition, goods, and gear, which were thought to be of great worth, cast away, and sunk to the sea ground on the coast of Mull, near Tobermory, in the Scots seas, where they lay, and still lie as lost; and the Marquis of Argyll, near whose bounds the ships were lost, having taken notice thereof, and made inquiries therefor, and having heard some doukers and other experts in such matters state that they consider it possible to recover some of the ships and their valuables, was moved to take and to cause pains to be taken thereupon at his own charges.

For this reason, the Great Admiral, with the King's consent, gives, grants, and disposes to the Marquis the said ships, ornaments, muntion, etc. of the Spanish Armada, and the entire profit that might follow, or that he had already obtained therefrom, with full power to the Marquis, his doukers, seamen, and others to search for the ships, and intromit with them, providing the Marquis were accountable and made prompt payment to the Duke of Lennox and Richmond of a hundredth part of the ships, etc. with deduction of the expenses incurred for their recovery, pro rata.

At about this stage of the story two points are made by those who maintain that the treasure in the *Florencia* is very great.

First, the Eighth Earl of Argyll is known to have been a person of considerable accomplishments, and a business man of no mean attainments. Also, he had in his possession, presumably, knowledge of the true character of the wreck.

Secondly, the records show that the Earl paid over to the King a sum equal to considerably more than the family had realized from the sale of the vast Kensington property, in exchange for the "Deed of Gifte."

The inference is clear enough. If the Earl was a good Scotchman and no fool, he knew what he was buying and didn't pay too high a price for it.

◇ ◇

In January, 1649, King Charles the First was beheaded.

On July 3, 1650 King Charles the Second landed in Scotland. It was the Marquis of Argyll who installed him in his royal palace at Falkland, and it was the same Marquis of Argyll who, on January 1, 1651, placed upon his head the crown of Scotland.

Meantime, however, the King was doing his share, in the form of promises. The following document is taken from the Royal Commission's Report on Historical Manuscripts, vol. 6, p. 606:

From King Charles II *to*
Archibald, Marquis of Argyll
St. Johns Town, 24th September, 1650.

Having taken into my consideration the faithful endeavours of the Marquis of Argyll for restoring me to my just rights, and the happie settling of my dominions, I am desyrous to let the World see how sensible I am of his reall respect to me, by some particular marks of my favour to him, by which they know the trust and confidence I repose in him; and particularly I doe promis that I will make him Duke of Argyll, and Knight of the Gartar, and one of the gentlemen of my Bed Chalmer, and this to be preformed when he shall think it fitt.

Whensoever it shall pleas God to restor me to my just rights in England, I shall see him payed the £40,000 which is due him, and this doe I promise upon the word of a King.

Charles R.

Argyll was to learn in due time what "the word of a King" could do for a man who owned a galleon of gold at the bottom of a quiet bay.

King Charles the Second had the Marquis beheaded in July, 1660.

The charge was treason. Friends of the Argyll family have always maintained that the real reason for the execution was the galleon. Several favorites of Charles wanted that gold.

Every great treasure for which men seek so diligently under the sea and in great chests beneath the earth is wet with blood and tears. The shining hoard in Tobermory Bay is no exception.

◇ ◇

The Ninth Earl of Argyll, another Archibald, was condemned to death on a trumped-up charge of "leasing-making," in order to get him out of the way of the avaricious noblemen who wanted to get at the galleon, but the young man escaped the penalty because he had some powerful friends at court.

From 1666 to 1670 efforts at salvaging the treasure went on, partly with the aid of a diving bell, invented about that time by a Swede. The wreck was found exactly where the maps of the time showed it to be, and a few relics were brought up. Among them was the gun designed and decorated by Benvenuto Cellini, heretofore referred to. Some gold was brought up too. How much, we do not know, but it was enough to arouse the royal avarice anew.

Charles the Second sent his brother, James, Duke of York, in 1677, to take the wreck away from Argyll. The Duke went in state to Tobermory, in a royal ship and with handsome writs and warrants.

The Ninth Earl of Argyll stood upon his rights and refused to be bluffed by mere royalty. Hadn't his father put a crown upon the head of the reigning King, and lost his own head for his pains? The Earl called for Scottish justice in the courts, and he got it.

He presented to the judges who were to try the case a Memorandum of Defense, setting forth that the "wrack ship" had been sold to his father for a goodly sum, and that it was a valuable piece of property, "a ship of 56 guns and with thirty millions of money on board."

Now, it is assumed by students of the case that this scion of a canny line of statesmen and business men knew better than to exaggerate the value of a piece of property which he was trying to keep the King from taking away from him. And it is further assumed that he knew what he was talking about.

Of course, it is not altogether clear what kind of money he was figuring in when he mentioned "thirty millions of money." It seems more than a pity that he didn't do himself the honor of being more explicit. But, since he chose to speak as loosely as most speakers and writers, it seems reasonable to suppose that he wrote in terms of Pounds Scots, the customary unit of money in that time and place. This, translated into American money of to-day, would place the value of the money cargo in the *Florencia* at about fifteen million dollars. Add to this the probable value of the silver and gold plate and other costly gear that may have been aboard the ill-fated galleon of Tuscany when she went to the bottom, and you have some clue to the reason why kings and noblemen have vied with peasants and barbarians in breaking heads and promises to get at that sunken treasure!

Argyll won the lawsuit against the Duke of York. The Earl, mindful of the chopping block upon which his father had lost his head, then wrote to the Duke, apologizing for being in the right. To which the Duke replied:

From JAMES, DUKE OF YORK
To ARCHIBALD, NINTH EARL OF ARGYLL.
London 8th September 1677.

My Lord of Argyll,

I have read a letter from you which came to my hands about 25th August, last, wherein you make a civil apology to me for justifying your pretentions to the Spanish Ship nere the Isle of Mull, which I cannot chuse but allow of, since it is naturall and reasonable for anyone to defend what they believe to be the right, and on the other side I doe assure you that I had very good reasons, grounded on the concurrent opinions of able lawyers, to believe my own title was the better of the two, and that I might very well endeavour by legall wayes to make it out.

But since the Lords of the Sessions have declared in your favour, I looke on the case as one of those intrique ones in law wherein wise mens judgments doe frequently diffir, and I make no reflection on what has passed anywayes to lessen or prejudice the esteem and kindness I have for you as being really your affectionat friend,

JAMES.

The Ninth Earl now resolved to make hay while there was any glint of sunshine, for he realized that political clouds could form quickly. He made a contract with a German engineering concern for the raising of the galleon's treasure. The contract provided that the crown, if found, was to be excepted from the division of spoils, and was to be reserved for the King of England.

The Germans had a diving bell, somewhat improved, they claimed, over the model used by the Swedes. Captain Adolph E. Smith was placed in charge of the work on the floats that were anchored above the wreck, and preliminary work was beginning beautifully when another cloud came sailing across the sky.

This time it was Clan Maclean. John Maclean of Kinlochalen and Hector Maclean of Torloisk marshalled a force of 130 clansmen, dug some trenches on the hill above the Bay, and began sniping and tossing heavy rocks at the divers.

These kilted hillbillies laughed at Captain Smith when he went across to them and showed them the royal warrant, vesting title to the wreck in the Argyll family. They explained that they claimed the wreck on the ground that their ancestors had made the situation that resulted in the resolution of the Captain of the galleon to hoist sails, and that it was one of their clan who had sent the ship to the bottom. Further, they claimed the wreck on the ground of foreshore rights. That is to say, the galleon had gone down, as one might say, on their ground. It was only a stone's throw from the shore, as they would prove to the satisfaction of the treasure-hunters by throwing stones at them from the shore and hitting them, and the shore belonged to the Macleans.

The divers refused to work while stones were being hurled at them, so there followed another lawsuit, won easily by the Earl of Argyll. The Macleans were enjoined from interfering with the work on the wreck, title to which was formally declared to be clear and cloudless in the Argyll family.

Just as diving operations were about to be resumed, the Earl was arrested upon order of James, Duke of York, who had written him such a lovely letter, and was tried on charges of "treason, leasing-making, and perjury." Montrose, notorious enemy of the Argyll family, was made foreman of the jury, and the defendant was found guilty and sentenced to death.

Here was plainly another attempt on the part of the King and his favorites to get the Spanish gold out of the *Florencia* for themselves.

Argyll was taken to London and permitted to escape to Friesland, where his father had bought a small place for refuge in just such emergencies as this.

The Earl was now officially declared a traitor in flight, and sentence of attainder, forfeiting his property to the Crown, was pronounced against him. So the royal gentlemen had got hold of the treasure of Tobermory Bay at last!

But not quite. James, Duke of York, started on another triumphal voyage to Tobermory Bay. He sailed in the frigate *Gloucester* of the Royal Navy in May, 1682, with men and machinery thought to be ample for the raising of the treasure. The *Gloucester* struck a sandbank off Yarmouth, and broke up in a storm. The royal treasure-hunter lost all his machinery, and counted himself lucky to get ashore on a raft, badly beaten by the waves. A good deal of James' enthusiasm for treasure-seeking vanished right there.

But the King presently revived the issue by publishing an offer of a fifty-fifty split for the salving of the *Florencia's* cargo.

Archibald Miller, of Greenock, Scotland, took the Crown up on its offer, and went to work in the summer of 1683 with diving bells and other equipment. He brought up the galleon's silver bell, three anchors, a capstan, rudder, and several guns. No coins were reported. Miller gave up the job, probably for lack of funds, and in the following year Joshua Maisee filed a petition for permission to "weigh ye wreck called ye Florence, at his own charge."

King Charles the Second died while this petition was pending, and the Duke of York became King James the Second. One of his first official acts was to have the Scottish parliament assembled in special session and to press through a bill confiscating to the Crown all the property of the Ninth Earl of Argyll. He was a persistent treasure-seeker, and through all the smoke of fervid politics he never lost sight of that tempting wreck alongside the Island of Mull.

Argyll thought his condition couldn't be much worse, and he believed he could set things right by force of arms. He joined the Duke of Monmouth in the ill-starred rebellion of 1685. He was captured at Inchinnan, and King James, who had written him that affectionate letter after the close of the lawsuit, ordered him beheaded at once on the sentence passed upon him theretofore for leasing-making, treason and perjury.

In the Argyll archives there is a letter, written by the Ninth Earl while he was waiting to be led to the block. Addressed to his wife, the letter reads:

Dear Heart:
God is unchangeable. He hath always been good and gracious to me, and no place alters it. Forgive me all my faults; and now comfort thyself in Him in Whom only true comfort is to be found. The Lord be with thee, bless and comfort thee, my dearest!
Adieu.

On June 30, 1685, the Earl's head rolled off the chopping-block. Thus one more heir to the treasure at Tobermory was put out of the way forever. He was the second of his line to pay the price so often exacted of those who strive to bring hidden gold to the light of day.

◇ ◇

But the fortunes of kings are often as uncertain as those of treasure-hunters. James the Wreck-Stealer did not remain King

of England long after the beheading of poor Argyll. A son of the
Ninth Earl of Argyll, an exile from Scotland, came back with
William of Orange and helped dethrone James. The King now
became an exile, and the new King raised the son of the beheaded Earl to the dignity of Duke of Argyll. All of the late
Earl's properties, including the wreck of the *Florencia,* were restored to the new Duke.

Work on the wreck was resumed, just as soon as the Duke
became settled at Inverary. The diving bell was used, and about
all the work that could be done with such apparatus was accomplished in a short time. But a diver could not leave the protection
of the bell. Cannon and gear lying on the decks of the wreck
were recovered, but there was no way of penetrating into the inside of the vessel.

When the possibilities of the diving bell had been exhausted,
the salvage work at Tobermory Bay languished. But in 1873 the
modern diving suit, in a somewhat primitive form, was experi-
mented with. The galleon had been on the bottom 285 years, and
she had sunk well into the mud. She had become heavily silted
over. Considerable difficulty was experienced in locating the
wreck.

The Duke of that day began a search among the old papers
of the family, and found a chart, dated 1730, which located the
"Spanish Wrack-Ship" in a line with two easily identified headlands. This chart was only approximately correct, however, as
was proved by an Admiralty survey in 1906.

Some timbers were brought up with the aid of hooks and
tackle, directed by a diver, during the 1873 operations. The oak
was found to be in perfectly sound condition.

In 1903 a ship's anchor was being drawn up from the bottom
of Tobermory Bay in the regular course of a day's work, and
tripped on some obstruction. When brought to the surface, the
anchor carried on one fluke a mass of wreckage, in which was
found a Spanish gold coin. The treasure fever spread quickly,
and soon a company, backed by Glasgow merchants, was hard at
work at the old job. In 1905 operations on a fairly modern scale
were carried on in the bay. Most of the available money was

spent in locating the wreck and in trying to remove the mud from above and around her with steam suction dredges. A great quantity of ancient arms, stone cannon balls, and a tall silver candlestick were brought to the surface, but the fortunes of the company engaged in the work were greatly damaged by a "dowser" who offered to find the treasure with a divining apparatus. Another such miracle man was employed to operate with a forked stick, and so the time and money of the company were spent. Eventually this company's grant expired, and the main treasure was still untouched, although some silver plate and other interesting bits of loot were brought up before the expiration of the contract.

The 1903 company held a sale of its salvage at the Stevens Auction Rooms, Covent Garden, London, in 1904. Several guns, one bearing the date 1563, and a good basket of coins were sold. The silver coins, mostly pieces of eight, brought about ten dollars each.

The next salvage company to undertake the job was called the Pieces of Eight Company, Ltd., and its existence was, indeed, quite limited. It was succeeded by The Tobermory Galleon Salvage Company, with a capital of about ten thousand dollars.

It was in 1912 that Lieutenant Colonel Kenneth Mackenzie Foss became interested in the salvage work and injected an entirely new spirit into the treasure-hunt. He got out prospectuses with pictures of the loot already recovered from the galleon, and sold stock in his enterprise. He was a hard worker and an enthusiastic devotee of the romantic project. He came to America, where he met Simon Lake, the submarine inventor. Lake had lately completed a treasure-recovery apparatus which is described in another part of this book. Foss was anxious to induce Lake to join his enterprise, or to arrange for the use of the Lake recovery apparatus in Tobermory Bay. This arrangement was never made, due to Lake's being completely absorbed in his submarine boat work. Foss made some addresses in the United States concerning his treasure-hunting project, and returned to Scotland filled with enthusiasm and determination to get up the Spanish treasure promptly and without interference.

Concerning the early part of his work in the Bay, Col. Foss wrote:

But it was not so easy; the two promontories unfortunately had no crossbearings given. Along the line indicated the water goes to a depth of 120 feet in places. Two other handlands, spoken of by the old local inhabitants, had soundings of 200 feet near them. The former depth even would have rendered salvage impossible. And the Duke's Chart did not coincide with the Admiralty Survey of 1906. I employed a steam trawler with a trawl to traverse the bay in the hopes of getting some trace of a wreck, but all in vain. While I do not mean to criticize the work of the former Syndicate, it seems to me that they moved about too much from place to place, and listened to too many legends and theories. So I divided the workable portion of the bay into a series of squares like a chess-board, and engaged a steam-driven boring machine, which took up cores six inches in diameter and eight feet long; they were sunk down to the "bed rock" of the bay, beyond which, of course, no ship could go. This went on for three months, and while I gained no positive information, I had the satisfaction of knowing for a fact the negative, viz., that the vessel was not within the area which had been bored day after day. Still, it was a tedious and costly process, and I was "maist despairin' " when lo! in the place where we, all along, expected her to be found according to the description of the wreck, viz., in 60 feet at high water, Diver Daniel Mackenzie, taking a submarine stroll one afternoon, kicked a hard substance with his boot, which, when dug clear of sand, was found to be a large piece of black African oak. This afforded the required clue. From thence on, we never let go, and though the "Pieces of Eight" Syndicate experienced many troubles subsequently, they were mainly those due to smallness of working capital, or else what all treasure seekers must expect to encounter, while human nature remains what it is. If there are "millions of money" in the vessel, there will always be people to be found who would like to block us, in the hopes that we would abandon the quest, and they might have a chance to succeed.

Before the World War stopped the salvage operations, Foss had recovered a good many gold coins, some guns, swords, and an interesting religious gold medal. The medal evidently had been worn around the neck of someone who perished when the ship went down, for it was picked up from among the disarranged bones of a human skeleton by a diver.

The workman, who was a phlegmatic chap and never showed any excitement in the course of his dangerous work, handed the medal to his employer, upon removal of his helmet, and said: "I got this coin among some bones down there. I don't know why, but I turned giddy when I was picking it up."

Well, it was spooky enough work, from a landlubber's point of view!

The "coin" was cleaned up, and was found to be a Catholic medal, bearing a remarkable relief head of Christ, and the inscription, "Ego Sum Lux M., Via, Veritas, et Vita." The M evidently stands for the Latin word Mundi, and the sentence reads: "I am the Light of the World, the Way, the Truth, and the Life." The medal was presented to the Princess Louise, wife of the Duke of Argyll, but the good lady did not live long to enjoy the mysterious relic. Experts who have examined the golden bit say the relief is copied from a head anciently reputed to be the only true likeness of Christ, which was cut upon a large emerald by command of the Emperor Tiberius Cæsar, according to a pious tradition.

Of course there has been speculation as to whether the skeleton from which this token was recovered may have been that of the beautiful princess who was to have been Queen of England. And you can weave your own romance out of the stuff of that speculation.

After the war, Col. Foss went to work again. He was more than ever confident of success. He located the wreck without much difficulty this time, and began dredging with a clam-shell dredge. He recovered, in 1919 and 1920, several pieces of eight, some pewter plates, stone cannon balls, pieces of badly rusted muskets and swords, and several valuable pieces of silver plate, probably part of the silver service used by the grandee who was captain of the galleon.

There were also some bottles of wine. And what a celebration might have been had with the aid of those bottles, had it not happened that the steel jaws of the clam-shell had broken every one of them and spilled into the Bay the precious liquid in which the gallant Spaniards had expected to drink the health of the Spanish Queen of England in 1588!

There was a pause in the work, due to lack of funds, but Col. Foss was tireless in money-raising and stock-selling, as he was in the actual salvage work, and soon the Bay of Tobermory was again alive with floats and divers.

Upon one of the floats the Colonel mounted a fire engine which he had obtained from some romantic municipality that was willing to contribute something to the cause. This gave a pressure of 125 pounds at an inch-and-a-quarter nozzle, and the stout stream was used to wash away some of the silt from the sides of the wreck. In manipulating this nozzle, Col. Foss tripped, and was struck by the full force of the stream. He was picked up as dead, and his internal injuries put a stop to the salvage operations for months.

When divers failed to bring up gold coins, gossip began to spread strange tales throughout the little town of Tobermory, which is always treasure-conscious. At the taverns it was whispered with knowing winks that someone was trying to discourage the enterprise so that those who had absolute knowledge of the exact location of the treasure might obtain the contract and bring up the gold in a short time.

These tales wore much semblance of probability, and they worried Col. Foss and the backers of his venture. In the little office of the treasure company the energetic Colonel fretted and fumed. He wished that he might learn to dive himself, but his injury had made that impossible.

Now, there was in the office Miss Margaret Naylor, the Colonel's energetic secretary. She was up to her ears in treasure lore, and as much interested in the project as she could have been had the recovered treasure been promised to her exclusively.

"I'll go down and see about it," she said.

And she did. She learned to dive in a few lessons, donned regular diving togs, and went below. Again and again she dived, until she was able to walk about on the bottom and make some examinations. Her findings did not justify the gossip that had stirred the village, but her diving work did attract attention to the project, and was the means of getting into the treasury sufficient funds to carry on the work for another short period.

Colonel Foss brought Miss Naylor to America, and she appeared in theaters and on lecture platforms in an effort to raise money for the treasure hunt.

In 1924 Miss Naylor took over the lease from the Duke of Argyll, and went after the treasure on her own account. The effort was short-lived, and the returns were small.

The treasure-hunters still come to Tobermory Bay every summer. One project succeeds another, but seldom does an enterprise get to the point of digging at the wreck. Almost any summer day you may meet in the tavern by the waterside some adventurer who needs only a small amount of capital and some modern American machinery to bring up a fortune in pure gold that would astonish the world.

Why have the treasure-seekers failed at Tobermory Bay?

Inadequate machinery, inadequate funds. These are the two chief causes of failure. As to the curse which is said to attach to all treasure that has blood on it, that is a matter that we can't go into here.

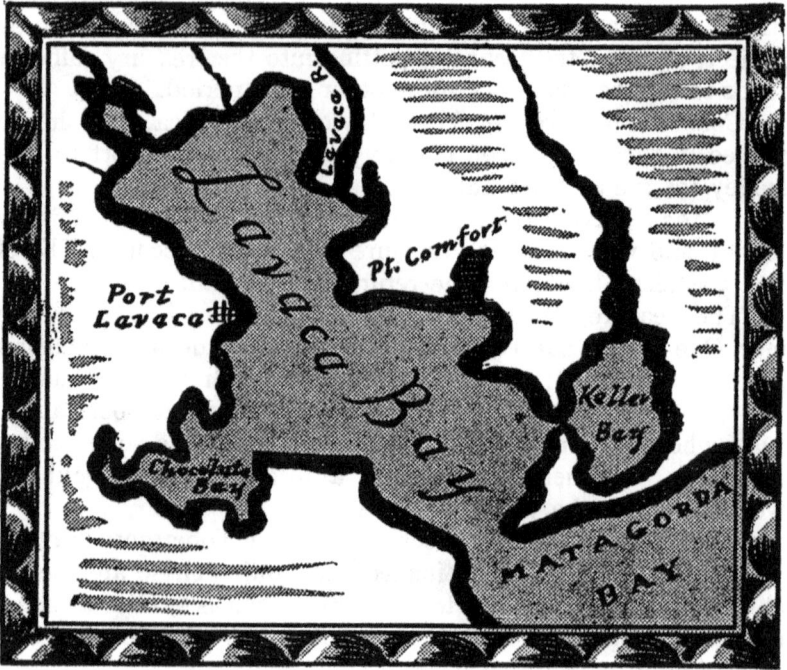

III. *Still They Dig*

I F THERE is a more romantic figure in American history than
that of Jean Lafitte, I cannot identify it. John Paul Jones
is invested with a more robust heroism, but there is less of
mystery, legend and romance about him. Lafitte lived and died
so recently that his personality has all the realism of contemporary history, yet the time and manner of his death are un-
known, and the legends that cluster about his life and death are
as numerous and as romantic as those that are associated with

King Arthur and Robin Hood. A good-sized library of Lafitte fiction could be assembled.

If Jean Lafitte actually placed all the cannon loaded with gold coins that are credited to his activities, he must have spent a lifetime sailing up and down and in and about the Gulf coast and exploring bayous, rivers, creeks and swamps, shouting lustily the while: "Heave ho, my lads! Over the side with another cannonful of gold! Easy does it! So! All hands aft to stuff gold into cannon! Carpenter ahoy! Break out another gross of muzzle-plugs for the guns!"

In Louisiana and Texas, many a boy has spent his adolescent years on the trail of very definite clues to the location of one or more of the big guns that Jean Lafitte is reported to have filled with money in such an obliging manner and concealed in some clever hiding place in a canebrake or swamp. But not nearly all the searchers for Jean Lafitte's treasure are boys.

A great deal is known about Jean Lafitte, but so much of it is obviously impossible that no writer has ever succeeded in separating the truth from the shadowy legend. Perhaps we shouldn't try too earnestly to reduce this heroic pirate and treasure-hider to the status of a mere notable in "Who's Who."

He was a native of St. Malo, France, according to one standard authority, although he is credited to Bordeaux, Garonne, Marseilles, and Bayonne by others. I lean toward the St. Malo story, because Jean Lafitte was just the kind of adventurer who should have been born in "The Nest of the Eagles," as that town of the corsairs was called. There was a brother, Pierre Lafitte, who was associated with Jean in much of the latter's Louisiana career. One persistent legend has it that Pierre was an adopted brother, and a son of an aristocratic French family that was ruined by the Revolution.

Sifting the Lafitte tales and piecing together the documents that bear the stamp of authenticity, one naturally concludes that the Lafitte career was divided into two principal parts, the treasure-getting and the treasure-burying epochs. I cannot imagine that such an expert treasure-burier as Jean Lafitte ever really scorned to bury a bit of gold, even during the earliest of his treasure-getting exploits. Nor did he ever neglect an opportunity to get more loot, even when his treasure-burying mania was full upon him. But until he was well along toward middle life, Jean seems to have been rather busy gathering the ingots.

He abandoned his berth as mate of a French East Indiaman at Mauritius when he was quite a young man, and became Captain of a privateer. He failed to observe the nice distinctions that separated privateers from pirates in those days, and presently found himself a full-fledged pirate. But he never rejoiced in the appellation of pirate, and throughout his life he resented the implication of piracy. When he was at the height of his piratical career at the mouth of the Mississippi he always managed to fly some sort of flag that would give color to his pretensions of respectability. Once an outspoken comrade of his laughed loudly at the term "privateer," and said something like this, "Let's quit pretending! We're pirates and we don't care who knows it, do we?" And Jean Lafitte, affecting shock, shot the fellow dead.

During his early privateering career, Lafitte performed several notable feats of skill and daring. The most amazing of these was his capture of the British East Indiaman *Queen*, in Indian waters in October, 1807. Lafitte commanded the twenty-six gun sloop *La Confiance*, with a crew of 250. He did not hesitate for an instant to attack the *Queen*, although she was one of the biggest armed India ships afloat, with forty guns and nearly four hundred men. The privateer was so small as compared with the tall Indiaman that it would have been impossible for Lafitte's men to board the prize in the usual way, climbing over the side. They would have had to climb so far from their low deck to her high deck that they would have been cut down easily, as one might scrape an attacking column of ants off the trunk of a tall tree.

Lafitte ran alongside the astonished merchantman, firing a broadside and making his men lie flat on their deck while the Indiaman replied with a withering broadside from her big guns. Before the smoke had cleared, the pirates were in the tops, tossing grenades and buckets of flaming pitch down upon the heads of the Englishmen.

While the enemy, discomfited by this sudden attack, fled aft, Lafitte maneuvered his little vessel so that her bowsprit extended over the gunwale of the merchantman at a point far forward, where there were no defenders. He then sent a boarding party over the bowsprit, and when the shock of the first attack was pressing the defenders back, he led a second boarding party in person. Turning a swivel gun upon the enemy, he threatened to wipe the whole crew out with its own grape shot, and soon he had the ship in his hands.

You may be sure that this one prize was worth a large fortune to Lafitte. He must have taken nearly a hundred prizes, mostly English, during his pre-American days. He was piling up the firm foundations of that fabulous hoard of gold which, according to treasure legends, he spent so many of his later days burying and stuffing into cannon for coastwise distribution.

When English merchantmen began sailing almost exclusively under strong convoy, Lafitte had to seek new cruising grounds. He forced the convoy system upon the British shipping of that day, as the German submarines did in a much later war.

Lafitte made for the West Indies, and then for Carthagena, the Colombian city which had set up a mock republic and lived by the piracies of the "privateers" she licensed. He stayed at Carthagena only long enough to purchase some supplies, including a stock for the flag locker, a commission to make war on the "enemies" of the Republic of Carthagena, and the friendship of a few high officials. He then departed on a cruise, and he succeeded so well in finding rich enemies of the toy republic that he had to look about for a convenient base of operations.

He found exactly what he wanted in Louisiana. That vast territory had recently been purchased by the United States. It was in charge of Governor William C. C. Claiborne, who issued many proclamations but was not taken too seriously by the inhabitants.

New Orleans and vicinity furnished a convenient center for the operations of smugglers. The hand of government lay lightly upon this frontier, and the people, having been handed about from one national ownership to another many times, could not be expected to burn with bright loyalty to the laws of their latest possessor, the United States. The people believed in smuggling and prospered by it. An American Embargo Act and an act to prohibit the importation of slaves were not exactly foreign laws, but they were laws with which the people of the Mississippi delta country did not warmly sympathize. Governor Claiborne was shocked at the indifference of the best people of New Orleans to the flouting of these laws, and he was outraged by the activity of what he considered the worst people.

The island of Grand Terre, sometimes called Barataria, about sixty miles west of the mouth of the Mississippi, was a favorite rendezvous of the smugglers. This is a long island, and behind it lies an expanse of water called Barataria Bay, and sometimes referred to as Lake Barataria. There are many islands in the bay.

Jean Lafitte first appears in the story of New Orleans as joint proprietor, with his brother, of a blacksmith shop, the site of which, between Bourbon and Dauphine streets, is always pointed out to tourists. The Lafitte tradition is so powerful in New Orleans to-day that no tourist ever leaves the city without acquiring something of an amateur interest in the romantic pirates who ran that blacksmith shop.

The Lafittes did not work in the blacksmith shop. Slaves did the work. The proprietors used the business as a means of getting acquainted. They were wealthy. That was quite apparent. They were gallant with the ladies. They had about them something of the air of old-world aristocracy, and the legend of noble descent wrapped them both around with a comfortable cloak of gentility.

Jean Lafitte soon appears at Barataria as merchant, agent, proprietor, banker, fixer, and a sort of ward boss. He was always well armed, and was known as an accurate marksman. He had powerful friends. He was immune from punishment. He was the friend and fence who transacted business with those who came in from the sea with cheap merchandise. He did not question the sources of the goods, and a little matter of a smear of blood on a barrel of Jamaica rum made the rum none the less valuable in his estimation.

The Big Boss of Barataria was still accumulating that store of gold and silver that was to be so widely buried.

Some of the merchants of New Orleans were pro-Lafittes because they were able to buy goods of him at very low prices. Others were anti-Lafittes because they had competing stocks on hand which they could not afford to sell at such ruinous figures.

Governor Claiborne was anti-Lafitte. He offered $500 reward for Lafitte's capture, and had notices of the offer posted all over New Orleans. When Jean heard about it, he went to town and had some handsome posters made, offering $15,000 reward for the capture of Governor Claiborne and the delivery of that personage into his hands. He had his posters pasted up beside the others, and had great fun posing before his admirers beside the pictures of him that the Governor had posted.

It is not known whether Jean ever went to sea as a pirate during this period of his lordship of Barataria. It seems probable that he was kept busy with the business ashore, but that he kept his own ship or ships going under the convenient Carthagena flag, without prejudice to the interests of other pirates who dealt with him in a large way ashore.

Lafitte demonstrated his ability as a promoter by establishing a regular auction of smuggled and pirated goods at Grand Terre. Bidders came from New Orleans and from all the country around. It was sometimes possible to buy goods at these auctions so cheaply that re-sale in world markets after payment of legitimate shipping charges was profitable. At one time, when the legislature was debating what to do about Lafitte and his colony of outlaws, the Big Boss held a well-advertised auction of 450 black slaves at his island stronghold.

The United States government became highly indignant at this flouting of its laws by a colony of foreigners. After two unsuccessful attempts to dislodge the pirates, the navy bestirred itself more earnestly. Commodore Patterson was sent with a well-armed flotilla, chased the Baratarians out of their lair, and captured a goodly quantity of loot. The Lafittes and their friends retreated to a wooded stronghold called Last Island, and waited for the storm to blow over.

When Pierre Lafitte was jailed by federal authorities, Jean hired the United States District Attorney, John R. Grymes, as chief counsel for the defense, Grymes resigning his federal post to take the case at $20,000 flat fee. When Grymes intimated that he might need able assistance, Lafitte hired, at an equal fee, Edward Livingston, formerly of New York, who was recognized as the best lawyer in Louisiana Territory. Pierre, of course, went free, and Grymes went to Barataria as the guest of his clients, to collect the fees for himself and his assistant. Livingston, who was a descendant of the famous Robert Livingston, co-partner with Governor Bellamont and King William in the ill-fated expedition of Captain Kidd, was too aristocratic to consort openly with the pirates and smugglers in their own homes. But he accepted the $20,000 gladly.

Governor Claiborne had been issuing some rather strongly worded proclamations about the Baratarians, in which he referred to the Lafittes as "banditti and pirates." When the former District Attorney returned from a week of feasting and celebration at Barataria, carrying $40,000 in a canvas bag, he issued a touching statement, saying, "What a cruel misnomer it is to call the most honest and polished gentlemen the world ever produced bandits and pirates!" When a colleague of the bar referred contemptuously to Grymes for having sold out to the pirates, the indignant attorney for the Lafittes demanded satisfaction, and got it. A duel was fought, and the lawyer who had had the hardihood to upbraid this sterling citizen was wounded in the hip, and had a limp for the rest of his life to remind him of the inadvisability of expressing what one feels about the well-feed employees of malefactors of great wealth.

The United States was engaged in the rather depressing conflict known in our histories as the War of 1812. The British naval forces entertained a project for the conquest of Uncle Sam's newly acquired Louisiana Territory. The pirates at Barataria, repeatedly condemned, denounced and outlawed by American federal and territorial officials, should prove valuable allies in opening up the mouth of the Mississippi and reducing New Orleans, the astute British naval councils believed. Advances were made to the Boss of Barataria through a Captain Lockyer. Jean Lafitte was offered a captaincy in the British navy, and some other inducements, for his aid in this enterprise.

For some reason that must always remain one of the mysteries of the Lafitte story, both Jean and Pierre hated England and the English. Jean temporized with the British Captain, and sent this communication to his old foe:

To Gov. Claiborne. *Barataria, Sept. 4th, 1814.*

Sir—In the firm persuasion that the choice made of you to fill the office of first magistrate of this state, was dictated by the esteem of your fellow citizens, and was conferred on merit, I confidently address you on an affair on which may depend the safety of this country. I offer to you to restore to this state several citizens, who perhaps in your eyes have lost that sacred title. I offer you them, however, such as you could wish to find them, ready to exert their utmost efforts in defence of the country. This point of Louisiana, which I occupy, is of great importance in the present crisis. I tender my services to defend it; and the only reward I ask is that a stop be put to the proscription against me and my adherents, by an act of oblivion, for all that has been done hitherto. I am the stray sheep wishing to return to the fold. If you are thoroughly acquainted with the nature of my offences, I should appear to you much less guilty, and still worthy to discharge the duties of a good citizen. I have never sailed under any flag but that of the republic of Carthagena, and my vessels are perfectly regular in that respect. If I could have brought my lawful prizes into the ports of this state, I should not have employed the illicit means that have caused me to be proscribed. I decline saying more on the subject, until I have the honor of your excellency's answer, which I am persuaded can be dictated only by wisdom. Should your answer not be favorable to my ardent desires, I declare to you that I will instantly leave the country, to avoid the imputation of having cooperated towards an invasion on this point, which cannot fail to take place, and to rest secure in the acquittal of my conscience.

I have the honor to be
your excellency's, etc.
J. LAFITTE.

The English brig, which was awaiting Lafitte's answer to the proposals of Captain Lockyer, grew tired of waiting off Barataria, and disappeared. Lafitte arranged for an interview with Governor Claiborne and General Andrew Jackson at New Orleans. Jackson had been even more vehement than the Governor in denouncing Lafitte and his pirates, and had made public declaration that he would never compromise with such villains to obtain their help. Now, however, both the Governor and the General were to sing a very different tune. They both realized that New Orleans would need every fighting man it could muster to save it from the British. And this gentlemanly, suave, courtly fellow who introduced himself as Jean Lafitte certainly didn't seem to be the kind of a person one should denounce and offer rewards for.

As the result of this interview, Governor Claiborne issued this proclamation:

The Governor of Louisiana, informed that many individuals implicated in the offences heretofore committed against the United States at Barataria, express a willingness at the present crisis to enroll themselves and march against the enemy.

He does hereby invite them to join the standard of the United States and is authorised to say, should their conduct in the field meet the approbation of the Major General, that that officer will unite with the governor in a request to the president of the United States, to extend to each and every individual, so marching and acting, a free and full pardon.

The story of the Battle of New Orleans is well known to readers of United States history. It was fought after peace had been made, because those immediately concerned did not get the news in time. The repulse of the British was complete. Jackson gained great glory. Americans rejoiced, because this was about the only land engagement of the war that gave them cause for pride and celebration.

The Baratarians contributed nobly to the defense of the town. They were used to desperate fighting. The reward offered them was amnesty for all their crimes, which were not few. They had charge of artillery units, and many stories of the battle are concerned with the heroism and determination of the pirates, smugglers, murderers and thieves who fought for America under the command of Jean Lafitte and Andrew Jackson on that famous day.

Many historians believe that it is not too much to say that the city might have been yielded to the British had it not been for these fighting Baratarians.

After the battle, the executive arm of the United States government kept its promise. Here is the proclamation issued by President Madison:

BY THE PRESIDENT OF THE UNITED STATES OF AMERICA

A PROCLAMATION

Among the many evils produced by the wars, which, with little intermission, have afflicted Europe, and extended their ravages into other quarters of the globe, for a period exceeding twenty years, the dispersion of a considerable portion of the inhabitants of different countries, in sorrow and in want, has not been the least injurious to human happiness, nor the least severe in the trial of human virtue.

It had been long ascertained that many foreigners, flying from the dangers of their own home, and that some citizens, forgetful of their duty, had coöperated in forming an establishment on the island of Barataria, near the mouth of the river Mississippi, for the purpose of clandestine and lawless trade. The government of the United States caused the establishment to be broken up and destroyed; and, having obtained the means of designating the offenders of every description, it only remained to answer the demands of justice by inflicting an exemplary punishment.

But it has since been represented that the offenders have manifested a sincere penitence; that they have abandoned the prosecution of the worst cause for the support of the best, and, particularly, that they have exhibited, in the defense of New Orleans, unequivocal traits of courage and fidelity. Offenders, who have refused to become the associates of the enemy in the war, upon the most seducing terms of invitation; and who have aided to repel his hostile invasion of the territory of the United States, can no longer be considered as objects of punishment, but as objects of a generous forgiveness.

It has therefore been seen, with great satisfaction, that the General Assembly of the State of Louisiana earnestly recommend those offenders to the benefit of a full pardon; And in compliance with that recommendation, as well as in consideration of all the other extraordinary circumstances in the case, I, James Madison, President of the United States of America, do issue this proclamation, hereby granting, publishing and declaring, a free and full pardon of all offences committed in violation of any act or acts of the Congress of the said United States, touching the revenue, trade and navigation thereof, or touching the intercourse and commerce of the United States with foreign nations, at any time before the eighth day of January, in the present year one thousand eight hundred and fifteen, by any person or persons whatsoever, being inhabitants of New Orleans and the adjacent country, or being inhabitants of the said island of Barataria, and the places adjacent; Provided, that every person, claiming the benefit of this full pardon, in order to entitle himself thereto, shall produce a certificate in writing from the governor of the State of Louisiana, stating that such person has aided in the defence of New Orleans and the adjacent country, during the invasion thereof as aforesaid.

And I do hereby further authorize and direct all suits, indictments, and prosecutions, for fines, penalties, and forfeitures, against any person or persons, who shall be entitled to the benefit of this full pardon, forthwith to be stayed, discontinued and released: All civil officers are hereby required, according to the duties of their respective stations, to carry this proclamation into immediate and faithful execution.

Done at the City of Washington, the sixth day of February, in the year one thousand eight hundred and fifteen, and of the independence of the United States the thirty-ninth.

By the President,

JAMES MADISON

JAMES MONROE,
Acting Secretary of State.

Jean Lafitte was a hero without an occupation when that proclamation was posted in New Orleans. He had made a glorious name for himself, but now the war was over and he found himself a respectable and famous citizen with no place to which to proceed. In those days there were no cigarettes to be endorsed, no gasolines or oils to recommend, and no syndicates to write for. Communications and transportation were primitive, and both broadcasting and lecture tours were out of the question. Jean Lafitte retired to the wilderness to meditate.

I suspect that it was at this time that the intrepid defender of New Orleans determined to start burying treasure. The insecurity of his situation in life must have been borne in upon him when he reflected upon his career, past and prospective.

To return to piracy or the bossing of pirates and smugglers in or near New Orleans would have been as inappropriate and embarrassing as it is for a United States Senator, defeated for re-election, to return to the practice of law or larceny in his home town. The neighbors would talk. There would be a certain indelicacy in the perpetration of any more of those picturesque insults against Governor Claiborne. The flavor of life had departed. Jean Lafitte hoisted his anchor and stood away for the New West.

He took possession of Galveston Island, where now stands the City of Galveston. He built a large house there and painted it red. He built lesser houses for his retainers, sailors, gangsters and hangers-on. He made Galveston. He *was* Galveston.

From this base, Jean Lafitte went out pirating. He issued statements denying his piratical character as of old, and he did not shrink from wrapping his piratical enterprise around with the Stars and Stripes. He said he chose this base because he wanted to be close to the United States, so as to render aid should the need for his services again arise. Jean Lafitte was growing old. He was living upon his war record, like some superannuated vaudevillian who might spend her declining years touring the provinces with the songs she sang to the men in the trenches. He was not ashamed to display his scars in the market-place.

Texas was the newest republic, and Patriot Lafitte, presenting his New Orleans credentials, was taken on as the Texas navy, or as a substitute for a defense at sea. This position, of course, merely cloaked the old pirate's real activities. A United States warship was sent to check up on the Hero of New Orleans. Lafitte sent out this communication:

To the commandant of the American cruiser, off the port of Galvez-ton.

Sir—I am convinced that you are a cruiser of the navy, ordered by your government. I have therefore deemed it proper to inquire into the cause of your lying before this port without communicating your intention. I shall by this message inform you, that the port of Galvezton belongs to and is in the possession of the republic of Texas, and was made a port of entry the 9th October last. And whereas the supreme congress of said republic have thought proper to appoint me as governor of this place, in consequence of which, if you have any demands on said government, or persons belonging to or residing in the same, you will please to send an officer with such demands, whom you may be assured will be treated with the greatest politeness, and receive every satisfaction required. But if you are ordered, or should attempt to enter this port in a hostile manner, my oath and duty to the government compels me to rebut your intentions at the expense of my life.

To prove to you my intentions towards the welfare and harmony of your government I send enclosed the declaration of several prisoners, who were taken in custody yesterday, and by a court of inquiry appointed for that purpose, were found guilty of robbing the inhabitants of the United States of a number of slaves and specie. The gentlemen bearing this message will give you any reasonable information relating to this place, that may be required.

Yours, etc.

J. LAFITTE.

Lafitte may have made good his bluff this time, but eventually a man-of-war, flying the flag the pirate had so lustily defended at New Orleans, hove to off Galveston Island and ordered Lafitte to depart. The nice collection of commissions from infant republics didn't impress Lieutenant Kearny, in charge of the warship. Lafitte's old friends at Barataria only lately had been captured, tried, and condemned to hang. The Pirate of the Gulf saw plenty of legible handwriting on the wall. He said: "All right, Lieutenant, I'll go." He went.

The stories of Lafitte's career from this time onward are various and divergent. The most dramatic tale has him killed on the deck of a British warship with which he engaged in a fight to the finish. Lafitte, according to this version, raised himself from the deck in his last minute of life, and struck with his dagger at the heart of the Captain of the vessel, who lay wounded beside the pirate. But, with appropriate dramaturgy, the blow was weakened, and the knife plunged into the Captain's leg instead, while the pirate fell back dead.

Another history, which has been verified to a considerable extent, brings Lafitte to his end by natural causes in a little port in South America.

A good many of the Texas treasure stories start with the escape of Lafitte inland when pursued by an American man-of-war. This version of the evacuation of Galveston Island has it that Lafitte did not leave quietly and mysteriously after the visit of the American lieutenant, but was chased by the man-of-war after proof had been discovered that Lafitte had plundered an American merchantman and sunk her in Matagorda Bay.

Much of this treasure lore centers about the lower reaches of the Lavaca and the Neches Rivers. The Houston "Post" printed a harrowing Lafitte treasure story upon the authority of Marion Meredith, of Port Neches, who said he was a principal in a treasure hunt which was guided by a proper map with a cross marking the exact spot beside the Neches River where the treasure is said to rest.

Meredith obtained the map from a man who had followed its directions, had dug a few feet at the spot indicated, and had been overcome by some mysterious compulsion which made him stop digging. This man told Meredith that the infallible marker by which the spot could be recognized was a fragment of heavy chain by which a ship had been moored to the river bank.

Meredith took with him a strong-armed friend who was good with a spade. They found the place and the abandoned spade of the poor fellow who had suffered from the strange compulsion to cease digging. Meredith dug, and soon dug up a skeleton of a human being. Then the other man dug, and when he was down in the hole eight or ten feet, suddenly was overcome by some strange horror. He dropped his spade and clambered out of the hole, nearly dead of fright and shock. He always refused to discuss the cause of his shock, but warned Meredith to stay away from the hole if he wished ever to sleep again. Years later Meredith met the man in Beaumont and tried to reopen discussion of the treasure trove. The digger turned pale at the remembrance of the incident, and swore he had never slept well since. He begged Meredith to mention it no more.

This inexplicable horror is a factor in many of the Lafitte treasure hunting tales.

J. C. Wise of San Antonio, Texas, did a lot of searching for Lafitte treasure to which he possessed a clue. Two of Lafitte's men who were with the pirate in his final getaway helped carry a treasure chest that was very heavy with gold, and buried the chest beside the Lavaca River, not far from the point at which Lafitte abandoned his vessel, the *Pride*. One of the two men who helped bury the treasure told a bartender in a New Orleans saloon his secret, when at the point of death. The other chest-bearer married and reared two sons. When Wise heard the bartender's circumstantial story, he hunted up the two sons of the treasure-burier who had married, and both, then quite mature, corroborated the story told by the dying pirate to the bartender.

Thus equipped with directions and verification, Wise set out to find a long brass rod, called a Jacob's staff, sticking upright in the ground in a meadow beside the Lavaca River, in a certain rather indefinitely defined region. A Jacob's staff was a rod used in surveying instead of a tripod, to support a compass. The certain mark of the treasure, estimated at a million dollars, was this staff, which had been driven into the ground above the iron chest by the defeated Lafitte. The pirate had taken other bearings, but these he had kept to himself. The end of the staff protruded from the ground only a foot or two.

Wise, in searching for data regarding the treasure, learned that the two sons of the chest-carrier who had married, had in their youth made a search along the Lavaca River for the treasure. They had searched carefully on a low-lying salt marsh meadow. They had gone away without finding anything, but persons in the neighborhood had heard from them that they were seeking the protruding end of a brass rod among the marsh grass.

Years later, a ranchman named Hill bought the ranch which included the marshy flat, and pastured horses there. A Negro was hired to herd the horses. The Negro, wishing to sleep one afternoon, idled through the marsh grass, looking for a root, stump or stick that might serve as a stake to which to tie his horse. He stumbled upon the brass rod with the little socket for the compass at the top, and, assuming that this thing had been put there by some strange providence that looked after his needs, he tied his horse to it and slept.

Afterwards, the herder pulled up the rod and took it to the ranch house, remarking upon the strangeness of such prairie stakes.

The ranchman, recognizing this at once as the Jacob's staff of the well-known Lafitte legend, was wild with excitement. But, with all the aid the bewildered Negro could furnish, he never was able to find the spot on the flat from which the staff had been pulled. And the plain was much too large to dig over.

Wise and two companions, following this clue, spent five days "working" the salt marsh with an electrical metal locating machine, but got never a "bite."

I have had many letters from Texans living near the Lavaca and Neches rivers, about the Lafitte treasures believed to be buried there. Some claim to know approximately where the treasure lies. They merely need a little capital to prosecute the search, and are willing to divide fifty-fifty. Others want no partners, but are anxious to be placed in contact with the owner of a reliable treasure locating device. Still others are pretty sure that the treasure has been dug up and carried away.

There is scarcely an island from New Orleans to Beaumont that does not have its tale of Lafitte cannon that were loaded with money and then craftily tossed overboard or hidden ashore by the romantic pirate.

A Beaumont newspaper in 1929 published a casual "Forty Years Ago" item bearing upon the gold-bearing guns of Lafitte. It speaks of the finding of some Spanish guns at Virginia Point near Galveston, thought to be part of the armament of the Texas war schooner *Tom Toby*. The forty-years-old item quotes the

Galveston "Civilian" concerning a hurricane in 1818 which drove ashore on Virginia Point several vessels belonging to Jean Lafitte. It is stated that these ships were destroyed, and that they flew the flag of Carthagena. The item concludes: "The discovery also of a huge iron chest at the point where the guns were discovered would seem to give credence to the story that some years ago a great amount of Spanish coin was taken therefrom and the existence of the guns kept a profound secret in the hope that more treasure might be found. We are inclined to believe the guns are from Lafitte's fleet, rather than from the *Tom Toby*."

Is it possible, then, that some of those famous cannon of Lafitte's actually were found and unloaded of their golden charges, some time in the 1880's?

Seven cannon with plugged muzzles were reported found by fishermen who were digging on Cayo Largo, off Batabano, thirty miles from Havana, in June, 1929. The Custom House authority at Batabano at once impounded the guns, according to a news story of the day, claiming that any gold that might be found inside must be divided with the government under laws governing treasure trove. The fishermen admitted this, but claimed that the cannon were theirs, and that they should be permitted to sell them as junk without their being tampered with by officials. The weighty questions of law thus raised may take generations to decide. Meantime, the government agents at Batabano retain possession of the guns, with sealed muzzles. Real Lafitte fans will maintain that the romantic Pirate of the Gulf alone could have been responsible for this rich cache of richly loaded cannon.

There are many recorded instances of individuals who have made careers of hunting for the gold that Lafitte buried or carelessly tossed overside in gun barrels. One of the most persistent of these treasure-seekers was a New Orleans printer named Newell. He had a chart showing where the treasure was buried on a small island. The chart had been given to Newell's father by a sailor whom the elder Newell had befriended.

The printer saved his wages in miserly fashion, and eventually bought a fishing smack and some camping and digging equipment, and went out in search of the island. After weeks he returned to work, broke, tired, but not discouraged. He saved his money for twenty years more, meantime becoming a butt of jokes among the other printers. He drifted into pronounced eccentricity. Then, as old age began to close down upon him, he set forth again, and in the summer of 1871 his body was cast up on the beach after a hurricane.

◇ ◇

Gardiner's Island, of course, must be included in any cross-marked treasure trove map. It is a tract of about sixteen thousand acres, seven miles long by three and a half miles wide. It lies off the north shore of East Hampton Township, within the two-pronged fork formed by the eastern extremities of Long Island, New York.

Jonathan Gardiner is the present owner of the island. It was transferred to him in 1926 by Lion Gardiner, who retains a life interest in the property. The present owner holds the island in trust for Winthrop Gardiner Jr., nephew of Lion Gardiner.

Ownership of the island is quite important. Gardiner's Island was granted to Lion Gardiner, first English settler of New York, by the King of England, as a manor and lordship, in 1639. Gardiner had bought the island from the Indians. The property has remained in the Gardiner family ever since, not a square foot of its soil ever having been sold. So far as I have been able to learn, it is the only piece of land that has descended intact through a male line of descent from an American proprietor of such an early date.

Although it is a widespread and popular belief that there is treasure buried on Gardiner's Island, I fear the treasure hunter will be unable to dig there for a good many years to come. The whole island is under lease to Clarence H. Mackay, head of the Postal Telegraph Company and associated enterprises, and the lease runs until 1940. Mr. Mackay uses the tract as a game preserve and shooting ground for himself and his friends. The approaches are by sea, and Mr. Mackay's trusty game wardens and caretakers would not be long about the ejection of any treasure hunter.

In the days when pirates flourished, Gardiner's Island was an obvious place to stop and barter. It was the first station on the way to New York. I do not know how the Gardiners regarded the swaggering gentlemen with ear-rings and bright sashes who used to anchor in their bay, but it probably would have done them little good to object to their presence. The island is large, and if pirates bound for New York really wanted to hold out on their owners or shareholders in the city, there was plenty of room here to bury some of the loot before dropping anchor in the Hudson river. If a pirate rather expected a fight or feared a hanging in New York, it would be wise and prudent for him to bury here a little nest-egg and make one of those romantic maps for use in case he should survive the fight or the hanging. Not that there was much danger of the pirate's being hanged in New York for piracy so long as he played "square" with the proper officials. But cogs would slip in New York in those days, even as they slip in some large cities to-day.

Several cogs slipped in the machine in which Captain William Kidd found himself fatally enmeshed in June, 1699, as he approached New York in the sloop *Antonio*, and hove to off Gardiner's Island. He had been abroad more than three years on a privateering and pirate-chasing mission. He had been forced into the enterprise by Governor Bellamont of New York and Col. Robert Livingston, one of New York's most prominent capitalists. Four Lords of the British Parliament and King William himself were shareholders in the project. It was to have been a great money-making business for the shareholders. Kidd was selected to command the vessel that was to bring in the money for the King, the Lords, the Governor and the Prominent Citizens, because he was known as an experienced, capable and honest sea captain. He owned a ship which was then trading between New York and European ports, and, as a means of forcing him to take command of the grand enterprise, he was threatened with refusal of clearance papers for his own ship from the Port of New York unless he undertook this task.

The expedition had been unsuccessful. Kidd had taken a few prizes and had accumulated a few chests of treasure during his three years out. But his vessel, the *Adventure Galley,* had been so badly built that she had gone to pieces on him. His crew was such a rascally bunch of hang-dog riff-raff that it had deserted almost in a body. Most of the seamen Kidd was able to get were old-time pirates or were pirates at heart, and when Kidd refused to turn pirate they deserted to the pirate Culliford, who was anchored in a port in Madagascar visited by Kidd.

In an altercation with a mutinous seaman of his crew, Kidd had hit the trouble-maker over the head with a tar bucket and the sailor died a few days later.

Kidd had started for Boston, where he was to report to Lord Bellamont, in a prize ship, the *Quedagh Merchant,* and in the West Indies learned that he had been proclaimed a pirate and that there was a price on his head. He stopped at Mona Island, near Porto Rico, a treasure island mentioned in Chapter IV of this book. His crew dwindled to a mere handful, and he had to abandon the *Merchant* and make the rest of the voyage in the sloop, which he bought.

Now there is a possibility that Kidd may have hidden some of his treasure in one of those dismal caves on Mona Island. There is no record of such disposition of treasure by Kidd, and the possibility of his hiding valuables on Mona Island is a speculation of my own. Kidd knew that he was proclaimed a pirate, and expected serious trouble upon his arrival at New York or Boston. He had to abandon his *Quedagh Merchant* and transfer part of his cargo to the little sloop. It would have been prudent and clever in such circumstances to lay away enough of the loot in a convenient cave to provide for the emergency that seemed to loom so threateningly ahead.

This was just what Kidd did when he reached Gardiner's Island. Lord John Gardiner boarded the *Antonio* when she hove to in the bay. He was met by Captain Kidd, who was very polite to him, furnished him with many good drinks, and then entrusted to the Lord of the Manor two black boys and a black girl, to be kept for him until his return from Boston, whither he was bound to see Lord Bellamont. Gardiner consented and took the slaves ashore. Next day he went back to the sloop, and he and Kidd had more drinks and more good conversation. Kidd presented Gardiner with some Bengal muslin and some other muslin, a bag of sugar, some cloth of gold, and sundry other presents. Kidd bought of Gardiner a barrel of cider and some sheep. Then he committed to Gardiner's care a box of gold, a chest of treasure, a bundle of quilts, and three bales of goods. All of this merchandise, except perhaps the quilts and other dry goods, was buried about a mile from the manor house.

"If I call for it and it is gone," said Kidd to John Gardiner, "I will take your head or your son's."

Poor Captain Kidd! He never called for the goods or the treasure. He was apprehended at Boston, and sent back to London to be tried, because it was essential that he be hanged, and piracy was not a capital crime in New England at that time. Kidd was given a series of mock trials at Old Bailey, and was convicted of murder and piracy. The murder was the justifiable killing of the mutinous seaman, and the piracy was the capture, by a duly commissioned privateer, of two ships that carried French papers, France being at war with England at the time. Kidd was railroaded to the gallows to save the faces of Lord Bellamont, the four Lords in Parliament, and the King. Kidd was probably the only innocent man among them.

Kidd was hanged at Wapping on May 23, 1701. It is the irony of fate and fame that his name became a synonym for pirate, and for generations children were taught that Kidd was the wickedest of all pirates, who made innocent men and women walk the plank. In recent years scholars have turned up in the British Museum the documentary evidence of Kidd's innocence of piracy. The documents were withheld at the time of the trials by persons in high places who were interested in having Kidd hanged.

The legend of Kidd's buried treasure grew with surprising rapidity. It probably originated in the burial of the consignment of treasure on Gardiner's Island. All of this loot was dug up and duly delivered to Governor Bellamont by John Gardiner, acting under the direction of agents of the Governor, who attended to the details of the digging and appraisal in person. This was done while Kidd was held in jail in Boston, awaiting transportation to England.

The first diggers for Kidd's treasure probably confined their efforts to Gardiner's Island. But, as the Kidd myth grew, and children and old women quaked at the popular tales of this man's barbarity, the treasure legend grew. It fastened itself to certain localities. In two hundred years it had spread almost all over the earth.

A great deal of digging for "Kidd's gold" has been done along the coast of Maine, particularly in the neighborhood of Wiscasset. There are tales, generations old, of gold deposited by Captain Kidd in a cave on Deer Isle on the Maine coast. This treasure, according to a tale which has gained much credence among all classes of Americans, was the foundation of the Astor fortune. There is a document of fifteen pages, typewritten, entitled "A Notable Lawsuit," purporting to tell the history of this treasure and of the Astor fortune. This document has been widely circulated, although for what purpose I do not know. Nearly everyone who is even slightly interested in pirates and buried treasure has a copy.

The story is a good one, but of course Captain Kidd never buried or hid any treasure on the Maine coast.

Much digging for Kidd's gold has been done on Long Island, on the Massachusetts coast, in Rhode Island, and even in Nova Scotia. In fact, when treasure-seekers can't think of any other name for that which they seek, they call it Kidd's treasure. Despite the modern revelations about Kidd's harmless life and false conviction, they are still digging for Captain Kidd's gold.

◇ ◇

After all the treasures, found and unfound, have been measured by the yardstick of estimation and weighed in the balances of imagination, it may be that the greatest treasure of all is buried in the hills of Hamadan, in Persia. It is not known to outsiders just where the treasure lies, and I doubt that the secret is known to anyone. But there are persistent rumors, borne by

Armenian rug sellers and refugees from the wrath of the Turk, that portions of this great treasure of the Hamadan hills have been melted down and cast into golden statues for Christian churches, and that some of these holy images have found their way to the great world outside the ancient domain of Darius.

The most reliable historical data places the depository of this great treasure somewhere within a radius of fifty miles of the ancient town of Hamadan. If you go there to dig, you may go by way of Bagdad, which is easily accessible from European points by railway. The town of Hamadan is 250 miles in a direct line from Bagdad, but you don't go by direct line. You proceed through the rising hills by motor car, and perhaps it would be just as well to buy a couple of serviceable donkeys for the last lap of the trip. There is a fairly good road leading up to the town itself, nine thousand feet above sea level, but for exploration of the rough country round a donkey is a great help.

It was on October 1, 331 B.C., that the forces of Alexander the Great met and vanquished the armies of Darius. This was the decisive Battle of Arbela, near the site of ancient Ninevah, beside the Zab River. Darius himself got away, and fled eastward with miles of baggage trains. He encamped in and about the town of Ecbanta, which is now called Hamadan. He remained here about a year, always expecting the inevitable advance of Alexander. Darius knew that his time was up whenever Alexander's army appeared, for his defeat at Arbela had left him only his baggage trains and a small guard.

During that year of waiting, Darius disposed of his treasure. When Alexander finally did advance against Ecbanta, Darius fled a short distance with a few men. Alexander, reaching Ecbanta, ceased pursuing his enemy, and started a search for the treasure. He found the corpse of Darius.

Now as to the extent of the treasure, and how it happened to be in the pack trains of the Great King behind the field of battle at Arbela. Gold was looked upon by the people of that time and place as a divine substance. Gold not only represented superiority, as it still does in the minds of millions, but its possession actually imparted divinity and immortality, if one had sufficient quantities of it. Hence the emphasis upon gold in connection with the person of the King.

Whenever Darius traveled, the whole store of the royal gold accompanied him. It was a convenient fiction that the presence of the gold near the King's person was essential to preservation of the royal dignity and divinity. There were no banks of deposit in those days, and if the King went to war or to a wedding, there was no one with whom he could trust the state treasure. Mere hirelings could not be trusted to keep the politicians and statesmen away from the treasure, without the presence of the King to encourage them. So it was the universal rule that the gold followed the King.

Darius went to war, but he never got very far away from the gold. The precious metal was done up in small packages, and these into larger packages, and these were packed upon the backs of donkeys, or piled into carts. A picked guard of faithful and powerful horsemen accompanied the treasure, which occupied a position at night just outside the royal tent.

When the battle was quite likely to be lost, the royal money guard, instead of rushing to the front and saving the day, faced about and trotted off with the treasure, the King in the midst of it.

The Empire ruled over by Darius was one of the wealthiest bits of royal property the sun ever shone upon. When Cyrus took over the Empire of the Medes, he acquired thirty thousand pounds of gold—pure gold—with it. There was much gold plate, probably worth millions of dollars, besides. Cambyses guarded every grain of this gold, and added to it the treasures he got from Egypt. Darius was a tireless collector of gold. From twenty satrapies he exacted every ounce of precious metal that could be wrung from the people. Annually, each satrap, in order to hold his job and keep his head on his shoulders, sent a train of pack animals to the King, with the gold that had been demanded of him. So the royal treasure grew and never was lessened.

Miners worked the veins of gold in the Altai and the Urals, panning the sand from the streams and digging deep into the rocks. There were rich sources of gold at hand, and there was plenty of cheap labor to produce it. And nearly all of the gold eventually reached the coffers of Darius.

It was this great treasure that Alexander wanted when he moved his unwieldy army through the hills, seeking the person of Darius. When Alexander reached Ecbanta and learned that Darius had spent the year there and had disposed of the treasure, he no longer sought Darius. He sent men with picks and shovels far and wide into the hills, but he did not find the gold.

That treasure in the high hills of Hamadan has attracted many a gold-seeker since 331 B.C. The Greeks and Parthians sent armies to hunt for it. The Romans were marching through Asia in 190 B.C. Crassus was the richest and most astute capitalist in Rome. When talk of dividing the Empire arose, Crassus, who knew all about the buried treasure of Darius near Ecbanta, let Pompey take Italy and Cæsar take Gaul. All he wanted was the golden hills of Hamadan.

The fact that Crassus was a treasure-seeker became common gossip in Rome. The day that Crassus set out for the East, the Tribune Ateius Capito publicly called down the curses of many Roman and assorted Eastern gods upon the gold-hunter and his family. Capito preceded Crassus to the gate of exit, and there stood throwing incense upon a brazier and calling out his denunciations, bad wishes, excoriations and curses.

Crassus didn't get the gold. At the door of a temple in Asia, the son of Crassus stumbled and fell. The father stumbled over him. This double fumble in so royal a family was looked upon by the Asians as a sure sign that the curses of the Tribune were beginning to work.

Crassus, despite this bad beginning in Asia, set out at once for Ecbanta and the gold. At Carrhæ he was killed and molten gold was poured down his throat by the natives, who were furious because this foreigner had come seeking the treasure of Darius.

In 45 B.C. Cæsar planned an expedition to the East to seek the treasure. At this time Rome was in bad financial condition, and money must be had from some external source or bankruptcy must be faced.

Cassius, an old friend of the unfortunate Crassus, had been quæstor in the days before Crassus set out on his fatal search for the treasure under the curse of the Tribune of the People. Cassius was determined that Cæsar never should possess the gold that Crassus had failed to get. At least so say those historians who are inclined to connect much of the history of the world with this greatest of all treasures.

Cassius, as every reader of the oration of Marc Antony knows, headed the plot which culminated in the assassination of Cæsar on the Ides of March. Antony himself spent much of his life trying to reach the hills about Ecbanta. Straight through those forbidding mountains he drove toward the coveted treasure, and twenty-thousand of his men died on Armenian soil. In 33 B.C. he concentrated sixteen legions in Armenia, and time after time retired defeated from his attempts to storm the high passes.

Gaius and Germanicus headed later movements to recover the treasure of Darius, and both died in the land they sought to rob of its hidden gold.

Nero sent an expedition to get the treasure in 66 A.D. He had been told of a cave in the mountains near Ecbanta, filled almost to the roof with gold and shining jewels. Nero's men, led by Bassus, the Carthaginian who had told the tale of the golden cave, spent many days digging in the rocky soil at that high altitude. Bassus was the butt of ridicule at first, but as the days wore on and the golden glory was nowhere to be seen, he heard many a threat of what Nero would do to him when he was taken back to Rome after leading Nero's men on a wild goose chase. Bassus wisely committed suicide.

Nero had a great expedition to recover the treasure of Darius in mind, and had plans drawn in detail. He committed suicide as the expedition was just about to get under way.

Trajan diverted a river to locate the treasure, which his engineers thought might be hidden in a cave that had no entrance except under the water. The ambitious undertaking failed.

If the treasure of Darius ever is found, it may astound the

world. Thus far it seems to have been protected by the high mountains, the patriotic natives, who combat treasure-seekers, and, according to the credulous, the ancient curse that attaches to all buried treasure.

What lives have been blasted, what hopes blighted, what blood poured out, in two thousand years of seeking for that gold of Darius!

But that's the way with buried treasure.

IV. *Cross Marks the Spot*

B UT did anybody ever actually recover any lost, buried or
sunken treasure?

This question is often asked by someone in a group
that gathers to listen to tales of treasure and pirates. He wants
his answer before the tale-telling begins. He flings his question
with a challenging inflection. You infer that he expects an eva-
sive answer and isn't going to stand for it.

The answer, of course is yes. In this book you will read of

many authenticated cases of the recovery of treasure, and of recovery operations that are even now in progress in various parts
of the world. But, before we begin marking the map of the world
with crosses to show where the treasures lie, it may be well to
cite the case of William Phips.

The story of William Phips is part of American and British
history. His portrait, in stunning robes of state, is in every well-
considered History of Massachusetts, and his tomb in the Church
of St. Mary Woolnoth, London, is one of those florid extrava-
gances with which the sculptors of the seventeenth century delighted to honor the great departed.

The inscription:

> Near this place is interred the Body of Sir William Phips,
> knight; who in the year 1687, by his great industry, discovered
> among the rocks near the Banks of Bahama on the north side
> of Hispaniola a Spanish plate-ship which had been under water
> 44 years, out of which he took in gold and silver to the value
> of £300,000 sterling: and with a fidelity equal to his conduct,
> brought it all to London, where it was divided between him-
> self and the rest of the adventurers. For which great service he
> was knighted by his then Majesty, King James the 2nd, and
> at the request of the principal inhabitants of New England,
> he accepted of the Government of the Massachusetts, in which
> he continued up to the time of his death; and discharged his
> trust with that zeal for the interests of the country, and with
> so little regard to his own private advantage, that he justly
> gained the good esteem and affection of the greatest and best
> part of the inhabitants of that Colony.
>
> He died the 18th of February, 1694, and his lady, to per-
> petuate his memory, hath caused this monument to be erected.

There you have the kernel of the story. William Phips won
wealth, fame, knighthood, and the governorship of Massachusetts
Colony by fishing a shipload of Spanish treasure out of the
Caribbean sea. The records, besides the wordy epitaph, are extensive and reliable. The diary kept by Phips during his treasure-
fishing expedition is preserved in the British Museum. There is a
detailed biography of the Governor, written by no less a person-

A WARNING TO YOUNG SAILORS

age than the Reverend Cotton Mather, a personal friend of the fortunate Phips. Mather, of course, tries to make a saint of the rough and profane sea captain, but the student of New England history, knowing Mather's weaknesses, can strip off much of the pious verbiage and uncover much interesting truth about this famous treasure-seeker.

Phips was born in 1650, poor and obscure, one of twenty-six children of James Phips and his wife, nameless in history. James was a gunsmith; William, one of his youngest sons, was famous as the salvor of great treasure; but the woman was just the wife of James and the mother of twenty-six.

William obtained a job as a shipwright's apprentice near his home, on Montsweag Bay, Maine. The town of Wiscasset, known in our time as the place from which Donald MacMillan sets forth annually on his voyages to the polar regions, was the closest settlement. Having learned something about building a ship, and having served his apprenticeship, William went to Boston at the age of twenty-two, worked as a ship carpenter, learned to read and write, and married.

There are many incidents in the career of the young man, as related by Cotton Mather, that tend to illustrate his character, but without reciting them here, we may sum up by saying that William Phips, on the verge of his great adventure, was a fully developed man of the sea, having made many voyages to the West Indies and up and down the North American coast. He was very tall and broad and stout, of reddish complexion, a stubborn, persistent, ambitious, fearless mariner, with much talent for leadership.

He had been hearing about "the Spanish wrack-ships" in the waters about Hispaniola (now Haiti) in the West Indies. Fishing for silver ingots in the shallow water had long been a favorite occupation of fishermen, unemployed pirates, and others of a romantic and adventurous nature. Phips was one of those young men whose earliest resolution was to become rich. From what he heard on his Caribbean voyages, there was a great opportunity for youth, persistence and hard work on some of those treasure-hunting expeditions.

About forty years earlier, a Spanish plate fleet, said to have consisted of sixteen vessels, had been wrecked in a terrific storm. Most of the ships had gone to pieces on the reefs at the Southern extremity of the Bahama Islands. The water was so shallow that naked divers, working from shallops and canoes, had recovered small fortunes from the wrecks.

In 1681 Phips made his first voyage in search of treasure. He did not succeed in locating a galleon's hulk, but he did pick up enough scattered ingots and coins to finance a voyage to England, whither he went with a great treasure story and a persuasive promotion talk.

After a year of wire-pulling, Phips reached the royal ear. King Charles II liked the glowing tale of piled-up silver bars, and turned over to Phips a frigate of the navy, the *Rose*, with eighteen guns to fight off pirates and a crew of 95 ruffians who classed as seamen. The King, of course, was to get a big share of the treasure.

Phips called at Boston to ship supplies, and he and his drunken sailors had the town in a turmoil for some days. Arraigned with some of his hoodlums before a Boston magistrate, Captain Phips stormed and cursed the court, and was heavily fined.

For several weeks the *Rose* and another treasure-hunting ship, the *Good Intent*, fished among the shoals for the Spanish treasure. When nothing was found, a mutiny blazed up, and Phips put it down with stern measures. While the bottom of the *Rose* was being cleaned at a neighboring island, another mutiny nearly ended the expedition. Phips, by quick strategy, managed to get the mutineers all in front of the muzzles of the loaded guns of the frigate, on an island beach, and bade them adieu. They begged to be taken aboard. Phips took them on, discharged them at Jamaica, and shipped another crew of roustabouts and ex-pirates.

Sailing again for the treasure shoals, Phips anchored off Tortuga and began an intensive campaign of information seeking. From an old Spaniard he obtained many seemingly reliable tips.

He sailed back to London with no silver, but with some charts that were decorated with sundry crosses.

King Charles had died. King James II took the frigate away from the treasureless treasure-seeker. Phips went about with his maps and charts and mysterious cross-marks and made quite a nuisance of himself, trying to force his way into the presence of every wealthy and powerful man of whom he heard. He got into jail and out again, and at length succeeded in obtaining financial support from the Duke of Albemarle and some of the Duke's friends. The terms dictated by the backers were almost as hard on the adventurer as the terms dictated by some modern backers of trans-oceanic flights. Phips was to receive only one-sixteenth of the treasure found, and the crew was to be paid wages only.

So Captain Phips set out in 1686 with the *James and Mary,* merchantman, and a tender.

When the expedition had been long on the spot marked by one of the most prominent crosses on the chart, a big silver bar, heavily encrusted with coral and sand, was brought to the surface by a native diver, and the harvest began. Phips had found one of the treasure ships.

The hold of the ship was down about forty feet, but easy of access. For a month or more the divers sent up pigs of silver, baskets of coins, and chunks of coral and sand which were broken up and proved precious cases for masses of gold and silver coins.

When provisions ran short and Phips began to note signs of a brewing mutiny, the *James and Mary* headed for London with thirty-two tons of silver and gold aboard. To stave off the mutiny, Phips promised the men bonuses, and he was able to make good his promise, for his proprietors were stunned into comparative generosity by the size of the silver cargo he brought home to them.

The fortune that fell to Phips in the division of the spoils was about eighty or ninety thousand dollars. That was a great fortune in those days. The story of the treasure ship spread rapidly over England, and Phips was the hero of the day. He was knighted by the King, and sent back to America as High Sheriff of Massachusetts.

He built a great brick house in Boston, and managed his difficult job with much skill. Returning to England, he spent some time with King William III, and was sent back to Massachusetts with a new charter and a commission as the first Governor of the colony. While he was out fighting a war, the Massachusetts conscience went on a rampage, and the Governor returned to find Salem and vicinity in the throes of the witchcraft mania. Phips put a stop to it by dissolving the court that was handing out sentences of death to helpless men and women.

Sir William Phips had many claims to fame. But it was the story of the Spanish treasure that they carved upon his monument.

◇ ◇

During all his years of statecraft, Sir William Phips longed to go back to treasure-hunting. He often expressed a desire to go down to the Caribbean and find the greatest treasure of them all—the golden table of Bobadilla.

Bobadilla was the Spaniard who was sent out to Hispaniola to displace Columbus and his brothers in the government of the New World, and who achieved an unenviable immortality by putting the great discoverer in irons. Bobadilla, who was a pompous, ostentatious, officious and dull-witted grandee, arrived on his new job while Columbus was in the interior of the island, settling some difficulty with the natives. As soon as the discoverer of the New World appeared, Bobadilla announced that he was now Governor, and showed his warrant of authority from the King and Queen of Spain. He then ordered the sixty-six-years-old Admiral ironed, and had much difficulty getting anybody to do the dirty work of riveting on the fetters. Columbus was sent back to Spain thus, a prisoner in chains. All Spain was indignant, and the King ordered the aged explorer set free. Columbus was summoned to court, and Queen Isabella wept when she saw him, in commiseration for his sufferings.

Columbus was sent back to the New World in charge of another expedition of discovery. It was his fourth and last voyage to the world he had opened up to Europe.

Arrived off Hispaniola on June 29, 1502, Columbus sent word to the Governor that his fleet needed repairs, and that a storm was brewing. He was refused permission to land.

Bobadilla had been summoned back to Spain to give an account of his stewardship. His fleet was even then about to weigh anchor. Columbus sent back a message, begging that the fleet then about to sail delay weighing for a few days, as a hurricane was surely coming.

Bobadilla vouchsafed no answer, but gave orders to hoist sail and put to sea. Columbus, confident that the storm was coming and would be a terrible one, hugged the shore with his little fleet, as he beat down the coast.

Now, Bobadilla expected to be called severely to account for his misdeeds during his term of office, not the least of which was his shameful treatment of Columbus. So he had spent the two years of his rule gathering gold, which he knew to be the great softener of royal anger. According to some accounts he had had all this gold cast into one piece, in the form of a table, which he planned to present with a great flourish to the King and Queen as soon as he should arrive in Spain. Could Their Majesties speak very harshly to him across that golden board? Bobadilla thought not.

So he set out, and two days after Columbus gave the warning, the hurricane struck, disorganizing Bobadilla's fine fleet and wrecking the ship that bore Bobadilla and the golden table. Bobadilla was saved, and the table, worse luck, was lost overboard.

According to Peter Martyr, whose work was known to and quoted by Sir William Phips, the golden table weighed 3,310 pounds. Mather, who doubtless spent many a long evening talking about this treasure with the Governor, had the impression that Phips knew just where to look for the precious table and planned to go and get it as soon as his days of office-holding were over. He died with the plan still unrealized, and if he left any chart showing the location of the table of Bobadilla, the chart is not known to exist to-day.

The inhabitants of County Cork, Ireland, have a saying, "Cows far away have long horns."

There are cows in one's own back yard, often enough, that are just as interesting and just as full of character and rich milk as any cows anywhere. But one is forever hearing about cows far away that are much more wonderful. Oh, they are cows indeed, those cows of Connaught and of Kansas, with their fine, long horns and their golden milk! What would one not give to behold them, and to be able ever after to boast about the cows far away with long horns!

It is so with buried treasure, and with most other mysterious things.

Buried treasure, in order to be worth going after, must be buried good and deep. Preferably, it must be far away, where the cows may be presumed to have long horns. It should lie in some tropical place, with palms and fronds and flying fish all thick and extravagant, like a Max Reinhardt setting.

And above all, there *must* be a wrinkled old map bearing, in some heathen script, these words:

CROSS MARKS THE SPOT WHERE THE TREASURE LIES.

Then, of course, there must be several crosses, with bearings indecipherably set down.

◇ ◇

For a really far-away treasure hunt, I recommend a jaunt to the islands of Tristan da Cunha, in the South Atlantic, where the cows, if there were any, should have horns as long as a treasure tale. If there is any more lonely spot than this on the face of the globe, I cannot think where it lies, unless it be Madison Square on a blowy night in January.

There are three islands in the group, the largest, Tristan, having an area of sixteen square miles. Inaccessible Island, twenty miles west of Tristan, is about the most aptly named island in the world, but is not otherwise notable. Nightingale Island, a mile square, is the smallest of the group, and is supposed to be the chief treasure depository.

There are at present 157 inhabitants, subjects of the King of England. There are no locks, money or firearms on the island, and none of the natives has ever seen a bicycle, automobile, telephone or other modern machine.

Tristan da Cunha is so far from trade routes that ships touch there only about once a year. Sometimes there is a missionary from the outside world, sent by some congregation that has much zeal and imagination. But the arrival of a stranger as a permanent resident would create a sensation on the island that might not die down for years. There is much inter-marriage, but the present generation seems as healthy and mentally alert as the natives of other islands in the South Atlantic.

The Tristan da Cunha group is almost halfway between Africa and South America, just a little nearer to Cape Town than to Buenos Aires. It is advisable to travel in your own yacht when you go there to dig for pirate loot. It might be well to take your own workers along too, and certainly your own supplies of food, medicines, machinery and tools.

Nobody lives on the square mile of volcanic rock called Nightingale Island, so you may disembark there, set up your camp, and dig and blast away to your heart's content, without greatly offending anybody. Even the whales have moved away from the neighborhood. They used to be numerous in those waters, and American whalers used to frequent the islands for supplies and land exercise. But for the last forty years the whales have ceased to list Tristan da Cunha as a winter resort, and latterly they haven't even regarded it as a blowing station. You might be lonesome on Nightingale or Inaccessible.

There are several large caves on Nightingale Island. Geologists say these caves, now well above sea level, were dug into the rock by the ocean waves, before the island was thrust up to its present height above the sea.

In the caves the treasure is said to be buried.

Who buried it? Dampier, Cavendish, and a party separated from one of Drake's expeditions are given chief credit for depositing the gold, in the accounts that have persisted through many generations of whalers.

When Francis Drake (not yet ennobled) went a-pirating around the world, he had a ship which has become a symbol of dashing adventure for generations of men. She was called the *Pelican* at setting out, but just before entering the Straits of Magellan, Drake changed her name to the *Golden Hind,* in honor of his English patron, Christopher Hatton, whose crest bore the figure of a gilded hind, running.

At various times during the long voyage, Drake had other ships in his fleet, although he finally reached port in England, after circumnavigating the globe, with the *Golden Hind* only. She was, let us not forget to add, well down in the water with her heavy load of gold and silver taken from Spaniards and Portuguese on land and sea. England was not at war with Spain or Portugal at this time, but Drake was not one to stand upon forms when there was rich booty to be won.

On the night of September 30, 1578, Drake, with three vessels, the *Golden Hind, Elizabeth,* and *Marigold,* had completed the stormy passage of the Straits, and the Pacific Ocean was before him. That night a terrible storm came roaring out of the south, cold, sleety, and ravenous for this dainty prey of three small English ships.

Next morning the *Marigold* was missing. She was a bark of thirty tons burden, mounting sixteen guns, and carrying a crew of about twenty, under Captain John Thomas.

History knows nothing more of the *Marigold* forever. So far as there is any record, she never returned to a European port. It is easy to conclude that she was swallowed up in the storm.

The wind and sleet in the Pacific continued. It blew for a month so hard that many of the most stout-hearted of these sailormen of Drake's were convinced that God was determined to put a stop to the plundering expedition then and there.

During the days immediately following the loss of the *Marigold,* the *Elizabeth* also parted company with the *Golden Hind.* Drake waited three weeks for her at the rendezvous that had been appointed for the vessels in case of separation in storm, and then proceeded sadly up the coast without either of his companion ships.

Now, the *Elizabeth* did not disappear forever. She was a stout vessel of eighty tons and sixteen guns, in command of Captain John Winter, with a crew of about sixty men. She sailed into the port of Ilfracombe, Devonshire, on June 2, 1579, nearly a year and a half ahead of the *Golden Hind* and Drake.

There is no room for reasonable doubt about the action of the *Elizabeth*. She deserted. According to John Drake, a nephew of the leader of the circumnavigating expedition, Captain Winter was imprisoned for this desertion, after Drake returned to England, and would have been hanged but for the intercession of Sir Francis.

Some of the most astute historians of the Drake expedition are far from convinced that the *Marigold* was lost in the storm. There are reasons for believing that she deserted, as did the *Elizabeth*, under cover of the confusion.

To go into the reasons for the desertion would take us far afield. But we cannot wholly ignore the incident of the execution of Thomas Doughty.

Just before entering the Straits, Drake had ordered the beheading of this Doughty, one of the gentlemen adventurers who had accompanied the expedition from England. The execution was considered a political move by many of the well-informed adventurers, and is still so considered by some impartial historians. The so-called "trial" of Doughty had many of the characteristics of a farce. The sentence of death, pronounced by Drake, was a great shock to many, including Captain Winter.

The iron will and forceful manner of Drake were stern obstacles to any who might wish to protest this high-handed procedure. But Winter knew what he could do about it. In the first good storm, he could, and did, turn about and make for England. He would sail no more with this man.

Now, the *Marigold* may have foundered. But the tradition of the South Atlantic whalers says that she did not. Instead, she went a-pirating on her own, and, in the course of much beating about upon a very big ocean, the little bark laid a course for African waters. Thus she came upon Tristan da Cunha, the tiny group of volcanic islands in mid-Atlantic. Her small crew settled down here for rest and recuperation, and in one or more of the caves of Nightingale Island they put away their handsome nest-egg of Spanish doubloons and pieces of eight. Later, some women were picked up here and there and brought to the largest of the islands, and a little settlement was started.

The settlement has never grown very large. There has always been a shortage of women. Once in a while one or two or three men, dissatisfied with bachelorhood in this lonely place, have gone aboard passing ships as hands, and have never returned. In 1885, fifteen men were drowned when a boat was swamped in a storm, and the proper balance of the sexes was nearly restored.

The tale I have told in accounting for the treasure at Tristan da Cunha is not verifiable as a whole, and, obviously, it cannot be disproved either. The stories of Cavendish and Dampier, who followed Drake in piratical voyages around the end of South America and into the Pacific, are romantic and stimulating. They lend themselves quite readily to the Tristan da Cunha treasure tradition, furnishing interludes not greatly dissimilar to the incidents of the *Elizabeth* and the *Marigold*.

The amount of treasure to be had at this lonely outpost of the South Atlantic is indeed speculative. But I have had hurry-up calls from my stockbroker concerning what he called investments that related to ventures no less speculative, and not one-tenth as appealing to the imagination.

◇ ◇

Block Island, a popular summer resort which is part of the state of Rhode Island, deserves a cross on any treasure-hunter's map.

It is midway between Montauk Point, Long Island, and Point Judith, Rhode Island, and is served by regular passenger ships, with frequent crossings during the summer season and less frequent service in winter. The island is eight miles long, and from two to five miles wide.

There is much good, romantic history connected with Block Island, beginning with the definite discovery of the place by

Adriaen Block in 1614. A settlement was established on the island in 1662. French privateers captured the whole island in 1689, and made it a base for operations on the Atlantic coast. Some of the treasure tales which still keep diggers busy along the sandy shores of the island are connected with these privateers. It seems not at all improbable that they may have buried some of their loot on Block Island. Again we must remember that there were neither banks nor safe deposit vaults available for the safe-keeping of such loot as the corsairs accumulated during their intensive raiding cruises, and burial in the earth was the obvious resort of pirates and privateers.

Joe Bradish was a pirate who made life a little livelier and a little shorter for a good many New England mariners in the last years of the seventeenth century. He was a native of Cambridge, Mass., and was reared as a fisherman and casual sailorman in New England waters.

He shipped as boatswain's mate aboard the hake-boat *Adventure* in London, in 1698. The *Adventure,* commanded by Captain Thomas Gulleck, mounted twenty guns for protection against pirates. She set out on a voyage to Borneo.

When the *Adventure* put in at a little cove in the East Indies for wood and water, Captain Gulleck and his chief officers, together with some of the men, selected as burden-bearers, went ashore on the little island of Polonais to hunt. Twenty-five men were left aboard, in charge of the boatswain's mate.

Bradish was highly elated to have temporary command of an entire ship. He talked about his importance with some of his men. A scheme was concocted whereby Bradish might become captain in fact. Common sailors might be elevated to important positions. The discussion set the Cambridge youth's head awhirl.

That night the cable was cut, and the *Adventure* put to sea. Captain Joseph Bradish, erstwhile boatswain's mate, was in command, and a fine pennant with a death's head on it was being made up by two sailors who were handy with the needle.

The first ship looted by the new pirates was the *Adventure.* They found in their own breadroom nine chests of Spanish dollars, and when the sharing was completed each common seaman had fifteen hundred of these coins, while Captain Bradish's share was nearly four thousand dollars. The fine broadcloths that made up much of the cargo were shared all around also, and the crew soon appeared at stations, dressed handsomely in broadcloth with trimmings of highly colored stuffs.

Captain Bradish never fought any hard battles. He captured prizes that offered no resistance. He wasted no money or men fighting useless battles. He hoarded his gold and jewels in canvas bags and chests near his bunk. Odd times, he sat on the floor and counted his money, or held his precious stones up to the light and gazed greedily upon them. Here and there, around the world, Bradish accumulated a goodly store of gems.

The *Adventure* stood off the eastern end of Long Island, New York, on March 19, 1699. Captain Bradish put off in the long-boat with several bags of jewels and a chest of money. He landed somewhere on or near Montauk Point. What he did with his treasure is not recorded, but he certainly put it away. Maybe some of those glistening jewels are still buried out on Montauk Point. So far as I know, there has been little or no search for them.

Captain Bradish sent off a pilot with directions to bring the *Adventure* around to Gardiner's Island which was a favorite refuge for pirates making the port of New York in those days. There was nearly always somebody on Gardiner's Island who would lend a hand to get stolen merchandise changed into ready cash.

The wind was contrary, however, and the pilot did not succeed in making the harbor. Bradish went back to the ship, after a day or two ashore, and made for Block Island.

Bradish sent two men over to the Rhode Island mainland to buy a sloop. The *Adventure* was becoming unseaworthy. Usually pirates were safe in Rhode Island, the officials and inhabitants there having made great profit by protecting and trading with sea-robbers. But these two were in ill luck. Perhaps they neglected to approach the right persons in the proper manner. Anyway, they were seized, charged with piracy, and jailed at Newport.

Captain Bradish removed more valuables ashore on Block Island, and is said to have buried them for fear of capture of the

Adventure by the governor's people. He went ashore himself, and prepared to defend Block Island against an attacking force, if that should be necessary.

Bradish now held a council of peace, and advised his men that the time was at hand for them to break up their pirate company and depart their several ways to peaceful occupations and enjoyment of their loot.

Two of the members of Bradish's crew decided to go pirating on their own. They bought two sloops that chanced to be passing Block Island, and sailed away. They transported Bradish and the others who elected land careers to various points along the Long Island coast. The pirates left the sloops by twos and threes, with their loot in gold and jewels in bags slung over their shoulders. At the little farms along the shore they bought horses, and most of them made their way on horseback to inland places, where they settled down to prosperous and apparently virtuous living.

The *Adventure* was sunk off Block Island before the pirates departed.

Captain Bradish went ashore on Long Island, with several helpers to carry his bags and chests. He went at once to the home of his old friend, Lieutenant Colonel Henry Pierson, member of the Assembly and close personal friend of Lord Bellamont, governor of New York. A quantity of money and jewels was left with Pierson, who came near getting into serious trouble as a result of his friendly relations with this pirate.

Bradish had news that his former shipmates were being picked up here and there for piracy. They had had too much wealth, and too little sense in the handling of it. They had made themselves conspicuous by their spending, and while in their cups had boasted in taverns of their successful piracies.

Ten of the Bradish pirates were seized at New London, upon orders of the governor of Connecticut. They had some eighteen hundred pounds of British money left when taken. Two or three were taken in Rhode Island, and they were made to confess where some of the treasure was hidden, and this was recovered by the authorities. Finally, Lord Bellamont, who was the bitter enemy of all pirates who would not share their spoils with him, captured three of Bradish's men in New York. These three not only gave up what money they had, but told about the treasure they had helped to carry to the home of Assemblyman Pierson.

Bellamont sent for Pierson, who came, full of explanations, and carrying one fat canvas bag, which contained some money and a great many jewels. These, upon expert appraisal, turned out to be imitation stones! Pierson, although in present danger of royal displeasure, did not produce the real treasure, unless he did so secretly, and with only unofficial knowledge of My Lord Bellamont.

Bradish was traced to Boston. There he was arrested and imprisoned in the stone jail.

Now, it chanced that Lady Luck, who loved a good pirate always, arranged that the keeper of this jail was honest Caleb Ray, a close relative of Bradish's. Nothing was said about this relationship at the time, but much was said later.

Bradish remained in his kinsman's keeping for two months, awaiting transportation to England for trial. He was not kept in irons, as was poor Captain Kidd. He was waited upon by his one-eyed personal servant, Tee Weatherly, who had been with him all through his pirating.

One fine morning in June the jail door was found wide open. Bradish and his bodyguard had departed.

Governor Bellamont made a terrible uproar about this escape of the pirates from the Boston jail. He was becoming a crusader against pirates, and was at this very time engaged in plotting to send Captain Kidd to his death in England to save his own face. He offered a reward of two hundred pieces of eight for the capture of Bradish.

An Indian sachem won the two hundred pieces of eight, and a hundred more for Weatherly. He betrayed both of the pirates, who had accepted Indian hospitality in the interior. In the autumn both pirates were again in the stone jail in Boston, with a new jailer over them.

Bradish and his accomplice were chained this time. Nevertheless, they managed to get their chains off twice, and once they

had nearly dug their way out of the prison when they were apprehended.

The British man-of-war *Advice* was sent to Boston for the
express purpose of conveying Bradish, Captain Kidd, and other
pirates, to London for trial. They were all tried about the same
time.

Bradish was found guilty of piracy in a speedy trial, and was
hanged in chains at Hope Dock, London, early in 1700. The
body was kept swinging there as long as there was any of it left
as an example to ambitious young seafaring men, and many a
rousing sermon was preached about it in the wordy pulpits of
the patient London of that day.

The story of Bradish's burying a considerable treasure on
Block Island was current during the time of the pirate's incar-
ceration and trial. It has persisted until to-day. A map with a
proper cross marking the burial place of the treasure is said to
have been left by Bradish to one of his accomplices who escaped
capture. This map-owner never returned in person to the island,
having died in England, whither he went to testify for his former
chief, according to the story.

Almost any summer, you can find men digging in the sand
dunes along the shore, wherever digging isn't too difficult.

If you can get the proper map with the cross-mark on it, there
should be much sport in exploring Block Island with a steam-
shovel.

◇ ◇

The submarine treasure field is as long and as broad as the
vast expanse of ocean itself. Hardly a ship or a scow goes to the
bottom without carrying something of value. And vessels have
been sinking beneath the water since long before the dawn of
history.

It is estimated by well-informed salvage engineers that the
tonnage that goes to the bottom every twenty-five years amounts
approximately to the total of all shipping on the seas in any given
year. In other words, the ships that will be lost or otherwise

removed from service during the next twenty-five years will equal in number all the vessels on the seas to-day.

Many ships are taken out of commission and broken up. But most things that float eventually go to the bottom. Davy Jones's locker is by all odds the richest treasure chest in the world. It covers seven-tenths of the earth's surface, and it has been receiving man's floating hopes and treasures, from the dugouts of the earliest sea-venturing savages to the noble liners that have gone down with lights and music or have been sunk by mines and torpedoes in war.

The harbor of Matanzas, Cuba, is said to be a fairly rich savings deposit vault, and thus far it has kept its hoard as safely as the most meticulous banking commissioner could require. In 1628 Admiral Peter Heyn, with a Dutch fleet of twenty-four well-armed ships, intercepted the Spanish plate fleet that was proceeding from America to Spain with the year's winnings from the American mines.

Fifteen of the Spanish vessels, including four large galleons, were chased into Matanzas harbor. The Spaniards knew they were beaten, and began throwing silver overboard. When gunfire from the pursuing Dutchmen became too hot for the treasure heavers, several of the great ships were set afire and scuttled. The crews swam ashore.

Despite conscientious efforts of the Spaniards to put all their bullion into the highly reputable locker of Davy Jones, Admiral Heyn sailed home to Holland with loot from that fleet that brought four million ducats into the Royal Dutch Treasury. That would be approximately nine million American dollars to-day.

How many millions lie at the bottom of Matanzas Harbor? One can only guess, but when you map your treasure hunt, you had better put a cross at Matanzas to mark the treasure that Peter Heyn did not get.

◇ ◇

Make a good, black cross also at the harbor of Quillebeuf, France. Quillebeuf is a small town, and very old. It is within easy reach of thousands of Americans who land at Havre every summer. Havre, you will remember, is a seaport at the mouth of the Seine, on the north bank of the estuary, and just inside the outermost cape. Go up the estuary twenty miles, and on the south shore, at the apex of a little promontory, you will find Quillebeuf.

There, under much sand and silt, lies the wreck of the *Télémaque*, and has lain since January, 1790.

Louis the Sixteenth of France was not nearly as dumb as antiroyalists of all countries would have one believe. When he felt his throne tottering, he began to prepare for what he conceived to be the worst possible fate—exile. He issued orders for the gathering of sufficient treasure to keep himself and his court for fifty years in a foreign land in the style to which they had become accustomed.

The man-of-war *Télémaque* was designated to carry the royal loot to a secret destination in a foreign country. No records extant give any definite idea of her port of destination. But whatever the port, she never reached it.

From the state treasury was taken all the gold and silver that could be levied upon for this most righteous purpose. Two wealthy abbeys were stripped of all specie, ornaments, and reserve treasure of every sort. Furniture and fittings of utmost royal dignity were requisitioned from palaces and monasteries. The *Télémaque* was well laden with everything that a royal court could desire during a long and prosperous prospective sojourn in exile. But as there was no accounting by Louis, no records were made of the loot loaded upon the ill-fated man-of-war.

The *Télémaque* sailed under sealed orders on the night of January 1, 1790. Three days later she went down with all hands, just off Quillebeuf.

Those were troubled times, and it was generally agreed that it would be most discreet to forget about the *Télémaque* and her unfortunate crew as soon as possible. There were other things to think about, such as the nature of the disaster that to-morrow might bring forth.

Sand rapidly drifted over the wreck. Amateur efforts to recover the treasure were made by fishermen and other mariners, but with slight success. Fifty years later, an engineer of Havre formed a company, and obtained authority to raise the wreck. The authority was good, but the engineering was only fair. Timbers, guns, and a few coins were recovered. Then the operation was abandoned for lack of funds.

The location of the wreck of the *Télémaque* is fairly certain and exact. Doubtless, permission to proceed with the salvage could be obtained from the French government without much difficulty. This is a fair project for a sporting salvor who won't feel badly hurt if he doesn't win.

◇ ◇

A very small cross should be made on Mona Island, about midway between Haiti and Porto Rico. Small, because the island is not more than seven miles from sea to sea at the widest point, and two miles wide where it narrows. There are about ten thousand acres in the island, but you won't have to turn it all over with steam shovels in search of the treasure.

Mona belongs to the United States and to Porto Rico. It stands in the middle of Mona Passage. It is apparently especially designed for the convenience of pirates wishing to lay up treasures for themselves upon earth. There are so many beautiful caves in the three distinct strata of rock that have been thrust up from the ocean's floor in times long past that no one has ever counted them all.

Some of these caves are high and dry; others are very close to the water. Several are weirdly lighted by a greenish phosphorescent glow that seems to come from the remoter cracks in the rocks. One of these mysterious caves is called Pirates' Cavern, and once you visit it alone at night, you can never doubt that dire deeds have been done there for gold. Stalagmites and stalactites stand all about in eerie grace, with green moss pendant from their arches.

The cavern is large with low passages that invite exploration. When you have advanced well into the interior, you may stop and listen, and you will hear a faint stirring, as of swiftly flowing water far away.

According to a tradition long current in the West Indies, Captain Jennings secreted his treasure in this cavern. To find it, they say, you must go back and below, down many winding passages, until you come to a place where a dark stream runs over a sort of natural culvert, leaving a dry grotto beneath.

Although many adventurous souls have searched the cavern, no one has made the slightest claim to having explored all its depths and labyrinthine passageways.

Captain Jennings won much loot; of that there is indisputable historical evidence. He was a Welshman, and rich in his own right. He went pirating for some reason that never was clear to his friends. Perhaps he did it, as did the notorious Stede Bonnet, to get even with a scolding wife.

When the Spanish plate fleet of 1714 was wrecked by a hurricane in the Gulf of Florida, salvage operations were undertaken by the Spanish authorities. As most of the vessels went aground in shallow water, the salvaging was done chiefly by divers without any special equipment.

Jennings had just outfitted a luxurious pirate sloop, and was looking for game. He heard of the salvaging operations in the Gulf, and steered thither from his home port in Jamaica.

He found 350,000 pieces of eight, all neatly piled on the banks, near the wrecks. The silver was waiting for a Spanish ship to take it to Havana. Jennings loaded it aboard his vessel, and sailed away.

This hoard, according to the story, was put away in a phosphorescent cavern on Mona island. Jennings, almost immediately afterward, took sixty thousand pieces of eight from a Spanish ship that was on her way to Havana, but the accounts handed down to us are not specific as to whether this pretty hoard was added to that already laid down in the cave. The Spanish ship that had been plundered followed Jennings to Jamaica, and her master made complaint against the pirate. However, the Governor of Jamaica was not unfriendly to pirates who behaved themselves and spent money freely in his domain, and Jennings was allowed to depart with his stolen cargo. It seems quite probable that he put his load of silver in the safe deposit vault below the whispering river of Mona Island.

Jennings reformed late in life, accepted the King's most gracious pardon, and lived happily ever after. But he was always closely watched by his neighbors and associates, and it is related that he never was able to go back to his treasure vault in his old age and carry away his loot.

V. *The Land of Spanish Gold*

PORTO BELLO, Panama, Carthagena, Nombre de Dios, Lima—these are place names that glitter with romance. So long have they been associated in the human mind with high adventure, golden galleons, painted sails, pieces of eight and yellow doubloons that the very sound of the names stirs in most imaginations vague memory-pictures of things we all might do if we didn't have to report for work in the morning.

The pirates, buccaneers, filibusters and sea-rovers under many names and flags, took rich booty from these romantic towns and from the country surrounding them. But I venture to say that there is more treasure still to be had in the Land of Spanish Gold than ever was carried off by the corsairs who preyed upon the towns and fleets of the Spanish Main.

The years between the discovery of America and the defeat of the Invincible Armada constituted a golden age for Spain. The years are indicated roughly by the two events mentioned. The great current of gold did not set Spain-ward from the New World, of course, until a few years after the first voyage of Columbus, but it was fairly beginning before the death of the Discoverer, in 1506. The plate fleets did not cease to drop anchor in the harbors of Cadiz, Vigo, Santander, Corunna and San Sebastian when the Armada came to grief in 1588, but that incident gave the corsairs and pirates increased confidence in their ability to take the treasure away from the crippled mistress of the western world, and it marked, as nearly as outstanding events in history can mark eras, the decline of the power of Spain.

That power was founded upon the gold of the New World. Spain herself was poor in natural resources, as she is to-day. High, mountainous, rocky, with vast stretches of wilderness unfit even for the grazing of sheep, Spain, in those golden days, sat on her proud peninsula and ruled the world in a more practical manner than Rome ever did in the height of her power.

The amount of gold and silver taken from the American mines and from the accumulated hoards of the primitive Americans during that age of Spanish power can never be estimated in terms of dollars or pounds sterling. No one ever will know how many shiploads of treasure reached the home ports or how many galleons, freighted with fabulous wealth, still lie on the ocean's floor. It is impossible to estimate how many such ships were captured from the Spaniards by pirates and privateers. And no adequate estimate has ever been made of the tons of gold and silver taken from the towns of the Spanish Main by the buccaneers and filibusters in their numberless raids.

The very fact that Spain had the gold and silver seemed to justify the robbers in their own minds and in the minds of most

TELL WHERE THE TREASURE IS!

of their countrymen. Sovereigns of countries at peace with Spain were not always averse to sharing in the loot taken by pirates of their own nationality. Preying upon the plate fleets of Spain was not looked upon by the general public in England, France and Holland as critically as Americans now look upon the business of bootlegging liquor into Americans ports.

◇ ◇

Perhaps the most notorious of all the buccaneers was Henry Morgan. He is called a buccaneer largely by courtesy, because that sounds a little more respectable than pirate. Henry Morgan has been much idealized in adventure books for boys and adults. He was whitewashed and elevated to a place of political power in his lifetime, and knighted by a British sovereign. The fact that he is called Sir Henry alone clears his name of all taint of criminality in the eyes of thousands of readers who are impressed by titles.

Henry Morgan was a particularly ruthless pirate, cruel, perfidious, ungallant, unprincipled, faithless, traitorous, unscrupulous. He was a villain without mercy, a robber without remorse.

But he was brave, and his courage had that dashing quality that characterizes so many popular heroes. He seldom fought against odds, usually having overwhelming numbers and the best armament on his side. But when faced by odds, he did not shrink. He had that ingenious quality of generalship which distinguished that other famous hero-pirate, Sir Francis Drake. If there was a wall in front of him, Henry Morgan could devise ways to get over, under or around it.

Practically all available histories of Morgan's life and piracies are by friendly hands. Most of them were written during the lifetime of Morgan, while he was enjoying his honors and spoils, or soon after his death. But even in the most fulsome of these efforts to build up a world hero there is discernible to the careful reader the true character of the noted freebooter.

Captain James Burney, of the Royal Navy, writing in the early years of the nineteenth century, well said:

"All the buccaneer histories that have hitherto appeared, and the number is not small, are boastful compositions, which have delighted in exaggeration: and, what is most mischievous, they have lavished commendation on acts which demanded reprobation, and have endeavoured to raise miscreants, notorious for their want of humanity, to the rank of heroes, lessening thereby the stain upon robbery, and the abhorrence naturally conceived against cruelty."

Spain claimed all of the New World except Brazil, which was given to the Portuguese. Spain's claim was based upon the discoveries of Columbus and those Spaniards who followed him, and was altogether in accord with the custom of the time. The custom has not changed even yet, as far as that is concerned. The American government has made it quite clear to the world that all the land looked down upon by Admiral Byrd while flying over the frozen wastes of Antarctica shall be American forever, unless some other power can prove that its explorers saw the land first.

However, the claims of Spain appeared extremely pretentious to all nations that were neither Spanish nor Portuguese. Why should the people of this rocky peninsula forever monopolize the wealth of the vast New World simply because an Italian named Colombo had chanced to start out on his fortunate voyage of discovery from Palos, instead of from Genoa or London or Bordeaux? True, some other nations had turned down this Italian navigator's pleas for assistance, but should that little error in judgment forever bar those nations and others from participation in the opportunities lying so temptingly spread out in the West? The answer, naturally enough, was: "Not if we can help it!"

But the might of Spain grew as the gold flowed in from America. More gold bought more ships and guns. Spain could afford to be extravagant. She had a wonderful start toward world domination before her enemies had fairly made up their minds about measures to be taken against her. Like every powerful people since the beginning of time, the Spaniards, once they had the gold, felt that they had been chosen of God to civilize and rule the universe.

The Spaniards had the notion of grandeur well developed, long before the discovery of the golden continents to the west. Perhaps the long era of Moorish occupation, which ended the same year that Columbus sighted San Salvador, had something to do with the growth of this notion, or it may be that the Spanish people are racially inclined toward grandeur because of the majestic mountains and brilliant sunlight, the luxuriant foliage and gaudy flowers that constitute an important part of their birthright. However it originated, this tendency to pomp and circumstance had much to do with the fall of the Spanish power.

The wealthy Spaniards loved ceremony, grand parade, soul-swelling music and triumphant architecture. These ideas went into the building of their ships. When they had plenty of money to build the kind of ships they wanted, the Spaniards built great, top-heavy galleons. They constructed on their ships of war and of commerce fine "castles" that were simply grand for show and for luxurious comfort, but quite impractical for wind and war.

The buccaneers and pirates who went out singly and in fleets to harry the Spanish commerce had no such ideas of grandeur, because they weren't Spanish and they weren't rich. They drove swift, light sloops and ketches that could harass and cripple the great, lumbering galleons as the sparrow delights in tantalizing and wearing down the soaring buzzard. In these light vessels the buccaneers slipped into the harbors of Porto Bello and Panama and wrought havoc before the captains of the galleons could weigh anchor or maneuver into a position of adequate defence. The advantage was with the swifter and more agile small vessels of the raiders and pirates. Sometimes the galleons could get their adversaries at the proper range and keep them there until enough shots were fired to decide the battle. But not often.

The buccaneers who preyed upon the Spanish fleets and towns had been organized into a confederacy long before the advent of Captain Henry Morgan among them. They were mixed French, English and Dutch, with the English element rapidly growing and threatening the elimination of the others.

The pirates of those days called themselves buccaneers, much as rum-runners of to-day might call themselves coastal traders, because the term sounded better than the word pirates. The importance of the label was stressed in those days quite as much as it is to-day, when undertakers advertise that they are morticians, real estate agents call themselves realtors, and show girls are introduced as ladies of the ensemble.

Bucaniers were the primitive meat-packers of Hispaniola. Most of them were marooned men who had managed to get to the forests of that part of Hispaniola now called Haiti, and, in order to provide themselves with food and pin money, killed the wild cattle they found there, and prepared the meat for market. The meat was smoked and partly cooked over a wood fire. There was a word, "bucan" or "boucan" or "boucain" among them, describing either the contraption erected for smoking the meat or the meat so prepared. Since most of these half-wild meat packers were Frenchmen, the word, probably Indian in origin, took on the French form, and the meat-smokers were called bucaniers. Later, when the English pirates of the Caribbean wished to give themselves a respectable name, they said they were "buccaneers," which was an anglicized form of the French-Indian word.

So Henry Morgan, Welshman by birth, was already recognized as a prosperous and daring buccaneer when he came sailing into the harbor of the pirate city of Port Royal, Jamaica, with six ships and much loot, recently taken from the Spaniards.

Morgan was then a young man, but well practiced in the business of piracy. He had come out to the Indies from England as a bond servant, as so many did in those days. He had served his time under a master in Barbadoes, and immediately upon his release had signed on with a pirate crew, a hand before the mast. Having made plenty of money on his own account while serving under a pirate captain, he went into partnership with several other prosperous seamen, and went to sea in his own sloop. Thus he rose to the position of affluence he held when he sailed into the pirate capital of the Western world with his six Spanish prizes.

Now Jamaica at this time was entirely under the domination of the pirates, although it was nominally a respectable British colony. The Governor of Jamaica was wont to give commissions to any pirates who applied to him and made the proper arrangements for returning to him one-tenth of anything they might take from the Spaniards. The commissions were a form of lawless license to rob at sea, and had about the same legal status as the writ of protection furnished a speakeasy proprietor by a police lieutenant or a recognized hijacker.

The chief of the buccaneer confederacy at this time was one Captain Mansvelt, a Dutch planter who had gone into sea-robbing when his crops failed on the Dutch island of Curacao some years prior to the entry of Morgan upon the scene. Mansvelt had shown such a genius for piracy and for organization that it was generally declared a shame that he had not hit upon his proper vocation earlier in life. He had succeeded, in a few years, in organizing the Brothers of the Coast, which was, at the height of its power, possibly the most efficient and powerful confederacy of thieves in all the history of the world.

Mansvelt liked this plucky young Morgan, and offered him the place of second in command in an expedition just fitting out for an attack upon the cities of the Spanish Main. Morgan accepted, and soon a fleet of fifteen sail, with more than five hundred pirates aboard, set sail for Santa Catalina, a small island off the coast of Nicaragua. This island, now called Catalina Harbor and belonging to Colombia, was called by the English Old Providence. Its position made it a desirable base of operations for the pirates.

The Brothers of the Coast long had had the idea of establishing an independent state of their own, situated where it would do the most harm to legitimate commerce. A pirate named Blewfields, who preceded Mansvelt in the organizing of pirate companies, had acted upon the idea to the extent of establishing permanent headquarters on a little island very close to the Main, almost directly west of Santa Catalina. The Nicaraguan state and city of Bluefields, figuring so often in news of American marines, are named for this pioneer pirate, the change in spelling being a normal geographical transition.

Mansvelt decided to set up the pirate state, with Morgan's aid, at Santa Catalina, so a descent was made upon the island. The plan failed because of a combination of circumstances. For one thing, the Spaniards from the Main came and stormed the garrison left by the pirates, and regained possession. Then, too, Governor Modyford of Jamaica, did not look favorably upon the project. He wanted the pirates to keep their headquarters in Jamaica, so that they might spend most of their winnings there and pay him his tithe. Mansvelt drank himself to death in a celebration soon after the taking of the island by the pirates, so there was no one especially interested in carrying forward the enterprise against opposition.

However, the island is important in this recital because it changed hands many times during the reign of the buccaneers, and is reputed to be the depository for much rich loot. A garrison, when trapped on the island, had no way to escape, but it was always possible to bury such treasure as had come into the hands of the inhabitants. Several times the change in ownership or occupation, accomplished by means of a general massacre following an assault from the sea, is said to have taken place when a considerable store of gold and silver had been accumulated behind supposedly impregnable defenses. Santa Catalina, St. Catherine's, Catalina Harbor, or Old Providence; however you call it, decorate it with a cross when you start cruising for treasure trove.

◇ ◇

Henry Morgan became chief of the Brothers of the Coast after the death of Mansvelt. One of his first schemes as High Admiral of the fleet was a racket worthy of a modern high-pressure uplift racketeer. From his headquarters at the capital, Port Royal, he sent out circular letters, addressed to the prosperous Puritan merchants of New England, asking for cash contributions to equip the fleet that was to keep popery and the Spanish Inquisition from ravaging the fair hills of Massachusetts and Connecticut. The astute admiral of the pirates had a "sucker list" supplied by merchants of Boston who were regular customers for Morgan's booty. Morgan was full of ideas. He never was known to despise the widow's mite, although he had plenty of experience in the taking of gold and silver by the shipload.

Twelve ships and seven hundred cutthroats joined Morgan's forces in time for an attack upon the Cuban town of Puerto del Principe. The place was taken easily enough, and the principal inhabitants tortured to make them reveal where treasure was hidden. While such gold and silver as could be located in this manner was being dug up, word came to Morgan that the Governor of Havana was sending a force to the relief of the town. So the pirates made preparation for a quick departure, meantime locking most of the inhabitants in the church, where they were left to die of starvation and suffocation. Five hundred cattle were driven to the beach, slaughtered and packed in barrels of brine, before the fleet sailed. Even though Morgan, the "buccaneer," had never done a day's butchering or meat-packing in his life, he had under his command at this time plenty of husky fellows who could butcher bullocks as readily as they could butcher men and women.

Sailing from Puerto del Principe with as much money as they could extract from the inhabitants under threat of death and the burning of the town, the pirates stopped at a small island for division of the spoils. Morgan reported a total of only fifty thousand pieces of eight taken, and the French buccaneers were disappointed and enraged. They left Morgan's fleet then and there, partly because of dissatisfaction over the division of spoils, and partly because of quarrels between individual French and English pirates.

Morgan soon recruited nine vessels and about five hundred men for an assault upon the town of Porto Bello, on the Main. Porto Bello at this period was the Atlantic terminus of the pack-mule trail over which the treasure of Peru was freighted from Panama, in preparation for loading upon the galleons of the plate fleet. Morgan thought he could not fail to take a handsome bit of loot in capturing such a rich town.

The assault was made at night. The first sentry was gagged, and the first fort was taken after a short but hot engagement. All the officers and men captured in this fort were locked up in a room in the building and blown up with gunpowder after they had surrendered. It is not surprising, therefore, that the soldiers in the next fort fought long and desperately.

Morgan tried a characteristic ruse. He had wide ladders built, each rung wide enough and strong enough to bear three men. Then he took possession of a nunnery and a monastery. At the points of the pirates' swords the monks and nuns were forced to raise the ladders against the walls and go over the top ahead of the raiders. Morgan thought the military governor of the place, who was personally in command, would refuse to permit his men to fire upon the religious, but in this he was mistaken. The governor ordered the utmost resistance to be offered, and the religious screen was no protection to the pirates, except in so far as the nuns and monks stopped bullets intended for the men behind them.

The fort was captured after a battle that lasted all day. The governor himself fought to the last, in spite of the promise of Morgan to spare him if he would surrender.

Meanwhile the inhabitants of the town had had ample time to hide their valuables. Many threw their money and jewels into the wells before fleeing with their more cumbersome possessions into the jungle. Others took their gold and silver with them, loading servants with as much as they could conveniently carry. In the forest, by the roadside, and in the depths of the jungle, the hoards were buried, to await the departure of the pirates.

The inhabitants of Porto Bello, even as early as this raid of Morgan's in 1668, had learned what to do with gold and silver as soon as pirates were reported before the town.

Morgan put to the torture every Porto Bello citizen he could find in the town or by beating the bushes outside. A favorite device of his was burning the feet of his victims. He also placed some of them in hammocks and built slow fires under them. In this way he obtained some information about the location of hidden treasure. But most of the victims were poor and knew nothing of where gold might be had. Morgan was fully satisfied to torture to death a hundred persons in order to obtain a mite of information from even one individual.

In this process of torture, and in the shooting of stray Spaniards who fled further into the jungles upon the approach of the pirate round-up squads, Morgan wiped out many families. Naturally, much of the treasure buried and secreted in wells by these people remains where they put it to this day. As Porto Bello was sacked in this manner several times during the reign of the pirates, it is to-day one of the very good localities for treasure trove in the Land of Spanish Gold. There is much more loot to be had out of Porto Bello now, in all probability, than there was taken away by Morgan. The pirate chief did manage, by torture and threats of burning, to carry away with him one hundred thousand pieces of eight, paid as ransom, and whatever loot he and his men were able to steal from the deserted houses.

The pirates stayed fifteen days, and their treatment of the women captured by them is the subject of regretful comment by Morgan's best friends among the chroniclers of this part of the super-bandit's life.

◇ ◇

Maracaibo to-day is a city of more than a hundred thousand inhabitants. It is an oil port, and fortunes are being made in its immediate vicinity.

It is situated on Lake Maracaibo, just inside the entrance straits, in Venezuela near the Colombian border. It is a very old city, founded in 1571. In the days of the pirates it was raided many times.

Lake Maracaibo is a large body of water, opening into the Gulf of Venezuela through the channel upon the upper part of which the city stands. The early inhabitants established at the upper end of the lake, three hundred miles above Maracaibo, a stronghold and place of refuge called Gibraltar. The place still supports a small village by that name.

Gibraltar served as an outpost for trading with the natives of the interior, and for a place to flee to when the pirates attacked Maracaibo, as they frequently did.

Lake Maracaibo is about thirty feet deep, but the channel running past the city, through which the tide and commerce flow in and out of the lake, is even now only seven feet deep at low tide, deepening to twelve feet when the tide is in.

In 1669, when Morgan sacked the city, the straits leading to the lake were even shallower. They were defended by forts to right and left. L'Olonnois the Cruel had raided Maracaibo several years earlier, and the defences had been strengthened since.

While assembling his fleet for this enterprise at Cow Island, Morgan cast covetous eyes upon a French vessel in the harbor. She was a noble ship, armed with twenty-four iron guns and twelve brass cannon. The freebooter urged the captain of the French vessel to join his expedition, promising rich loot. The Frenchman declined with profuse thanks, saying that some of his countrymen who had served under the great pirate had not found the enterprise they took part in quite as profitable as they had expected it to be.

When cajolery failed to win over the Frenchmen, Morgan invited the officers to take dinner with him in his cabin. They accepted, and at the close of the meal found themselves clapped into irons. Morgan's men had taken possession of the French ship, confining the surviving French sailors below decks.

But the master pirate reaped no benefit from this bit of treachery. He staged a great jollification dinner aboard the captured ship, and while the dinner was in progress one of the Frenchmen below blew the vessel up. She went down with the loss of all of Morgan's celebrators and nearly all the French prisoners. Unluckily for the people of Maracaibo, Morgan himself chanced to be on his own flagship at the moment of the explosion.

Several days later, Morgan had the bodies of the victims of this disaster fished out of the water, all jewelry and money removed from their persons, and the bodies thrown back to the sharks.

When the pirate's little fleet arrived before the entrance of the lake on which the city of Maracaibo is situated, Morgan placed his best fighters in small boats, which were rowed to the shore under the fire of the outer forts. The pirate ships stayed out of range while the first land skirmish was in progress.

The defenders of Maracaibo had laid their plans with full

knowledge of the character of the enemy they were confronting. They had heard of the tortures that the merciless Morgan had inflicted upon the soldiers and citizens of captured cities. The entire civil population of the city departed for the deep forests as soon after the beginning of the assault as practicable. The citizens first gathered all the available gold and silver, carefully concealing it under the direction of the city authorities. Some insisted upon taking their treasure with them.

The soldiers had orders to fight to the uttermost limits of their endurance. They were warned, furthermore, that if they surrendered themselves into the hands of the pirates they had nothing to look forward to but death by torture. These warnings helped to explain the condition of the city when Morgan entered it.

The pirates scaled the walls after repeated assaults. Fighting on both sides was desperate, and no quarter was given or expected.

The soldiers of Spain resisted as long as they could, and then retreated. With few exceptions they did not allow themselves to be taken prisoners.

Morgan found Maracaibo a deserted city. He quartered his men in the Cathedral, and gave orders to have some of the fugitive citizens captured and brought before him.

Searching squads were dispatched in every direction, and about fifty unfortunate families were captured and returned to the city.

Without regard to the protestations of the prisoners that they were all poor people, and that the rich had been able to provide themselves with means of transportation that got them farther out of range of searching parties, Morgan subjected every captive to unmitigated torture.

Stout cords were bound about the foreheads of men and women alike, and slowly twisted until the victims fell unconscious from pain. An old man who was suspected of being a rich merchant, though he protested that he was only a servant, was tortured in the public square for eight days. On the eighth day he was suspended by his fingers and toes to four tall stakes, and a slow fire was built under him. Strange to relate, the old man survived, and was allowed to go when he promised to raise twenty-five thousand pieces of eight for his ransom.

Maracaibo was a disappointment to Morgan. The buccaneer resolved to follow the precedent set by the villainous L'Olonnois and extend his operations to Gibraltar. He assumed that much of the wealth of Maracaibo had been transported to the other city.

The assault upon Gibraltar occupied several days, and was, of course, eventually successful. Again the prize was a deserted city. Again the searchers were sent out, and the scenes of torture were re-enacted. This time the efforts of the pirates were more richly rewarded. A goodly shipload of treasure was obtained, and Morgan prepared to return to Jamaica.

But the power of Spain had been aroused, and three great warships were waiting beyond the harbor of Maracaibo.

With consummate strategy, Morgan managed to pass the batteries of the city, which had been remounted and remanned, during the night. He met the well-armed Spanish fleet without fear.

One of Morgan's ships had been converted into a fire-ship. She was loaded with tarred logs and other inflammable materials. Twelve men were placed aboard her, and she was steered in advance of the pirate fleet, directly for the Spanish flagship.

The fireship was alongside the great Spanish man-of-war before the Spaniards realized that she was not an ordinary pirate vessel. The twelve men lashed their ship to the flagship's side. Then they set her afire and leaped into the sea.

Thus the Spaniards lost their principal vessel before the action was fairly begun. One of the remaining ships of war ran herself aground, and was burned by the Spaniards. The other was captured by the pirates.

The Spanish galleon that was burned contained a considerable treasure. Morgan knew of this from a prisoner he had taken, so he risked much in order to search the wreck. He found that most of the booty had sunk to the bottom, but he recovered 15,000 pieces of eight from the stern, which was only slightly below the surface. Many of the coins were melted into a great mass by the heat.

For those who care to follow Morgan, picking up treasure that he left behind, the wreck of the burned galleon is an item not to be neglected. Contemporary accounts describe the location of the battle with enough detail to give a very good clue to the probable location of this wreck and treasure.

◇ ◇

In 1670 the Kings of Spain and Great Britain signed a solemn treaty, known as the Treaty of America, whereby both sovereigns undertook to respect one another's rights and territories in America, and to see to it that no depredations against the ships or settlements of one another were made by their respective subjects.

Morgan heard about this when he got back to Jamaica with booty amounting in all to 250,000 pieces of eight. He straightway announced that he intended to proceed upon another cruise against the rich towns of the Spanish Main. The Governor of Jamaica, as usual, coöperated with him officially as well as unofficially.

This expedition was thoroughly planned and well equipped. Morgan had acquired such prestige as a leader of robbers that thousands of unemployed pirates and bandits of every description who gathered at Port Royal from all parts of the world flocked to his standard. From among them Morgan chose two thousand men whom he embarked in thirty-seven vessels. Meat was provided for the expedition by a mass drive against the wild cattle of Hispaniola.

Morgan's Panama expedition probably comprised the largest army and the most numerous fleet ever assembled under the command of a pirate.

After some preliminary fighting, the fleet cast anchor off the town and castle of Chagres. This was as far as the vessels could venture up the river. Having taken possession of Chagres and left a guard unit in charge there, Morgan and his army started across the Isthmus on foot, January 9, 1671.

The trip across the Isthmus, through the tropical jungle, occupied nine days, and for picturesque romance and hardship there are few military expeditions that rival it. There is no record of the casualties of those terrible nine days and nights, but it is improbable that Morgan had more than a thousand men when he arrived before the city of Panama.

The Spaniards had ample warning of the approach of the pirates. They had removed almost every bit of food and all domestic animals from the route over which the attacking army had to travel. Morgan found towns along the way, but they were all deserted and most of them were burning.

For six days and nights the footsore pirates were almost without sustenance. Had the Spaniards been just the least bit more careful in the removal of food, it seems probable that Morgan never would have reached Panama. He took no provisions along, foolishly expecting to find plenty to eat on the route.

On the fourth day of the march, the pirates found a deserted Spanish camp, and made a meal of the leather bags that had been left behind. The pirates soaked the leather bags in hot water, pounded them to a paste on a rock, and roasted the paste before an open fire. This was not a luxurious meal, but it sustained life in the bodies of most of the marchers until next day, when they found two bags of corn-meal that had been hidden in a cave.

Two bags of meal and a few leather patties do not make very ample rations for an army of more than a thousand men that is marching through tropical jungles.

The pirates were in a desperate condition when, on the sixth day, they found a barn filled with corn. They ate the corn as it was, dry and raw.

This was all the food the pirate horde was able to get until the ninth day of their miserable journey, when they came within sight of the steeples of the city of Panama. Here they captured a few dogs, cats, and mules, all of which they ate with great relish. They had also a little raw beef before entering battle.

When men are hungry and there is food on the other side of a wall, men will fight. These pirates were not ineffective fighters when they were well fed. When they were starving no army could stop them.

The Spaniards at Panama were well prepared for the attack. They had plenty of the best artillery that the wealth of Spain could buy. They had thick walls, well manned. The number of their well-fed and well-trained soldiers was more than ten times the number of the pirates.

The Spaniards also had twenty thousand cattle, mostly wild bulls from the South American pampas. These animals were driven by negro and Indian slaves directly into the ranks of the advancing buccaneers. It was the belief of the Spaniards that the wild cattle would disorganize the attackers and make them vulnerable to a military movement.

The onset of the wild cattle proved a hopeless fiasco. The bulls weren't wild enough. In fact, they were not half as wild as the pirates.

Morgan led his men through the woods, and assaulted the city where it was least prepared to defend itself. When the pirates had killed and eaten enough of the wild animals to make them strong for the battle, they advanced through the bewildered ranks of the cattle and threw themselves upon the defenders of the city with irresistible fury. The Spaniards, who had made a brave sally against the invaders, were completely routed.

With the loss of not more than a hundred men, Morgan was within the city. The Spaniards fled precipitately.

Morgan's first order to his men was this: "Don't touch the wine. I have secret information that it is all poisoned."

The wine wasn't poisoned. But Morgan knew his men. And he had heavy work for them to do.

That night the city of Panama was one brilliant flame against the calm tropic sky. In the morning there was little of the town untouched by fire.

Morgan's stay in the ruined city lasted three weeks. During that time he proceeded with his usual tactics to force the citizens to disclose the hiding places of their treasure. He was more successful at Panama than he had been at Porto Bello or at Maracaibo. The number of persons tortured to death by Morgan and his men at Panama ran well into the hundreds.

When the pirates started back toward Chagres, they carried their spoils on one hundred and seventy-five pack mules. Six hundred prisoners were taken along to be sold as slaves. The total value of the loot taken from Panama will never be known, because Morgan was so crooked that not even his financial backers ever knew the extent of his winnings. But it must have run into millions of dollars.

This much, however, is certain. Most of the treasure of Panama was kept safe from the plunderer. How safe, only the revelations of the last few years have made clear.

The warning of Morgan's approach reached Panama at least a month before the pirate and his men appeared before the city. All the church plate and the national treasure were securely hidden during that time. The wealthiest families departed early from Panama, taking no chances. They had heard about Porto Bello and Maracaibo. They took their treasure with them, or buried it safely before they departed. When they returned, the town was a smoking ruin. It was never rebuilt. As this is written, the ground is being cleared for a great national park, and soon tourists will swarm over the ground that was soaked in the blood of Morgan's victims.

One of the most persistent and probable tales of Morgan's treasure has to do with five certain boxes of gold, said to have been taken from the general loot on the first day of the march back to Chagres. Morgan had kept close to himself these five boxes of pure gold, lashed to the backs of five mules. On the evening of the first day out of Panama, the pirate chief personally selected three men whom he ordered to lead these five mules, with their loads, immediately and quietly, and follow him. The perfidious robber chieftain led the men to a certain spot, perhaps an hour's march from the trail. There he made them dig a hole and bury the gold. With his own hand he slew the three diggers. Then he made a map, giving the bearings of the spot as exactly as he could. He turned the mules loose and went back to camp and to bed.

Within the last few years, several expeditions have sought this gold that Morgan buried. In the fall of 1927 two expeditions, each headed by a Morgan claiming to be a descendant of the notorious pirate, set out for Panama to find the hidden gold.

One of the treasure-hunters was Louis Morgan, of Victoria, Texas, son of a prominent lawyer. The other, heading a rival party, was Donald Morgan, of Providence, R. I., who carried on researches in England and Wales to discover, if possible, authentic clues pointing to the exact location of the treasure. Each party was supplied with a map with the cross properly affixed to the site of the treasure chests.

There was some blowing of trumpets when the expeditions set forth. If they returned, they did so quietly and in small detachments. No report of any treasure discovery came from either camp.

But we must go back to Morgan for a few minutes.

Arrived at Chagres, he perpetrated the crowning feat of his iniquitous career. He cheated his own cutthroats of the reward that was due them under their agreement with him.

Morgan distributed, upon the demand of his men, a reward amounting to about fifty dollars per man. The pirates grumbled. Morgan sensed impending mutiny.

In the night the wary buccaneer loaded his loot upon the three seaworthy vessels in the harbor, and put aboard skeleton crews made up of his most trusted adherents.

When morning dawned, the men on shore found themselves marooned. Looking out to sea, they saw their perfidious commander sailing away with the loot that they had won with so much sweat and blood. The deserted pirates were mad with rage.

Standing in the shadow of the ruined fortress of Chagres, the marooned men hurled imprecations against their betrayer. But they were helpless. Morgan made his way back to Jamaica with the richest cargo of gold and silver that was ever stolen by mortal man.

A charge of piracy was afterwards lodged against Henry Morgan by his political enemies in Jamaica. The bold buccaneer was taken back to England, tried, acquitted, and released to receive the acclamations of his enthusiastic admirers in the homeland.

It was then that Henry Morgan was knighted by Charles the

Second. He was sent back to Jamaica as deputy governor of the island, charged with authority to wipe out piracy from Caribbean waters.

Sir Henry Morgan served his King in Jamaica well, and he grew constantly richer and more powerful. He died, full of years and honor, and was buried with royal pomp and mourning.

◇   ◇

Far and away the most intensive and effective treasure-hunting job of modern times is being done by Lieutenant George Williams, a British subject, most of whose activities have centered around Panama. Williams is a lone worker. His equipment consists of a radio treasure locating machine, a few shovels, a pick or two, and as many Negro laborers as required. He isn't incorporated. He doesn't sell stock in his ventures. He will not take a partner. He has nothing to sell. And he digs up golden treasures that would turn the head of King Crœsus himself.

Williams has been in the treasure-hunting business ever since the close of the World War, when he retired to civilian life, practically broke. But during the war he had been experimenting with radio and the locating of metal under water. He continued his experiments privately after returning from the service. He spent all the money he could earn, carrying on these experiments. He landed at Panama with his electrical machine for locating metals under the earth, but he had no money in his pockets. He went out and located and dug up enough gold to get himself started. He demonstrated for the officials of the Panama government, and obtained a permit to hunt treasure trove.

Williams, who is 33, married, father of a tiny daughter, is a racing enthusiast. Out of his gold diggings he has bought a string of horses and a string of racing dogs. He makes headquarters at Ancon, Panama Canal Zone, and enters horses and dogs in all the meets, backing his own runners extravagantly. Perhaps you have heard that it would take a gold mine to support a man who bets on the ponies. Williams indulges his betting passion quite freely. He has more than a gold mine to support his fancy. He has the accumulated hoards of ages, taken from the world's richest gold mines in the long ago.

I am going to tell you a good deal about Williams, because I think he has the most romantic job in the world. Who has not day-dreamed about digging up gold? Who has not longed for a chance to dig here and there and everywhere in the Land of Spanish Gold? Williams does it! Not as pastime or an occupation for a winter vacation, but as a life work. And he doesn't go at it in hit-or-miss fashion. He has a machine which, he says, locates the treasure without error.

In a recent letter to me, Williams described his machine. It is well to remember at this point that you can't buy the invention from Williams, and he is not in the business of manufacturing the machine for sale. He has just one. He had another. It was stolen from on board a ship on which Williams was having it shipped to a new field of endeavor. But the thief left an important part of the instrument behind, and could not operate without this missing part. Williams never heard from the thief, and concluded that the useless instrument had been destroyed when it failed to locate treasure for the person who had stolen it.

The Williams machine is similar in many respects to other instruments that are being used with more or less success by mineral and oil prospectors. It consists of a transmitter of electrical impulses and a receiver. The impulses are transmitted into the earth, and are picked up by a receiver attuned to the same wave-length. "If no metal is in the earth," says Williams, in his letter to me, "the lines of force have a free passage, and will give off a negative sound in your earphones." But suppose the waves encounter a metal, say gold. The waves presumably pass around the gold, thus interrupting their free normal flow back to the receiver. This makes a sound in the earphones which is easily recognizable by an experienced operator, and may be detected by one who is not experienced.

But to Williams, who has lived with this machine for years, a certain sound in the phones says "Gold!" just as plainly as though the word were heard as pronounced by the human voice.

That must be a rather jolly sound, I should say. I venture the opinion that the prospecting adventurer often hears it in his dreams, as another man in a more conventional way of life may hear the dulcet strains of a charmer's soprano.

So much superstition, fakery and pseudo-science have been associated with the locating of water and minerals under ground that the critical reader who is unaware of recent developments in this field is likely to be suspicious of this recital of treasure-hunting as soon as a treasure-locating machine is mentioned.

Everybody has heard of water witches who claimed to be able to tell you right where to drill your well or drive your pipe for a good supply of sparkling water. Usually the wonder-worker held a forked stick, one fork in each bare hand, horizontally in front of him, as he walked along the ground. When over the water, the antics of the stick informed the operator. The stick bent downward or turned to one side, or otherwise spoke to the man who knew how to make it work.

The divining rod has taken many forms and has borne a shady reputation among scientists. Generally it has had strong support from farmers and country folk, and has been looked upon as a rank fraud by city people. Owners and operators of an endless variety of divining rods, from the earliest times, have claimed to be able to locate metals as well as water. The literature of the divining rod, the water witch, the doodle-bug and the prospecting machine is extensive enough to fill a large library. There is a surprising lack of agreement among supposedly scientific writers as to whether any divining rod or water witch has ever really located water or metals. The Smithsonian Institution has gone on record against the probability of any such mysterious power residing in the rod or in the water witch. This pronouncement was issued before the advent of the modern radio devices, however. And besides, the Smithsonian was mistaken about the identity of the inventor of the airplane.

Since the World War, numerous devices for locating oil and metals underground have been invented, and very extensive oil prospecting is now done with the aid of some such devices. The locating machines are used in connection with geological surveys, and their indications are taken seriously by great oil corporations.

Several of the machines now in common use in prospecting are similar in principle to the one used by Lieutenant Williams in his treasure hunting.

But Lieutenant Williams has no case to prove. He goes after the treasure, and thus far he has been remarkably successful in getting it. He is extremely unconcerned about anybody's opinions as to whether his machine is any good.

One of the first finds made by Williams was at Old Panama. After examining the legends and histories, he decided that a most likely place for treasure was in, under or about the ruins of the old Cathedral of St. Anastasius. This church was destroyed by Morgan in the general sacking of the city, and the site was covered by jungle growth when Williams began his explorations. The picturesque ruin of the square bell tower remained to point the way to the treasure-seeker.

It took until November, 1926, to clear away the political and arboreal entanglements that surrounded the ruins. In that month, Williams set his machine down where the floor of the old Cathedral was still visible in patches. Don Rodolfo Chiari, President of Panama, was present, with a staff of his high political officers.

Williams had been informed that he might demonstrate his machine for the officials, but that any real searching for treasure must be done under a concession which would cost ten thousand dollars.

The earphones, after a few trials, indicated the presence of gold below.

"Gentlemen," said the audacious English adventurer, "if you will be so good as to permit the men to dig here, you will see something handsome."

Permission was given. The next two hours were trying ones for the treasure-seeker. If he failed this time, he could not expect the President to listen to him any further. And he had no money to buy a concession. It was important that he make a great demonstration.

To relieve the tension, Williams took a spade and went into the little excavation himself. He dug rapidly and carefully.

Presently his spade struck something bright. Williams knew how Sir Francis Drake had felt when he stood in "that goodly and great high tree" upon a Panama mountain, and gazed out toward the Pacific, where in imagination he saw the treasure ships he hoped to loot.

A handsome chalice of solid gold rolled to the feet of the sweating Englishman!

Summoning all the nonchalance of his English ancestors to his aid, Williams picked up the golden goblet, shook the clay from within it, and, stepping to the surface, smilingly presented it to President Chiari.

"The first fruit of our harvest, Mr. President," he said. "May it be the presage of many golden days for you and the Republic!"

Williams was made. The ecstatic President could scarcely contain himself, and the cabinet lost all semblance of a deliberative body. Williams was given the treasure-hunting concession out of hand, with no down payment whatever. The digging went on, that day and during several following days. Then Williams went back to England to obtain the equipment he thought he must have for regular operations.

Meantime he was studying old documents and plans of the ancient city of Panama, the site of which is five miles east of the present Panama. The town had extended along the ocean front for approximately a mile. Williams found an old secret chart that indicated extensive tunnels that had been cut under the city, apparently to serve as hiding places for treasure and refugees during attacks by pirates. The main tunnel ran from the treasury, under the Cathedral, to an underground chamber beneath the Santa Ana convent, thence, at an acute angle, to San José convent.

The old treasury was near the sea. When Morgan's pirates were coming over the walls of the city, the Spaniards were letting the sea into the tunnel system. How they did it, no one now living knows. There had been several lootings of Panama before that time, and the Spaniards had learned some valuable lessons. According to a long understood plan of action, the treasures of the state and church, together with as much private treasure as it was possible to gather in a short time, were placed in the tunnels and underground chambers, and when no hope of saving the city remained, the tunnels were flooded by a system known only to a few Spanish officials.

Morgan never recovered any treasure out of the flooded tunnels. There is no mention of any such hiding place in any of the records written by the pirates. Probably Morgan came and departed without ever hearing of the tunnels. If he had known of them, it is improbable that he could have worked them for their treasure despite the guardianship of the sea.

Williams started his work, upon his return to the job under the duly signed concession, at the Cathedral. He recovered a fine equipment of church plate and sacred vessels.

In this first find under the church were a silver sanctuary bell, remnants of a solid gold, jewel-studded reliquary, gold paten, six gold cruets, a large gold platter, a richly carved gold door, apparently from the tabernacle of the high altar, an incomplete monstrance, and several other items. These treasured appurtenances of the sanctuary must have been hidden hastily by the priests, even as the pirates were running through the town and becoming more and more enraged by the deserted condition of it. All the priests found in the city were tortured to death or summarily shot by Morgan's men, so there was never anyone to tell the succeeding generations of Spanish worshippers where they might find the resplendent altar furnishings. More than two hundred and fifty years were to elapse before the amazing miracle of radio should call forth the consecrated vessels from their hiding place.

After the hiding of the treasure by the sorely pressed Spaniards, there were many changes that would have made it difficult, one might surmise, even for the spirits of the departed ministers to find the things they had hidden so securely. When the Cathedral was burned and looted, the walls collapsed and the floor caved in. Later there were earthquakes that collapsed the walls of most of the tunnels. And Nature is given to a peculiarly extravagant sort of forgiveness in the tropics. Jungle growth can change the face of a deserted city in a year so that it would hardly be recognized by its former rulers. In two and a half centuries Old Panama had been thoroughly overgrown, and the powerful roots of great trees twined themselves about many a delicately wrought golden crucifix and jewel case beneath the deserted streets of the old city.

Williams read that the tower of the Cathedral had once contained a chime of seven silver bells. More likely, the number was eight. When he had cleaned out the first treasure trove, the enthusiastic young man began searching for the bells. He sought these relics in every direction from the part of the tower that is still standing, and after weeks of work was rewarded by finding one of the bells, badly crushed by the crashing tower, and still bearing the marks of the fire that was set by Morgan. The other bells were not found. It is possible that they were carried off by Morgan. It is possible that they were dug out of the ruins by the returning Panamanians after the desecrating pirates had departed, and recast for use in a new church in the new city, or sold for their metal value. And again, it is within the bounds of possibility that they may have been removed from the tower as soon as the pirates appeared before the city, and hidden in one of the secret tunnels yet to be excavated.

Exploring the jungle about the ruins of the bishop's house near the Cathedral, Lieutenant Williams got the message from his earphones that carries the great thrill; the sound that means there is gold beneath. Only one foot below the surface, the men uncovered an earthen jar containing a double handful of gold and silver coins, all minted prior to 1671, the year of Morgan's raid.

Further excavations around the foundations of the bishop's house uncovered a large stone slab with a circle carved into its surface. Lifting the slab carefully, the workmen were face to face with an entrance to a secret tunnel which led under the house of the bishop. This discovery was made as darkness was closing in, and the treasure-hunters had to go to bed that night without knowing what was within the long-deserted tunnel.

Next day, the work was found to be arduous and slow, for the mouth of the tunnel was blocked with many rocks and quantities of clay. But as the wreckage was cleared away, a stone stairway, cut into the solid rock, was followed to a depth of twenty-five feet, where the tunnel led away horizontally.

As the bottom of the stairway was reached, the workmen came upon a veritable museum-ful of Spanish pottery of the seventeenth century. A surprisingly large number of the pots were taken out without crack or blemish. Many, of course, were broken when found.

Several of the more important pieces of pottery bore ecclesiastical symbols, the crossed keys of the papal insignia being, in.many cases, beautifully wrought upon the surface of the pottery before glazing. Black, green, and red are the chief colors of the decorations.

It seems likely that the Bishop of Panama maintained a potter or two who worked in a shop near his house or upon the Cathedral premises, and that many of these interesting pieces are the handiwork of this highly skilled artisan who was "by appointment to His Lordship, the Bishop of Panama." Evidence of this is found in several pieces of half-finished pots, one pot that was unglazed and only partly painted or colored, and one bowl containing unused bits of pigment and balls of potter's clay that had been put away with the marks of the potter's fingers upon them. It seems probable that the frightened potter, in the general panic, hid away for safe-keeping, here in the secret tunnel beneath his patron's house, the most valuable of the earthenware objects he had made for the Bishop, and with them the work he had in hand at the moment.

Perhaps the luckless potter postponed his departure from his work to the last minute. I can see him now, rushing below stairs with the pots under his arms, and the precious little bowls that he had modeled so lovingly, in his trembling hands. The pirates are coming! God save us all! Well, our soldiers will soon drive them out, for they are nothing but Englishmen after all, so I will take this work with me, and may the Lord grant me patience until I can get back to my work on this beautiful vase for Our Lady's altar! Here I'll be working this good clay with my hands, and I will sit here on the lowest step of all until the Bishop—God bless him and keep him safe—shall call me with the news that our men have chased the heathen pirates into the sea!

I think the potter waited long. Some poor, crumbling bones were found there upon the floor of the tunnel, beside the pile of beautiful pottery, two and a half centuries later, by a mild young Englishman who worked with a strange device with a magic power to see under the earth.

Again the work of clearing away the wreckage proceeded, and it was found that the pottery had rested upon a sort of landing. The shaft that had been cut into the solid rock went down to an extreme depth of 65 feet. This lower shaft probably was a cistern.

Working into the tunnel that led off from the shaft, the excavators found that this work had occupied many men for many months, for the tunnel walls had been strengthened by the application of a thick layer of concrete, into which had been mixed millions of copper nails. This was reinforced concrete as the Spaniards of Panama knew it in the seventeenth century.

The tunnels were not mere passageways, but there were recesses, some deep, others shallow, in the walls. In these recesses were found most of the valuable objects that were recovered. One of the curious items, which eventually should find its way to some museum, was a wine jar shaped like a graceful bird, and appropriately colored. A small hole in the top admits air while the wine is being poured through the concealed spout in the bird's tail. Perhaps this was the masterpiece of the unfortunate potter who brought his artistic materials into the tunnel when the sack of the city began. At any rate, it had been placed carefully in a well-protected place where it remained safe and sound through the floods and earthquakes and varying fortunes of two and a half centuries. It fared far better than the bones of the artisan who fashioned it.

Many other beautiful vases, bowls, pots and jugs were found —hundreds of them—in holes and recesses in the tunnel walls.

A branch of the tunnel reëntered the bishop's house after branching off from the part first excavated by the treasure-hunters. It entered the basement of the house through a door, over which was affixed a nicely modeled clay figure of a man's head, with what the finders took to be horns on the temples. The eyes are of pure silver, and three ingots of silver are imbedded in the forehead. The significance of this curious piece of workmanship will be a problem for some antiquarian to solve.

It would seem that many of the men who were wounded in defending the bishop's house were carried down into the basement and through the secret door into the tunnel, for here were found the remains of many skeletons with rusted swords and other armament about and among them. One of the highly prized finds is the silver sword hilt, with elaborately fashioned wrist-guard, of some grandee who perished thus miserably and vainly, far beneath the city that was being burned and destroyed by the pirates. Perhaps you can picture that final scene in the dark tunnel, where the sorely wounded men must have lain long, perhaps untended, waiting for the succor that never came. Those who would have helped them had been slain by the marauders.

In all, three silver hilts were found, and two swords that were but little damaged by time, and were bright when withdrawn from their scabbards. These were the swords that had not had a chance to drink the blood of the enemy. The bloody blades rusted away, leaving only their hilts of silver.

A handsomely wrought gold pitcher, with a gold bowl to match, were found near the skeletons. The handle, curiously enough, is fastened to the pitcher with copper rivets. A gold bowl, similar to a soup tureen nineteen inches in diameter, was found here also.

Some of the jugs and bowls of glazed pottery have silver inlaid into the designs in lumps as big as the end of a man's thumb. There are six or eight gold wine jugs, many gold and silver drinking cups, somewhat resembling loving cups, and forty-five silver spoons.

A candlestick of curious design and ingenious workmanship was found in the tunnel leading to the bishop's house. It is of silver, with large base and top, and jointed so as to permit of its being taken apart into short lengths. Thus the candlestick could reach a height of five feet or more before the altar on feast days, or it could serve as many short candlesticks, distributed about the altar.

A mysterious object recovered from a niche in one of the tunnels is described as a candle-holder by the treasure-hunters, but it may never have been intended to hold a candle. It is made of gold, and when found resembled a circular, flat box, without a lid, fifteen inches in diameter. Much prying and twisting revealed that this little box was made in three parts, two of which somewhat resemble the doughnut cutters that the grandmothers used to use, with outside rim and inside tubular extension to make the doughnut hole. These tubular parts led the searchers to believe that the contrivance was a candle-holder. Inside the little box was a roll of parchment, bound around with about ten feet of fine gold wire. The parchment had suffered from some deteriorating agent, probably salt water, despite the great care that had been taken to preserve it. It went to pieces in the hands of the investigators.

A censer of peculiar shape, not at all like the swinging censers commonly used in Catholic churches, was recovered. It is gold, and cylindrical in shape. It would not have been recognized as a censer, except for the grains of incense, partly burned, found within it.

A swinging censer of gold and silver was found, as well as several mitres, such as are worn by bishops on solemn ceremonial occasions. These mitres, partly ruined by the ravages of time and dampness, must have weighed very heavily upon the heads of their wearers, as the framework that remains is of solid gold, and exactly the shape of a complete mitre. It is presumed that these gold mitres were at least partly covered by fabric when they were new. One of the mitres, so complete that it could be worn to-day without any trimmings of fabric, has the date 1641 in one place, and 1643, followed by the letters "O. P." in another place. The letters identify the mitre as the property of the Franciscan fathers, according to information obtained by the treasure-hunters from a Franciscan college in Cincinnati, Ohio, to which Lieutenant Williams has promised the relic.

Part of a bishop's crozier, of gold set with jewels, was among the fragments brought to light.

Working through the tunnels leading downward and in the direction of the sea, the adventurers came upon salt water that rose and fell slightly with the tides. It was found impossible to proceed farther in this direction until extensive engineering work has been carried out. The Panama government, in preparing the whole area of the old city for a park, expects to find the sea inlets and close them up. It seems probable that the entire cost of clearing the ground and establishing the park will be paid for out of the proceeds of the government's share of the treasure.

By making smoke smudges in the tunnels, far beneath the jungle that covers the ruined city, Williams found several outlets to the surface in widely separated parts of the old town. Some of these outlets were opened up with very considerable labor, and always with the result that valuable pottery and treasure items were found.

The richest find of a whole treasure-hunting season was obtained by fishing and dragging in one of the water-filled tunnels. This is a ball, apparently of solid gold, seven inches in diameter, representing the terrestrial globe surmounted by a gold cross.

This find caused great excitement among the Panamanians, because of what it might presage, as well as what it is worth. There is a tradition, supported in part by written history, that somewhere in the ruins of the ancient city of Panama lies hidden a solid gold life-size image of the Blessed Virgin Mary, cast at Porto Bello out of nuggets brought in by the Indians, and presented to the Governor of Panama.

Now a conventional figure of the Mother of Jesus, often seen in European Catholic churches, represents her holding the Child in the crook of her left arm, and holding in her right hand the symbolical figure of the globe surmounted by a cross.

The golden globe found in the tunnel shows unmistakable evidence of having been fastened to something at its base.

Optimistic Panamanians believe that this globe is the one the Golden Virgin of Panama held in her right hand; that it has been broken away from the statue, and that the solid gold statue itself will be found somewhere near the spot at which the globe was recovered.

All the treasures dug up by Williams at Panama have been stored in a place selected by the Panamanian government. They are held there and officially valued at the end of each contract period, when Williams is paid his share of the proceeds. Occasionally some of the treasures are exhibited in the city of Panama for the delectation of tourists.

◇ ◇

Not all the treasure to be got out of the ground in Panama and other Central American countries was buried by pirates or by victims of pirates.

The people who inhabited this region before the coming of Columbus—possibly hundreds or thousands of years before that time—knew a good deal about gold and silver. They knew how and where to get these valued metals, how to work them, and they had much the same sort of respect for them that has been noted all through the history of man, wherever and whenever the dawn of civilization has been perceptible.

These people, about whom we know very little indeed, practiced burial of gold and costly objects with the bodies of their richest or most honored men. It is a common human trait to wish to put away with the body of the loved one something of great value, as a sort of tribute to the worth of the person who has passed away. It is as if the survivor might say, "Here, I'll throw in all this gold too! What does it amount to in comparison with the dear body that is being laid away forever!"

Perhaps the motive for burial of gold and precious property with the dead has been merely this. Twentieth century Americans are too good at business and accounting and the practical aspects of life and death to bury any considerable treasure with their dead. But even they, when they can afford it, buy silver handles for the caskets that contain the bodies of their departed friends and relatives. Some, indeed, pay more for the things they bury with their dead than many a hard-working person can earn in a year or two. And Americans are "sensible."

These primitive Central Americans weren't a bit sensible. When a chief of state or religious affairs died, he was laid away with a blanket of beaten gold about him, or, if it was not expedient to indulge in this funereal extravagance, at least a sheet of gold was placed under the head of the dead chieftain, and a similar sheet under his feet. Various precious objects of gold and silver were arranged in the grave before the body was abandoned to its last long sleep.

No one now knows how far these expensive burial customs extended, either in time or in geographical space. But Lieutenant Williams, with his gold-locating machine, is making progress in clearing up the historical mystery and in gathering in the treasure.

There seems to be no active opposition to this exploitation of the burial places of the pre-historic Central Americans on the part of anyone important enough to matter. The religion professed by these departed first citizens of ancient Panama was forgotten long ago, except by a few primitive tribes that still live in abysmal ignorance of modern civilization and modern creeds, far in the interior jungles.

Fifty miles from the city of Panama, in a straight line, is the border of the Panamanian state of Cocle. The state is only forty miles long and twenty-five miles wide. But for all these short distances and brief directions, it isn't easy to get to the treasure in Cocle. Means of communication are such as you are able to make, and the jungle is deep and dank and rather well stocked with ravenous mosquitoes, poisonous spiders, and dangerous snakes.

Lieutenant Williams has a treasure-hunting franchise that covers the ancient graves of Cocle, and he has been using it to great advantage. Williams has a wholesome respect for venomous reptiles, but he has no fear of ghosts that are a thousand or more years old, and the inscriptions he has found on precious objects taken from the graves are in a language that probably was forgotten before Columbus was born. If there are threats and curses, the explorer prefers to know nothing about them.

The most valuable finds made by the treasure-seeker of Panama among the graves of the ancient civilization have been made in carefully sealed caves. The work proceeds slowly, because of the inaccessibility of the region, and because it is impossible to do any work at all during the long and violent rainy season.

The only town in the state of Cocle is Penonomé, the capital, which has 13,000 inhabitants. The other settlements are small native villages. But Cocle is liberally, not to say extravagantly, supplied with rivers. There are rivers swift and rivers slow, rivers wide and rivers narrow, and all of them go roaring down to the sea when the rainy season starts.

The biggest river is called, as are so many rivers in Latin America, Rio Grande, or Big River. At a certain spot on the bank of the Rio Grande, three and a half hours' horseback ride from Penonomé, local legend said there was a hidden cave that had been used as a burial place for important personages, ages ago. Williams went out with his locating machine, tested out the region, and finally located metal at a point twenty feet below the edge of the high bank of the river. The workmen had to maintain a toe-hold on the steep river bank while they dug horizontally inward through hard clay that was almost rock. Picks were required for loosening this clay.

After tunneling in a distance of ten or twelve feet, several pieces of ancient pottery were found, and from then until the entire burial cave was excavated there were finds that kept up the excitement and buoyed the hopes of the workers.

The bones of five important personages were found within this primitive mausoleum. Each skeleton lay upon thin gold plates, and each of the grand personages had been laid away with a great gold ring fastened in his nose.

These gold nose-rings are of considerable interest from an archæological point of view. Similar rings heretofore found, not in association with skeletons, were known to most of the wise men of the universities as rain gods. Somebody deduced or presumed that these objects were worshipped as gods that could make rain. The five chiefs of the Cocle tomb on the Rio Grande come forth with the indisputable information that these strange objects are simply nose-rings. It seems likely that they were used for burial only, as they are rather too cumbersome for lifetime wear. The nose-rings look something like glorified small dog collars, and were fastened to the noses of the dead with a stout gold wire that was made something like a modern key-ring. A design of frogs is carved in the broad surface of each ring.

Great quantities of beads, mostly arranged in necklaces, were found in the tomb near the skeletons. There were also numerous gold frogs with peculiarly long tails. These objects ranged from an inch to an inch and a half long, and some of them had the gold tails looped over the back and grotesquely held in the mouth. It would seem that the early inhabitants of this swampy land held the croaking frogs in high esteem.

Under the head and feet of each of the skeletons were thin circular gold plates, each a foot and a half in diameter. Under the head of one of the ancient heroes was a battle-axe, with the gold plate laid over it. What doughty warrior was this, whose sorrowing people laid him to rest in this somber cave so long ago, with his honored head pillowed upon his trusty weapon? It is improbable that we shall ever know.

Eighteen hundred pieces of pottery were taken out of this tomb undamaged, while thousands of pots were broken in the excavating, or had been broken long ago by the weight of earth upon them.

Further excavations along the steep banks of the Rio Grande, and elsewhere in the states of Cocle, Veragua and Chiriqui in the Republic of Panama, have brought forth skeletons and treasure quite similar in character to the items found in this first tomb to be located by the electrical machine. The Republic is storing up a very fine state treasure for itself, and Lieutenant Williams is supporting racing horses and dogs that run now fast, now slow, but always with assurance that the source of their next meals is amply provided for.

◇ ◇

One of the disconcerting features of many legends about buried treasure is that they may be true; the treasure may be there where the cross marks the spot, but it may be humanly impossible to recover the loot.

Taboga Island is a beautiful spot, only about ten miles out in the Pacific from the City of Panama. The sides of the island are mostly steep and rocky, making approach by any kind of boat dangerous. On the island are many caves. There are treasure legends clustering about these caves. One of the most persistent of these legends says that Henry Morgan hid some of the loot he stole from his own men in a cave on this island.

Many natives of Panama know just where the gold of Morgan is hidden, they say. They can find the cave for you. If you pay them enough, they will find a cave without too much difficulty, but when you get there, you have, after all, only a cave.

Lieutenant Williams plans a thorough exploration of all the caves on Taboga Island, but I have a fatalistic feeling that he will leave this little chore for one of the last on his treasure-hunting program. He went to Taboga once.

Having survived the perils of landing on the rocky coast and getting his radio gold-finder up the rocky side of the island, the adventurous young Englishman found himself at the mouth of a cave which, his guide assured him, was certainly the very one in which Morgan had hidden his ill-gotten gold.

The opening of the cave was about five feet high and three feet wide. Inside—blackness.

Williams led the way, the guide now admitting that he was unacquainted with the terrain within. There were two or three flashlights in the party, and these made feeble breaks in the blanket of darkness in the great cavern.

Presently the air was so full of flapping bats, disturbed by men and flashlights for the first time in centuries, that it seemed doubtful whether the exploring party could go on. The squeaks of the bats and the flapping of their myriad wings made an eerie chaos in the weird atmosphere of Morgan's Cave.

When it was found that one could go forward in spite of the bats, simply by ignoring an occasional collision with one or more of them, the party made some progress. Suddenly the flashlight in Williams's hand revealed a gigantic snake, lying on a ledge of the damp wall, in the act of rearing his ugly head to strike at the intruders. The men stepped back, and the snake slid along the ledge toward his home in the cavern's roof.

The explorers went sixty feet straight ahead before coming upon what they took to be the rear wall of the cavern. The air was hot and very foul. Not much time could be spent here. Williams set up his instrument, and soon heard the sound of the golden voice in his receivers. The workers had to retreat to the outer air for ozone before proceeding with picks and shovels.

The excavation work was very brief. Only one piece of gold was recovered, and it was a nose-ring, such as had been recovered from the burial caves of Cocle.

With this one bit of treasure, the searchers were glad enough to escape from the foul cave and make their way back to the mainland, completely exhausted from their labors.

Williams looked at his nose-ring and said: "Perhaps it's only another burial cave anyway. But some day we'll go back and make a thorough search for Morgan's treasure."

The native workers shifted uneasily on their feet, and looked at the ocean in a non-committal manner.

◇ ◇

There is another source of treasure in Panama. A few finds have been made, and many more are to be made, along the Cruces Trail.

It is pronounced crew-sees, accent on the first syllable, and means crosses. It is the old trail that winds across the Isthmus of Panama from the old city of Panama on the Pacific side to the city of Porto Bello on the Atlantic side. It was called Cruces Trail because the Spaniards who first broke it through the jungle erected crosses and crucifixes at the principal turns and places of rest.

There is little doubt that there is treasure in great volume along the route taken by the trains of pack mules that carried across the Isthmus a stream of gold and silver over a period of nearly three centuries.

The Spaniards developed a system of handling the treasure that came out of the mines of Peru. The mines were worked by Indians under Spanish taskmasters. The gold and silver, after smelting, were concentrated at Lima. During the dry season, the pack trains were started north to Panama, and then across the Isthmus along the Trail.

This stream of gold had long ceased to flow from coast to coast, and the old Trail had been partly swallowed up by jungle growth, when the California gold rush became the world's sensation in 1849. The pack trains began moving again toward Panama with supplies for the new Californians, and toward the Atlantic coast with heavy loads of gold.

More than forty million dollars in gold passed over the Cruces Trail on pack animals during the years of the California excitement.

Robbing a pack train was not a difficult feat in the days of the Forty-niners. Many an ambuscade was carried out successfully by the desperate highwaymen who made headquarters in Panama. Sometimes there was a battle in which lives were lost on both sides, but generally the ambuscade was such a sudden and complete surprise that the guardians of the gold surrendered without a struggle.

There are many tales of burial of gold after these holdups. The robbers, anxious to make a quick escape, would bury the loot, make a map of the terrain, and return for their heavy burden later if they had good luck. Sometimes their luck was bad.

The governments of the United States, France, Great Britain, Peru, Brazil, Denmark, and Ecuador joined in a diplomatic protest to the government of Panama against the robbery of passengers and treasure trains crossing the Isthmus, under date of January 26, 1854. The government of Panama was reminded that it levied a charge of two dollars per head upon all persons crossing its territory, but failed to give even a dollar's worth of protection. It was pointed out that vast quantities of treasure had disappeared along the Cruces Trail and that many foreigners had been murdered. It was known to everyone who took the trouble to investigate, said the joint note, that criminals and toughs from all over the world had gathered along the Trail to reap the golden harvest.

But nothing was done by the Panama government that tended to check the crime wave. So the foreigners most interested, led by the Americans, organized a protective body called the Isthmus Guard, headed by Ran Runnels, a bad man from Texas.

Runnels supplied himself with a few good Texas cowboys and a nice collection of cowponies, ropes and rifles. The bandits of the Cruces Trail were found hanging from noble palm trees with surprising frequency. Banditry slackened and became unfashionable. The Governor of the region and the government of Panama looked on with amazement at this efficient but wholly extra-legal enforcement of law. But no protest was made.

Lieutenant Williams has made a start along the Cruces Trail, but has had no time to follow up his first discoveries.

At one spot, where there was a sort of jungle hummock, the locating machine gave a positive report of treasure.

After listening for some time and making several moves on a slightly raised spot in the jungle beside the old Trail, Williams started his men working with spades and picks and machetes. He was sure he had a find.

The tangled growth was cleared, and digging uncovered the tiled floor of an old Spanish house. In the center of the floor was a tile design of the arms of Castile and Leon. This portion of the floor was carefully removed, and beneath it was found a box containing thirty-two gold coins and seventy-two silver ones. The dates on these coins were all prior to 1804. There were doubloons and pieces of eight, and a few scattering coins of other denominations.

Further excavation uncovered valuable gold and silver utensils.

But there is a big job ahead in the treasure search along the Trail. The Panama government now proposes to make a trans-

Isthmian automobile highway, for the convenience of tourists, along the route of the historic path of the treasure-bearing burros. While the engineering work is proceeding, the search for treasure will not be neglected.

VI. *Blackbeard and His Treasure*

NO REAL pirate has been credited with burying more treasure than Blackbeard. The reputed locations of Blackbeard treasures range from the Isles of Shoals off the coast of New Hampshire, to Trinidad off the coast of Brazil.

The search for Blackbeard's hoards in many localities has been undertaken with increased zeal since Christmas Day, 1928, when it was discovered that a treasure chest buried by Blackbeard about the year 1716 had been dug up and carried away.

Plum Point is a narrow neck of land in Beaufort county, North Carolina, where Bath Creek flows into the Pamlico River. The end of the Point, low and sandy, is cut off from the mainland by a marsh, so that it is practically an island.

For more than two hundred years the story of a treasure chest, buried on that point at night by Blackbeard and his men persisted. The low ground had been dug over many times during those two centuries. Never a month passed without some digging there by treasure-seekers, or by idlers and trappers of the vicinity who just thought they'd like to get rich if the getting wasn't too difficult.

Many earnest diggers had heard the story in detail, and had given much time to their searching for that treasure chest. They had dug deeply and widely. But it was impossible for any one digger to cover the whole surface of the Point in a reasonably active lifetime, so the diggers, one by one, became discouraged or disillusioned and went away.

On the Christmas Day just mentioned, two trappers were crossing the Point to examine some traps they had set in the marsh. They stumbled over large brickbats scattered on the sand, and at once were awake to the fact that something had happened on the Point.

The broken bricks were scattered near a freshly dug hole. They had been taken out of the hole. About eight feet down was a brick vault that had been broken open on top and at one end. In a minute or two the trappers had forgotten their traps in the excitement brought on by realization of a tremendously sensational fact.

Blackbeard's treasure chest had been found and carried away!

The bricks were very old, larger than bricks now commonly used in building, and hand-made, with rounded edges. The portion of the vault remaining told the story eloquently.

The top of the vault had been rounded, somewhat in the shape of a roof, and the bottom, still intact, was a flat floor made of three courses of bricks. The sides were mostly intact. Only enough of the vault had been broken away to make possible the extraction

TREASURE ABOARD

of the treasure chest, which had been raised out of the hole, apparently by tackle rigged on a tripod of poles.

The floor of the vault had been laid by the hiders of the treasure, the chest lowered upon the floor, and the walls and top then built up with bricks and plenty of mortar, around and over the chest. The chest had been a little more than three feet long, possibly forty inches. It was about thirty-two inches wide and about the same depth. Mortar had been smeared freely in the hasty laying up of the bricks, and had been squeezed into the inside walls of the vault. This mortar retained a perfect imprint of the chest, with its handforged iron straps criss-crossing one another and the large round rivet-heads studded thickly.

There were foot-tracks of three men who had unearthed the chest. There was a trail indicating that the heavy chest had been dragged, mounted upon a plank, from the hole to the river bank, where it evidently had been loaded into a boat.

So the long-sought treasure of Blackbeard had been dug up and carried away! The news caused a sensation in Bath and vicinity that has not yet subsided.

Who got the treasure? How did they know exactly where to dig for it? Why had all the other searchers missed it all these years? The lucky ones had dug straight down, at a spot close to a very old tree. They had had to cut some of the roots of the tree to get down to their treasure trove. The signs indicated that these treasure hunters had known exactly where to dig, for there had been no fresh spade marks anywhere on the Point except where the chest had been dug up.

And what did the treasure chest of Blackbeard contain? There is much speculation on this point in North Carolina. Some say the chest undoubtedly contained thousands and thousands of doubloons and pieces of eight, diamonds and golden goblets. But others repeat a story of Blackbeard that is told by the oldsters of Bath.

◇ ◇

Blackbeard was known in the records of the courts as Edward Teach and Edward Thatch. In Bristol, England, where he was

observed growing up "for the gallows," as many of the neighbors
said, his name was Drummond. Most of the court records I have
perused, in following the maturer career of this gentleman, called
him Teach, and by that name he was known ashore in Bath
Town and neighboring settlements. There are numerous families
named Tinch still living along the shores of Pamlico Sound, and
some of these claim to be descended from Blackbeard. Considering the known facts of the pirate's history, it would seem probable that he must have a great many descendants somewhere, and
the very numerousness of the Tinches would appear to lend color
to their claim.

Much of Blackbeard's reputation in song and story is due to
his consummate showmanship. He had a fine sense for drama,
and he made up for his part better than any other pirate who
ever lived.

Most of the successful pirates liked to dramatize themselves.
They were fancy dressers. In an age when other seafaring folk
went about in rather sober garb, the more dashing pirates wore
scarlet and green and yellow silk, romantically tailored, and affected large earrings, heavy gold rings on their fingers, and
cocked hats in many colors. This fanciful style of dress had much
to do with getting recruits for pirate fleets, just as the shining
trappings and plumes provide long waiting lists for the various
companies of guards that add so much to the royal pageantry for
the remaining monarchs of Europe.

Blackbeard made up for his rôles just as meticulously as
Edwin Booth ever did. He wanted to be known as the Terror of
the Seas, and he tried to live up to that characterization. At
sea he let his black whiskers grow. He let his black hair grow.
He was abundantly supplied with coarse hair and beard, and when
the shaggy growth was flourishing, in the midst of a piratical
voyage, the pirate was rather a fearsome looking fellow. Indeed,
according to some of the passengers of ships boarded by him, he
looked much more terrible than any conventional impersonator
of the devil.

He was tall. Some accounts of his depredations describe him as
six and a half feet tall, but this may have been a natural exag-

geration, due to terror. He was very broad-shouldered and his arms were long, like an ape's, so that his hands hung down below his knees when he was seated. His long reach with a cutlass and dagger had much to do with his remarkable success as a pirate.

Captain Teach was at his best in a charge, leading a boarding party of cutthroats down the deck of an unfortunate merchant ship that had resisted his command to surrender.

On these occasions he was a terror to write letters to the papers about, if ever you should live through the scene. Many survivors of captured crews did write such letters, some of which were published as warnings against ocean travel.

Before climbing aboard the recalcitrant vessel, Blackbeard was wont to don a long sash of scarlet silk, wrapped once or twice around his waist, and passing over one shoulder, somewhat like a glorified Sam Browne belt. In the waistband were stuck three pistols. Three more were slung in the shoulder sash. Another usually was in the giant's left hand. Two or three short knives were in the belt, close to the right hand, and sometimes an extra cutlass was in a scabbard slung from the left side of the belt. The Terror carried a naked cutlass in his right hand, and generally appeared on the enemy's deck carrying a knife about two feet long between his teeth. The plenitude of knives was a part of the Terror's technique. He could throw a knife of almost any size or design very accurately, so as to bury it in the heart of a person across the deck from him.

Blackbeard made the most of his whiskers on these occasions. He made them up for the show according to his whim and according to their length. If they were very long (and they sometimes reached below his waist) he was wont to plait them with black ribbons and stick burning slow matches into the plaits, just for the infernal effect upon the terrified beholders. The slow matches of those days, used to light the priming charges of the cannon, were somewhat equivalent to the punk sticks used by American children on the Fourth of July in places not yet cognizant of the safe and sane Independence Day.

The Terror of the Seas often stuck slow matches under his hat, so that the burning ends were dangling about his face, when his whiskers did not provide suitable nesting places for these little ornaments. The whiskers were really more effective when grown out to about a foot in length, for then they were very bristling and terrible, sticking out in all directions and presenting a peculiarly fiendish appearance. The whiskers grew high on the pirate's face, so that his fiery eyes seemed to gleam out from the midst of them, especially when the coarse hair from the head straggled down around the face.

While he held the knife between his teeth, the Terror looked formidable enough, but when he had thrown it he was ready for his best act—the charge down the deck. Captain Teach was almost brokenhearted when he captured a prize if he could not put on this act.

He led the charge. He did not permit any of his men to go before him, but the villains did not keep many paces to the rear. If there was a crew making a desperate last stand on the deck with a few armed passengers to reinforce the defenders, Blackbeard was pleased. A few weeping and praying women, with children at their sides, added just the touch of melodrama that this superb actor demanded for the exhibition of his best histrionic art.

He bellowed; he roared; he let out infernal yells. Towering above every human being on the deck, he advanced with long strides, swinging his cutlass in his right hand, shooting with his left, or striking with a clubbed pistol. Was there a sturdy group of defenders in the waist of the ship? Blackbeard was upon them with a horrible yell, his great mouth wide open, his eyes flashing hatred and murder, his cutlass dripping hot blood. Left he struck; right he slashed, ahead he kicked with his great feet or butted with his head.

Stout-hearted, indeed, was the group that did not break and run for cover before the swinging cutlass of the monster reached its outskirts.

When up to his best form, Captain Teach used to like to dispose of the women and children who chanced to be on deck, just to make the scene complete. If the fight did not demand all of the leader's immediate attention, he loved to make quick excursions to the sidelines, pick up a woman or a child in his great left paw, and stab repeatedly into the yielding flesh with a dagger, then quickly throwing the murdered person over the side and rushing back to the main business of the moment. This sort of thing always had an effect upon the opposing fighters. When the defenders of the ship saw their women and children thus wantonly butchered, they often desired to surrender, hoping to prevent further slaughter of this kind.

Sometimes Captain Teach would call off his murderous crew the moment the boarded ship struck her flag in token of surrender. If he was so minded, he would become all at once the soul of polite gentility. With his great form soaked in blood and his hands dripping gore, the Terror would salute the ranking officer of the prize, and remark lightly upon the weather or upon the outstanding features of the fight, as a victorious captain of a football team might exchange gossip about the game with his defeated rival.

"By my soul, Captain," he would say, " 'twas a hot bit of a scrimmage, was it not? I hope we have not put you out with our uncouth ways, this hot day! My men are country fellows, mostly, and 'tis little they know of courtesy or of respect for a fine fighting man like yourself. Will you join me on my sloop yonder for a cool pot of ale or a noggin of rum? Faith, we'll drink to the ladies, if there be any of them left alive after this little misunderstanding we've had! Come, Captain; your hand!"

If the humor was strong upon him, he would forbid his men to shed another drop of blood, and would force the captured officers, and often some of the women passengers, to go to his cabin and drink with him.

On other occasions, he would give no quarter, and would not cease butchering or call off his men until every captured person had been slain and thrown overboard. He was a fellow of violent moods, and loved to observe the effect of these moods upon his own men and his victims.

He ruled his men with an iron hand. He was feared by all of them. He took advantage of every opportunity to keep that fear alive.

One of Blackbeard's most confidential lieutenants was Basilica Hands, generally set down as Israel Hands by chroniclers of Blackbeard's exploits. Stevenson's coxswain in Treasure Island took his name from this villain. Hands was faithful to Teach, and a valuable fighter. But the boisterous Captain went too far with Hands just once.

Blackbeard was drinking in his cabin with Hands and Richards, his first mate. Two loaded and primed pistols lay on the table in front of the Captain. Hands and Richards were across the table.

Suddenly, Teach blew out the candle, crossed the pistols under the table, and pulled both triggers. Richards was uninjured, but Hands was shot through the left knee. When Hands complained bitterly over such wanton deviltry, Blackbeard shouted: "Aha, you bellyache over a little thing like that? Well, if I didn't kill or maim one of you fellows once in a while, we'd never know who is Captain here!"

Teach was Captain, all right, but that little demonstration was to cost him more than he could have suspected. Hands nursed his wound and his grievance long. He was a cripple for the rest of his life.

One of the classic stories of Blackbeard, told many years later by Basilica Hands in a London tavern, concerns Captain Teach's demonstration of hell. There had been some little talk about hell among the group of favorites in the Captain's cabin. Eternal damnation was a thing much argued about in those days before hell went out of style in the pulpits.

"Come, my bullies," said Blackbeard, "we'll make a little hell of our own, right here in my cabin. Since we all must go to the brimstone country soon, it's no harm to get the smell of the stuff in our nostrils now. I tell you, I'm not afraid of hell. Brimstone is like incense to me."

So he ordered a pot of sulphur (then generally called brimstone) brought in and lighted under the table. The window and the door were closed tight, and a jolly endurance contest was on. The four men who were the Captain's guests in the little cabin hell sputtered, choked and coughed. But whenever one of them staggered toward the door, Captain Teach was there to bar the way and to fling the suffering villain back into his chair. It seemed to be great fun for the Captain. He roared with mighty laughter when one of the victims declared they would all die unless the door were opened at once.

"If we die, we'll never know it, boys!" he shouted. "We'll be in hell anyhow, with our lungs full of brimstone. Why, Richards, I believe we're dead already, and smoking in hell! Don't you remember, bully, that you were hanged at Execution Dock for a bloody pirate, and you and I have just met here in hell? Don't cough so, my brave lad, you have only a million years to spend in this room, and then we move on to the broiling cage!"

When the door finally was flung open by Blackbeard, his victims were nearly asphyxiated, but he was in a hilarious mood, laughing and slapping his long thighs with glee, and drinking great beakers of hot rum to clear his throat.

Captain Teach had, besides great physical strength and size, a supply of sagacity and a knowledge of a certain type of human character that might have made him, had he been born two hundred years later, a great captain of industry or a successful Secretary of the Interior. He knew his men. He was not far wrong when he said that he had to shoot one of the boys now and again to demonstrate his leadership.

A tale that was told by Teach's men ashore after a certain long cruise concerned the presence of Satan aboard ship. The men swore that they had been out two weeks and had become thoroughly acquainted with one another, when a stranger made his appearance on the ship, from nowhere. They had not had contact with any other vessel. But here was this stranger, dressed handsomely, in red silk, some said, walking about the vessel, looking her over, as though appraising a piece of property. The tall, courtly stranger did not mix with the men, and he was not seen speaking to any of the officers except the Captain, with whom he seemed always to be on familiar terms. The men put their heads together and decided immediately that this was none other than the Devil himself. Sometimes they saw him aloft in the crosstrees, looking off toward a little dark cloud and making peculiar motions with his hands. In such cases, they said, the wind invariably rose, and there was, at least figuratively, the devil to pay. It was the opinion of the hands that there was the devil to pay quite literally, for the handsome stranger, smiling mysteriously, was seen to betake himself to Blackbeard's side in the height of one such storm, and the two went below together. When they returned to the deck, an hour and a half later, the storm began to abate. The pirates thoroughly believed that Blackbeard's infernal partner had forced a settlement from the "old man," and they chuckled to think that somebody could make old Blackbeard himself come to terms.

What planning and stage-setting that little scenario of the devil aboard ship must have cost the redoubtable Blackbeard! You see the dramatic genius of the fellow.

Captain Teach kept a log, just as legitimate captains always have done. One little fragment of that log has survived:

> Such a day! Rum all out. . . . Our company somewhat sober. . . . A damned confusion amongst us . . . rogues a-plotting . . . great talk of separation . . . so I looked sharp for a Prize . . . took one with a great deal of Liquor aboard . . . so kept company hot, damned hot . . . things went well again.

◇ ◇

The story of the treasure of the Isles of Shoals is associated with Blackbeard. It can be told here, before we go into the recital of the main facts of the pirate's career, since there is much variation in the stories told by different chroniclers as to the period in Blackbeard's life in which the incidents relating to the Isles of Shoals occurred.

Captain Teach, according to those who attempt to explain certain traditions of the Isles, was operating off the coast of Scotland during one of his brief absences from American waters. Lying off the west coast of Scotland, awaiting the scheduled passage of a richly laden East Indiaman, Teach's pirate sloop was hailed by a lone man in a rowboat.

The little boat came alongside, and a Scotch seafaring man came up the rope that was tossed to him, hand over hand. The visitor had no difficulty in finding Captain Teach, who seemed to be expecting him. The two conferred in Blackbeard's cabin for three or four hours. Then they appeared on deck, very friendly, and Blackbeard called his officers together and introduced the stranger:

"Boys, here's Sandy Gordon, a pirate that can show a lot of you tricks in spilling blood.

"He's going to be with us for a while and we're going to work together, even after he gets a ship of his own.

"You know my rule on this ship against women. We want no women aboard, except in the Captain's cabin, and we don't want them there often or long. But I'm making a little exception to the rule. Captain Gordon is going to bring a lady aboard as his guest for a little while. She'll have the cabin next to mine, and all hands are to keep clear of that cabin until Gordon and his lady go aboard their own ship."

The officers and men aboard Blackbeard's vessel were not much pleased with this news, but they managed to hide their dissatisfaction from their boss. Women caused trouble aboard ship. That was part of every pirate's creed. Nearly all articles signed by captains and crews of piratical vessels in those days forbade the presence of women on the ship. Blackbeard maintained the same rules, except as to his own personal women. When it suited him to keep a captured woman aboard for a few days, he did so, usually throwing her overboard with his own hands when he thought the time appropriate. It was observed that the men were always harder to handle during or after one of these romances, for they were plainly and wickedly jealous of their Captain, and would not suffer him to violate the rule against women were it not that they were afraid to oppose him in anything. They had seen too many men choked to death by the powerful hands of Blackbeard.

So there was talk, but not loud talk, among the men of Blackbeard's crew when, the night after the arrival of Sandy Gordon aboard, the vessel put close in toward shore, and Sandy, with one of Blackbeard's men, rowed up the little inlet toward a quiet farmhouse. Before daylight the boat returned. The third passenger was a fair-haired Scotch girl, whose feet and hands were bound.

The fair passenger seemed to be unconscious. She was carried to her cabin.

She was Martha Herring, and she had been in custody of Pirate Sandy Gordon for several weeks, afloat and ashore.

Sandy had been a mariner from earliest boyhood. He had served as ship's carpenter on many peaceful voyages. Sailing to and from the Guinea coast aboard slavers, he had observed with satisfaction the large profits made by his employers. Sandy was pleased because he had no intention of remaining a ship's carpenter all his life. He, too, would make profits.

But he was in his late twenties, and still a ship's carpenter, when he sailed aboard the *Porpoise,* under Captain John Herring, to capture some of the Algerine corsairs who were doing great damage to English shipping. The *Porpoise* was an armed merchantman, privately outfitted on a private business venture. There were profits in capturing Barbary corsairs sometimes.

Now, as in the case of the memorable schooner *Hesperus,* the Captain had taken his little daughter, to bear him company. But in this case, the Captain's little daughter was quite eighteen years of age, and Captain John Herring soon learned to his sorrow that one does not take one's beautiful daughter along on pirate hunting expeditions. Captain Herring never did it again.

Sandy was young himself, and the good ship *Porpoise* was not more than four days out of the port of London when Sandy Gordon was seized with a great fancy for the Captain's daughter. Neither history nor legend tells us how the beautiful Martha responded to the attentions of the amorous young Scot. But this we know: Captain Herring was indignant, furious. He gave Sandy warning. And just then Sandy began to realize that he was a very fearless young man.

Sandy sought out the beautiful Martha in the Captain's cabin. The Captain entered.

There followed some rather trying hours for Sandy.

Suffering from the effects of seventy-two lashes on his bare back, Sandy lay in irons in the ship's hold and meditated. In thirty days one may do a lot of meditating, especially if one be alone and in irons.

When our young hero was permitted to resume his duties aboard the *Porpoise,* he was very quiet and orderly in his demeanor. Also, he was very friendly with certain of his shipmates. Sandy was plotting mutiny.

Before the first Algerine corsair came in sight, the mutiny broke.

It was a dark night, and Sandy had the mid-watch. A shot from his pistol was the signal. The mutineers, constituting an active minority of the crew, rushed to their bloody work.

The Captain was dragged from his cabin, bound, and lashed to a gun. The mate, who attempted to protect the Captain's daughter, was shot through the head, his blood streaming over the unconscious girl.

The Captain was wounded more than twenty times by handspikes wielded by his mutinous men. But Sandy saved him from death.

"Belay that, lads!" cried Sandy, "I've a bonnie score to settle with this mon, ye ken!"

Most of the sailors were spared at Sandy's command. They could be used with profit in the business just ahead.

Sandy himself wielded the lash upon the back of the helpless Captain. Seventy-two!

"Now," said Sandy, "ye may rest a wee bit."

At the end of an hour, Sandy laid on seventy-two more lashes. And so it was continued at intervals of one hour until there was no life left in the body of the unfortunate Captain.

Sandy took charge of Martha and did not permit any member of the crew to approach her. He kept her locked and guarded in her cabin while her father was being whipped to death.

When Sandy called his crew together in council, he was all dressed in red. He had appropriated the full dress uniform of Lieutenant Meeks of the Royal Marines, who had been in charge of the fighting force aboard the *Porpoise* that was to overcome the Algerines.

Sandy liked himself in the red uniform. He had suddenly become a striking figure. He proclaimed himself Captain of the ship, and announced that all nations were his enemies.

Those of the crew who did not instantly agree with everything the Captain said were thrown overboard without ceremony. And then the Captain posted an astonishing set of rules that he had been writing ever since he had been released from solitary confinement. The rules set forth that on this pirate ship there was to be no division of plunder, share and share alike, as was the custom among all other pirates.

The expedition was the property of Captain Gordon. It was his private business venture. The profits were to be all his. The expedition was a closed corporation, and Sandy owned all the stock. The men were to be paid wages, twenty-five per cent more than wages paid on merchantmen. Wounded men were to be compensated according to a prudent scale of insurance. Dissenters were to be thrown overboard.

When the men read the new regulations, there was quite a bit of throwing overboard to be done. But Sandy attended to it, efficiently and promptly. He pointed out to his mate that this was the most economical method of disposing of undesirable persons, since there was no wear and tear on tackle, and no expenditure of powder. Thereafter drowning was made the official form of execution, for enemies as well as for shipmates.

This first piratical cruise of Captain Gordon's was brought to a close off the Scottish coast, after several prizes had been taken. The men mutinied against Sandy's parsimonious policy. They wanted to share in the profits of the business, and Sandy held that such an arrangement was contrary to sound business principles.

The men won the argument, and Sandy, his lady, and his efficiency program were bundled over the side into a rowboat. They had landed and set up a very restricted form of house-keeping in an old farmhouse. Sandy had had some difficulty in keeping Martha from deserting him. He had solved the problem by knocking her unconscious and tying her up from time to time.

Captain Teach and a small party of his men had come upon the distressed pirate and his unwilling consort while ashore one night, seeking water and Scotch liquor. Blackbeard had been affected by the brawny Scotsman's tale of adventure, enterprise and maltreatment.

"Come aboard me, and we'll see how good a pirate you are," said Teach. "If you prove as good as your boasting, I'll see you outfitted, and maybe we can do business together."

That was the beginning of a profitable partnership.

A week later, Blackbeard fought a jolly battle with a tall East Indiaman, homeward bound for London. She was a rich prize, and well worth fighting for. But she was well defended too. It was a fine opportunity for Sandy Gordon. He recognized the situation as one that might make possible a prosperous career for him. He fought like a wild beast, and when the two vessels were lashed together, Gordon and Blackbeard were side by side in leading the boarding party that swept the Indiaman's deck clear of defenders.

Out of the survivors of the crew, Blackbeard picked a few, and inquired of them whether they would like to sail this ship under Captain Gordon, under the black flag, and under strict agreement concerning an equitable distribution of the spoils.

None of the men refused. Articles were drawn up, and Blackbeard forced Sandy to consent to the usual clauses concerning a share of the loot for every man.

"A muckle waste, I call it," said Sandy, "but do as ye will."

A rendezvous was appointed for the Isles of Shoals, and an approximate date set down for a grand celebration there. The men of Sandy's new crew were promised that no woman would be permitted aboard ship after the rendezvous. Until that time, Captain Gordon should enjoy the unusual privilege of retaining his fair companion.

The two pirate vessels parted company, each going its own way.

Gordon's first impressive prize was a great Spanish galleon. As soon as she was sighted, explicit instructions were given out to every member of the crew of the *Flying Scot*, as the great ship had been named by Sandy. Each man knew exactly what was expected of him.

But Sandy's men behaved themselves better than their master

had hoped. Their lives were not so precious to them as the average reader, comfortably perusing these lines, might suppose.

Some months at sea as a common sailor, under the conditions prevailing in the early years of the eighteenth century, had a tendency to make life seem of no great importance. If a man could die fighting, he generally did so with great gusto. A good fight was likely to end forever the spiritless ennui that pervaded the life of the sailing ship.

The galleon fired a broadside when she was in position to do so, but she tried her best to run away. She was quickly overhauled.

The *Flying Scot* was lashed to the side of the galleon and a boarding party fought its way to the broad deck that was half filled with panic-stricken Spaniards, hopeless of victory but determined to sell their lives dearly. Most of the Spaniards were tossed overboard, after the first rush of the boarders had caused the defenders of the galleon to throw down their arms.

Captain Gordon, prodigious in his scarlet trappings, prudently boarded the galleon some fifteen minutes after the first of his men had started the battle. He was in time to save the Captain, the chaplain, and half a dozen sailors, from immediate death. These unfortunates were tortured until they revealed the amount of treasure on board and the secret places in which most of it was stored. Then they too were thrown overboard.

Careful check of the treasure showed that Captain Gordon was indeed a wealthy man. He had more than a million dollars' worth of gold and silver out of this vessel.

Other good captures were made, and Sandy's crew soon was recruited to full strength by the simple expedient of giving captured seamen their choice of piracy or instant death.

It was six weeks after the capture of the galleon that Sandy Gordon was called upon to exercise his genius for thrifty administration in an extraordinary crisis. There was a fearful storm. The pirate vessel was heavily laden with the Spanish treasure. She was making no headway against the tremendous seas that poured over her deck and threatened to send her to the bottom.

Sandy called the entire crew to prayer. While the service of supplication was in progress, a picked squad of ruffians rushed upon the kneeling sailors, bound twenty of them fast, and threw them overside.

Thus lightened, the *Flying Scot* weathered the storm.

Martha accommodated herself to her new station in life, when she gave up hope of altering her condition materially by rebellion. She appeared on deck during a fight one day, and bound up most tenderly the wounds of her lord and master. From that day forward she had the run of the ship, and the men, without too much politeness, suffered her to go where she would without molestation.

The *Flying Scot* arrived at the Isles of Shoals some weeks ahead of Blackbeard and his crew. She carried a heavy cargo of treasure. On Star Island, the day after arrival, division of the treasure was made. The crew separated into groups, and many burial parties were organized. Each group swore its members to secrecy, and in each little treasure company there was an understanding that the survivor or survivors were to take all, in case of the death of some members.

Captain Gordon and his fair companion betook themselves to White Island, and there, according to the surviving legend, their treasure was buried. They had a small house constructed for themselves here, and during the remainder of the stay of the pirates at the Isles of Shoals these two enjoyed a honeymoon. Although the partnership had started off badly and bloodily enough, the remarkable adaptive powers of the young woman were such as to make a honeymoon on the Isles a romantic and almost idyllic interlude.

When Blackbeard and his crew arrived, there was more burying of treasure, and some other burials too, for Captain Teach took it upon himself to kill three of his men in a little academic argument about the disposal of certain valuable pieces of plate that had been taken from a Spanish ship.

There were long business conferences between Gordon and Teach, and the general belief of the men was that these conferences resulted in further enrichment of the Captains at the expense of the crews, but no one ever was able to make any proofs of any such collusion.

Blackbeard did not tarry long at the Isles of Shoals. He had no honeymoon on his hands, and did not shave off his whiskers. He was soon off to sea again.

A week or two later, a lookout sighted a sail. Sandy Gordon assembled his crew and lifted his anchor. The men were eager to take a prize, loot her, and return to the Isles to finish their holiday. When Martha was about to embark, Captain Gordon was reminded of his promise, in his contract with his men, to have no women aboard after reaching the Shoals. Reluctantly Sandy led Martha back to their little house on the hill on White Island. According to the legend of the Shoals, he made her swear a terrible oath that she would stay there and guard the treasure until his return, however long that period of waiting might be.

The strange sail proved to be a British warship, looking for pirates. The battle was long and bloody, and when it was over the *Flying Scot* was a sinking hulk, drifting in toward the Isles of Shoals. So far as known, the only pirates who escaped death in the battle were hanged at the yardarm of the victorious man-of-war.

Old frequenters of the Isles of Shoals tell the story of a wraith-like figure in white with streaming blonde hair that may be seen on stormy nights on a low point of White Island, looking off to sea.

Treasure hunters should put a large cross on the Isles of Shoals. But those who are afraid of ghosts had better keep away from White Island.

◇ ◇

For a time the careers of Blackbeard and Stede Bonnet were intermingled. Near the mouth of the Cape Fear river, close to the tip of the peninsula formed by New Hanover county, North Carolina, as it dips toward New Inlet, is a spot marked with a cross by many treasure-hunters, for here Bonnet, near the end of his career, is said to have buried large quantities of treasure. And Bonnet, unwillingly enough, was associated with Blackbeard in the latter's most prosperous days of treasure gathering.

Major Stede Bonnet went pirating because he couldn't stand his wife.

In movies one goes down to the sea in pirate ships only because one's king has abused one, made a slave of one, and deserted one in trouble.

Stede Bonnet's King had used him well. He had given him a life job in the Royal Colonial Army in Barbadoes, and, when Bonnet had reached middle age and the rank of major, His Majesty had been pleased to retire him with honor and half pay.

No, Major Bonnet hadn't anything against his King. But if the King had known the Major's wife, Bonnet might have had royal clemency when he needed it sorely.

Major Bonnet, after retiring from the army, became a professional prominent citizen of the city of Bridgetown, Barbadoes. He was rated a wealthy man. Probably he had taken a flyer now and again in colonial shipping enterprises while serving his time in the army. He was a dignified personage; a man of property and education. I can imagine him a vestryman of the quality church of the city, a position which, in that place and at that time, was equivalent in glory to the post of Grand Exalted Ruler of the Elks in our own epoch.

But Stede Bonnet couldn't stand his wife. She is set down in the annals of Bridgetown as a harridan most horrible. Poor Bonnet had managed to maintain appearances and uphold his social standing as an army officer and a man of substance as long as he was busy bossing troops. If he heard foul language at home in the morning, he could take it out on the men during the day. He could order extra maneuvers in the hot Barbadoes sunshine, and his temper could thus be kept under.

But when he retired from the army and the affairs of war, he wanted peace and quiet—and he had to go pirating to get them.

We have no detailed record of the domestic battles that so racked his morale, but it is recorded by the historians of those troubled days that his neighbors and associates pitied him, and did not blame him, concluding that his reason must have been unsettled by his wife's appalling nagging.

In the spring of 1717, he began looking about for a vessel. Having plenty of money and being of unquestioned standing, he found no difficulty in buying a fine sloop and arming her with ten guns. No one questioned his purpose. Nobody in Bridgetown knew Mrs. Bonnet quite so well as her husband knew her, so nobody suspected that he was preparing to sail forth to slay hundreds of surprised Christians, inwardly gloating because each victim of his cutlass was a vicarious sacrifice, standing for the revolting Mrs. Bonnet.

On a dark night that spring Major Bonnet sailed out of the harbor of Bridgetown as owner and captain of the pirate sloop *Revenge*. Commentators have been puzzled that a clever and well-educated man of quality should show no more originality in naming his ship. There were more than a dozen *Revenges* sailing the seas under black flags at that time. Every second pirate felt it necessary to pretend that he had a score to settle with the nations of the world. If you were going pirating and had no imagination or originality, you called your ship the *Revenge* to indicate that you had been put upon and were going to get even.

But Stede Bonnet had imagination. He was going out for revenge. He could imagine how his querulous wife would feel when all the neighbors crowded about to sympathize with her because her husband hadn't been able to stand her any longer and had gone off to sea under the skull and cross-bones! Oh, the Major had his revenge!

Unluckily, he did not know port from starboard. He had never been to sea, except as a dignified passenger, uncurious about the gear that made the ship proceed from point of departure to destination. Now he found himself captain of a fine sloop, and the only order he knew how to shout to his seventy salty ruffians was: "Forward! March!"

When the crew discovered that their captain was ignorant of the uses of a belaying pin and thought that aft was the name of a cabin, mutiny was narrowly averted. The spectacle of the commander, very seasick and altogether at sea, consulting with the first mate as to the best method of getting from south to north when the wind was south-southeast, was one to wring the heart of any respectable mariner. That any man with ambition to become a real pirate should serve docilely under such direction was beyond the scope of the imagination of every cutthroat aboard the *Revenge*.

Major Bonnet won his first and most praiseworthy victory at sea when he demonstrated to his men that he was really captain of the ship and knew how to enforce obedience, even if he didn't know a pennant from a pinnace. He had his men soundly flogged, flogged again, served with a double ration of rum, and again flogged.

That was language a good sailor could understand. The Major had failed for lack of a firm hand in managing one establishment. But he wasn't married to the crew of the *Revenge*, and he didn't have to be a gentleman any more unless he wanted to be one.

One of the first captures made by him was the ship *Turbet*, from Barbadoes. He put the crew into boats and, after taking out most of the merchandise, set fire to the ship. One may well fancy that this rough conduct was indulged in to give the wife a good scare. When the sailors from the *Turbet* got back to Barbadoes, how they must have regaled Madame Bonnet with tales of the fierce pirate she had nourished unawares! No doubt the good woman's blood ran cold when she remembered how often and how dangerously she had tempted this raging monster, supposing him to be hopelessly domestic and thoroughly harmless.

Stede Bonnet is the patron saint of all henpecked husbands. Suppressed homelovers should call upon his name before they go forth to roister.

Standing off the Virginia capes for a short cruise, he took half a dozen vessels, mostly from Scotch ports. In most cases he detained the prize only long enough to transfer the loot. Then he let her proceed, after taking a few precautions to make her progress slow and uncertain. But occasionally, no doubt to celebrate his freedom from matrimonial bondage, he would stage a party. He gets credit for inventing the game known as walking the plank. In fact, it is the opinion of many learned historians that he was the only pirate who ever actually indulged in it.

According to tales told by survivors, Bonnet did, upon occasion, rig a wide plank sticking straight out to sea at the port gangway. But this was done only when the captured vessel carried a large passenger list.

When an ordinary crew was to be dispatched to its reward, Bonnet's trusty men, who had learned to obey cheerfully that they might be long-lived upon the earth, waded in with heavy cutlasses, and the job was accomplished as expeditiously as is the laying low of a half-acre of sunflowers by a Kansas farmer armed with a sharp and heavy corn-knife. But passengers required more delicate attentions. Passengers were apt to be finicky. The ladies, sadly overdressed and undernourished, used to faint below decks at the sound of hacking cutlasses making contact with sturdy frames. Stede Bonnet's men looked decidedly foolish, lugging unconscious ladies up the ladders to toss them ungracefully overside.

So the plank was rigged, and it proved a blessing. Timid passengers were blindfolded and marched in single file to the plank, and then permitted to continue marching just as far as the limited accommodations would allow. That surprised step into space, followed quickly by a splash into salt water below, furnished unrivalled entertainment for the bully boys of the good ship *Revenge*. Major Bonnet, they swore, was a jolly tar, despite his limited knowledge of the art of navigation.

Favorite survivors of the first cruise off the Virginia capes were taken to New York, whither Bonnet shaped his course so as to dispose of his handsome load of mixed merchandise. All these survivors were men. No women had been spared. Major Bonnet's experience in life had not made him partial to the dainty sex. The happy prisoners were landed quietly at Gardiner's Island and the word was sent around that a bloody pirate was in port, awaiting customers. New York was then an excellent market for pirated goods, and well-behaved pirates who were not unreasonable in their relations with public officials and public-spirited merchants were made to feel that it was a friendly port of call.

Bonnet sold his cargo and bought provisions, gave his men a bit of shore-leave, and sailed away. He next appeared off the bar at Charleston, where he instituted a sort of benevolent blockade.

He took an inbound brigantine from New England, under command of Thomas Porter, and another Barbadoes vessel, a sloop laden with rum and commanded by Joseph Palmer. The sloop was burned after the crew had been set adrift, as in the case of the previous Barbadoes capture. Bonnet was bound to have the good news travel back to the home folk that there had been a real he-man once in charge at the home of Mrs. Bonnet.

After cleaning his sloop and taking on water at an inlet on the North Carolina coast, he sailed southward, and dropped anchor in the Bay of Honduras, which was then a favorite meeting place for pirates.

Here the redoubtable Major fell in with Blackbeard.

Major Bonnet had acquired a great respect for his own executive ability during the months since he had escaped from his fair commander-in-chief in Bridgetown. He called upon Blackbeard on board the latter's ship, and suggested that the two of them, being the best pirates afloat, should join company and effect a merger. He pointed out that the *Revenge* was an uncommonly graceful sloop, for which he had paid a fancy sum of money.

When Blackbeard heard that Bonnet had paid for his ship, he was desolated by gales of merriment. Continuing the conversation but a little way, the gay old dog discovered his guest's regrettable ignorance of nautical affairs. Although he had spilled a goodly measure of blood and sailed north and south with his own planks under his feet, Major Bonnet was still a major, and not a captain in very truth. Also, he still called a ship's ladder a stairway.

Blackbeard called his trusted mate, Richards. He ordered him to take command of the *Revenge,* and informed Major Bonnet that he was to act in a clerical capacity aboard Blackbeard's own ship. The two vessels would sail in company, but both must be in command of pirates who knew their salt water. If Bonnet should behave well and make no disturbance, he might live—and learn.

The proud army man made the best of a humiliating situation. He became chief bookkeeper for the piratical enterprise of

Ed Teach. He ranked as a sort of apprentice pirate. And he learned the trade under a master.

Stede Bonnet learned much from Blackbeard. The two vessels sailed north along the coast, and were joined by others, attracted by the marvelous name of the bewhiskered terror. Soon there was a fleet of three sloops and a full-rigged ship, the latter carrying forty guns. The fleet was manned by four hundred husky blood-letters. Major Bonnet was studying piracy in no mean academy.

He made several cruises under Blackbeard, and was permitted to take part in the fun whenever he showed any progress in his work. After a few months of this training, he was competent, in the opinion of Professor Blackbeard, to take out a ship under his own command.

Blackbeard disbanded his fleet at Topsail Inlet, in North Carolina, and took a sabbatical year ashore. After all, time was passing, the jolly old throat-slitter was as rich as a king, and there were no ladies to speak of at sea. So the master gave his apprentice permission to take his own sloop, the *Revenge,* and go out on his own account.

Now, George the First, by the grace of God, King, had recently issued a grandiose pardon to all pirates who would surrender to authorized pardoners and obtain a certificate of good character. George was getting into another war, and wanted pirates in his royal navy, or at least in the privateering business. Most pirates were only privateersmen devoid of a good and official war, and they were always eager to sign any sort of document that would add the King's license to their own determination to live by blood-letting.

Bonnet left the *Revenge* at Topsail Inlet and journeyed to Bath. He surrendered to Governor Eden, expressed his unwavering loyalty to the King who had given him his lifetime job in the army, and begged to be permitted to serve His Majesty as a legalized privateer against the Spaniards. This permission was readily given, and Stede Bonnet became once more, for a short time, officially a patriot. He obtained clearance papers for St. Thomas.

He had no crew, but he knew how to get a good one. Blackbeard, just before disbanding his fleet and going in for respectability, had marooned a shipload of men on a barren island, not far from the Inlet, so as to avoid having to pay them for their services. Bonnet picked up these poor devils and gave them jobs, on condition that they would serve him forever, particularly in punishing their ungrateful master, Blackbeard.

He had determined to go out after Blackbeard, if he could find him afloat, and prove how well he had learned piracy from the master. He had many a score to settle with the baleful old ogre, and he had all of the rescued seamen as stout partisans in his desire. The most able and intelligent of these men was David Herriot, who had had a vessel of his own in honest trade, and had been captured by Blackbeard in the Bay of Honduras. He had become a pirate, and a good one, when there seemed no way out of it. He had served under Blackbeard, but he had become attached to Bonnet, and had secretly commiserated with the latter during his enforced clerkship.

The Major made Herriot sailing master of the *Revenge,* which he now named the *Royal James,* in honor of the current pretender to the English throne. These jolly pirates were pretty good politicians in their way, and several of their captives testified that Bonnet and his men were wont to drink damnation to the King and a health to James, the Pretender, whenever they started out to loot a cargo of rum.

The first cruise of the revivified *Royal James* was up the coast of Ocracoke Inlet, where, gossip said, Blackbeard and his favorite henchmen might be found aboard a small vessel, holding council concerning the division of their spoil.

Bonnet declared he could not go to sea as an honorable pirate until he had settled scores with Blackbeard and punished the bewhiskered old fakir for his sins. This got a great hand with the crew, and for weeks the *Royal James* scoured the sea and the inlets in search of the old boss. Had the two forces joined battle, a lot of trouble later on would have been avoided, for undoubtedly they would have wiped each other out. Stede Bonnet, by that time, was a match for any pirate who sailed the seas; even for his devoted instructor.

But weeks were wasted, and Blackbeard, like Evangeline's lover was always about a day's sail ahead of his pursuer, without knowing that he was being pursued. Bonnet finally gave over the wild goose chase, and went into ordinary commercial pirating.

On this cruise he called himself Captain Thomas, and compelled his men to address him so. He put an antic disposition on in other respects also. Whenever he robbed a ship of her cargo, he insisted upon giving something for the goods taken. He carried a good many barrels of rice of no great value, and usually he made the captain of the captured boat a present of several of them after transferring his cargo to the *Royal James*. On one occasion Bonnet gave his prize an old rusty cable, and when he took twenty barrels of pork out of a Virginia sloop, he traded two barrels of rice and a hogshead of molasses for the goods, without asking consent. He took another Virginia vessel that had nothing aboard but a few combs and needles and such-like accessories of the toilet. Bonnet gravely transferred some pins and needles to the *Royal James,* and ordered two barrels of bread and a barrel of pork hoisted over the side and transferred to the captured ship, which was then told to go on her way.

Back and forth between Cape Fear River and St. Thomas he cruised, taking plenty of vessels and demonstrating to the world that a hen-pecked army officer, given a fair chance, could rehabilitate and assert himself. He became, in the absence of Blackbeard from the sea, the most talked-about pirate afloat.

In August, 1718, he arrived in Cape Fear River aboard the *Royal James,* and accompanied by two sloops recently taken in action. The *James* was leaking badly, and she was careened. The men were set to work at the repairing and cleaning job, and when timbers were needed they stole a shallop and tore it up to supply the necessary materials.

During this time Bonnet is reputed to have gone ashore with a small squad of men and buried three chests of treasure.

It was very hot weather, and the job lagged. Meantime the report had spread to Charleston that Bonnet was in the river, preparing for a descent upon the city. Charleston had suffered much at the hands of pirates, and the authorities there were quite generally unfriendly to the rovers, although in New York pirates were able to live in the style to which they had become accustomed and were seldom molested.

Fortunately for Charleston, there were public-spirited rich men in the town. Most noteworthy of these citizens was Colonel William Rhett, receiver-general of the province. Colonel Rhett's descendants are still prominent in Charleston, and they have accumulated a family tradition that is worthy of their pride. They have not forgotten the example set by their ancestor in 1718, when their fine old city was threatened by Bonnet and his pirates.

Colonel Rhett went to Governor Johnson and asked permission to fit out an expedition against Bonnet at his own expense. The Governor was happy to comply, since the province itself was helpless, and there were no warships along the coast. Rhett had learned that Bonnet was ready, or would soon be ready, with his three vessels, well armed. He was given a commission, and presently fitted out and manned with fighting Carolinians two sloops, the *Henry*, of eight guns and seventy men, and the *Sea Nymph*, of eight guns and sixty men. Rhett went aboard the *Henry*, and on September 10 sailed across the harbor to Sullivan's Island, to complete his preparations. Sullivan's Island (miscalled Swillivant's Island by an early pirate historian and his later paraphrasers) plays a further part in Charleston's history, for it was on it that Fort Moultrie was built years later.

Rhett took supplies aboard, and on September 15 crossed the bar of Charleston and set out to capture his pirates. He wasted several days in the pursuit of rumors, but finally arrived at Cape Fear on the evening of September 26.

As soon as he entered the river, he went aground on the sandbar with both his sloops. The Carolinians could see the topmasts of the pirate fleet, beyond a bend in the river bank. Simultaneously, Bonnet's watchers brought him word of the hostile-looking vessels at the mouth of the river, and the pirates prepared for action.

At dawn Bonnet hoisted his anchors and sailed down the river to meet his enemy, all sails set. Rhett had got off the sandbars, and, weighing anchor, went to meet the pirates. Their two sloops took positions upon either quarter of the *Royal James,* and forced her aground. The Carolina sloops themselves grounded only a few minutes later. The *Sea Nymph* was out of range, but the *Henry* was within pistol shot.

At the outset of this extraordinary struggle, it appeared that the god of battles was with the pirates. Both the pirate ship and the *Henry* careened on their sandy beds, both leaning in the same direction, and in such manner that the deck of the Carolinian was wholly exposed to the pointblank fire of the pirate, while the latter's deck was sheltered from the fire of Rhett's guns by the tipped-up hull.

Nevertheless, Rhett began pounding away with all the guns he could bring to bear on the pirate.

For five hours the combatants awaited the tide that would float them, meantime using both large and small arms as well as they could. Rhett's deck was swept by merciless musket fire, and his men had to be satisfied with inflicting what damage they could on the pirate's hull.

Whoever got first afloat would win the battle. That was understood by everybody on both sides. So Bonnet and Rhett watched the tide flow in for five hours, and never has a tide meant more to men than did that tide in the Cape Fear River to all those gallant lads, pirates and pirate-chasers, on that September day in 1718.

There was a good deal of droll mockery back and forth between the two ships. The pirates waved a red flag at the Carolinians, and kept asking Rhett to come aboard. This the stout Colonel from Charleston was fully resolved to do, if he could get afloat before being destroyed.

The *Henry* began to float first! The pirates were sorely alarmed, and some of them demanded that their chief surrender at once. But Bonnet wasn't that kind of a pirate. He had surrendered too often in the great house at Bridgetown. He told his men that he would fire the magazine himself if any man attempted to surrender.

But the debate continued among the pirates, although Bonnet took his stand on the deck, two pistols in his hands, and tried to shoot all the defeatists.

The *Henry*, now altogether afloat, made for the *Royal James*, and Rhett gave the order to board.

Bonnet was beaten. His men prevailed. They ran up a white flag in spite of their chief, and the defeated freebooter received Colonel Rhett on board the *James* and gave up his sword like a genuine Major of His Majesty's forces in distress.

Rhett lost twelve men killed and eighteen badly wounded. The pirates suffered rather fewer casualties.

Colonel Rhett sailed into Charleston harbor amid public excitement comparable to that of Armistice Day. He brought with him not only his own two sloops, but also the *Royal James* and the two Bonnet sloops that had remained out of the fight. He brought Stede Bonnet, the most redoubtable pirate afloat, and thirty of his men.

Bonnet and his pirates were delivered to Provost-Marshal Nathaniel Partridge, who was obliged to turn the rank and file of the men over to the military for safekeeping in an army guardhouse, since there was no adequate prison. Major Bonnet at once made an impression upon his captors. It was evident that he was a fellow of quality, and the South Carolinians could never be guilty of confining such a personage along with the rag-tag of the piratical world. So Major Bonnet was invited to be the guest of the marshal at his home, but with the formality of two guards at his door.

David Herriot, loyal sailing master for Bonnet, also managed to get himself transferred to the marshal's home, and Ignatius Pell, one of the pirates who had agreed to turn King's evidence, was lodged there to keep him from being killed by the other pirates. Thus the marshal had a full house.

Major Bonnet had behaved himself in such magnificent fashion that he quite captured the imagination of many good residents of Charleston. He was a good-looking man, dignified and gracious, and it was known that he was not understood at home. What wonder that the town was soon divided into pro-Bonnets and anti-Bonnets! There were some major disturbances in the city while preparations for the trial were under way, and there was a considerable demand that this gentleman pirate be permitted to go his way in such peace as he could muster.

The pro-Bonnet movement finally settled down to a plot for the pirate's delivery, and this was effected, apparently by bribing the guards. Herriot, the faithful, went along, and a party of Bonnetites was waiting with a boat. This was on October 25, three days before the trial of the pirates was scheduled to begin.

Governor Johnson immediately offered a reward of £700 for the recapture of Bonnet and Herriot. He sent out the hue and cry, replaced the provost-marshal with a person who was thought to be less susceptible to the blandishments of gentle manners, and called Colonel Rhett into conference.

Rhett was never found wanting in time of need. He set out at once with a small party, and trailed the fugitives to Sullivan's Island, where they had been forced by rough weather and shortage of supplies to land.

Bonnet and his little band of faithful followers were hiding in the brush among the sandhills. They were surrounded and fired upon, but made no effort to defend themselves. When Herriot fell beside his master, Bonnet seemed to lose all his fighting ardor. He surrendered and was taken back to Charleston. This time he was put in close confinement.

Meantime, the trial of the other pirates was under way before a special admiralty court, presided over by the notable Nicholas Trott, one of the most picturesque tyrants who ever graced the bench.

The pirates had a grand trial, with an imposing bench crowded with twelve prominent citizens who acted as judges under the presidency of Trott. The defendants were not allowed counsel. Trott frequently interrupted the proceedings to denounce them, and he spoke to the prisoners as one might to so many very naughty dogs. All but four of them were found guilty, and sentenced to be hanged.

Bonnet was captured before the trial of his men was completed, but he was not brought to trial until two days after his old companions in arms had been hanged at White Point, near

Charleston. The bodies of the pirates were buried between high and low water, in a marsh.

The hanging of his men transformed poor Bonnet. Once the most swaggering and daring of the sea rogues, he now became a shaking, shuddering coward, abjectly pleading for his life. Facing death in a bloody fight at sea, he had been invincible. Bullying his crew of brawling brutes, he had shone as a master whom the worst of men feared to cross. But now, as his merry men swung lightly in the soft November breezes, and he himself faced judgment, he became even more craven than the Major Bonnet who had suffered quietly so long under the lash of a shrewish wife.

The same court that had tried his men tried Bonnet, and Tyrant Trott again presided. He was not so rough with the chief as he had been with the common seamen; not for a moment, indeed, did anybody forget that Bonnet was a rich man and a gentleman.

But the pirate chief was not allowed counsel. Occasionally he ventured to speak in his own defense, and when he did so he spoke humbly and as a broken reed.

"May it please Your Honors," he said, "and the rest of the gentlemen, though I must confess myself a sinner, and the greatest of sinners, yet I am not guilty of what I am charged with."

Trott interrupted to ask him what he had to say in answer to the witnesses who had testified to having been captured by him.

Bonnet, with the straightest face in the world, replied that he had never taken any part in the seizure of a vessel, except when he was acting as Blackbeard's clerk. He explained that when piracies were committed by the men under his charge, when he was sailing in his own ship, it happened because he was asleep in his cabin, and had no knowledge of what the men were doing.

Trott's charge to the jury was a much better speech for the prosecution than either of the prosecuting attorneys had made. He wound it up with this cynical play:

"So I think the evidence have proved the fact upon him: but I shall leave this to your consideration."

The verdict was guilty, and the sentence was that Bonnet be hanged.

Trott, in passing sentence, read a long document in which he quoted Holy Scripture for more than an hour to prove that the prisoner would go direct from the scaffold to Hell, to take his "part in the lake which burneth with fire and brimstone, which is the second death."

December 10 was named for the execution of the sentence. Bonnet spent the time until then pleading for his life and planning for a reprieve. He sent a message to Colonel Rhett, who had twice captured him, begging the gallant Colonel to do something for him.

Rhett admired and pitied the fallen pirate. He admired him as a gallant fighter and a pleasant gentleman, and he pitied him in his present plight, because he had heard the story of the scolding wife in Barbadoes who had driven this estimable fellow to destruction.

Rhett comes very near being the hero of the story. He actually came forward and tried to persuade Governor Johnson to permit him to take Bonnet to England for another trial. He offered to be surety for the prisoner (and this after Bonnet had once escaped!) and likewise offered to furnish the ship to take him to the other side.

Rhett worked for nothing and always turned up when needed, but he is one hero whose city hasn't forgotten. In one of the old churchyards in Charleston, within a few feet of one of the principal streets of the town, I found his grave, covered by a great granite block on which is carved:

> In Hopes of a Joyful Resurrection
> Here rests the body of
> Col. William Rhett,
> late of this Parish,
> Principall officer of His Majesties Customs in
> this Province.
> He was a person that on all occasions promoted the Publick good of this Colony and severall times generously and successfully ventured his life in defence of the same
> He was a kind Husband, a tender Father, a faithfull Friend,

a Charitable Neighbour, a religious and constant worshipper
of God
He was borne in London 4th Sept. 1666
Arrived and settled in this country 19th Novemr. 1694
And dyed suddenly but not unprepared 12th Janry. 1722
in the fifty-seventh year of his age.

Good old Rhett! He would have taken Bonnet for a ride to the
motherland in the hope of saving a fine pirate and a noble swasher
of bucklers, of whom he knew the world had all too few! But
Governor Johnson would have none of it. Someone produced an
insulting letter to the Governor, which, it was claimed, Bonnet
had written the night before the battle on the sandbars at Cape
Fear. In this bit of bravado, Bonnet boasted that if he should
win the fight he would take up his station off Charleston and burn
every vessel coming in or going out. Bonnet must hang, declared
Johnson.

Now Bonnet reached the depths. He wrote to Governor Johnson an abject letter, in which he humiliated himself far below the
level to which a brave man commonly is supposed to descend,
even in the gravest emergencies. He said, among other things:

...I intreat you not to let me fall a Sacrifice to the Envy and ungodly
Rage of some few Men, who, not being yet satisfied with Blood, feign
to believe that if I had the Happiness of a longer life in this world, I
should still employ it in a wicked Manner, which to remove that, and
all other Doubts with your Honour, I heartily beseech you'll permit
me to live, and I'll voluntarily put it ever out of my Power by separating all my Limbs from my Body, only reserving the use of my Tongue
to call continually on, and pray to the Lord my God, and mourn all
my days in Sackcloth and Ashes to work out confident Hopes of my
Salvation, at that great and dreadful Day when all righteous Souls
shall receive their just rewards.

This crawling in ashes went even further. The fearsome pirate
begged that he might be permitted, after severing his arms and
legs from his body, to go far inland, out of sight of the sea, and
there serve the Governor in some menial capacity for the rest of
his life. His parting benediction to the Governor was:

Now the God of Peace, that brought again from the dead our Lord
Jesus, the great Shepherd of the Sheep, thro the blood of the everlasting Covenant, make you perfect in every good work to do his Will,
working in you that which is well pleasing in his Sight, through Jesus
Christ, to whom be Glory forever and ever, is the hearty prayer of

Your Honour's
Most Miserable, and
Afflicted Servant,
Stede Bonnet.

But the Governor was not impressed. Perhaps he suspected
that the jolly freebooter did but jest, and that respite would but
increase his chances for escape and further depredations.

So on the appointed day Stede Bonnet was hanged at White
Point, and buried in the sand, between the rising and falling of
the tide. When he was brought to the gallows, he was but semi-
conscious. Fear had practically killed him before the noose was
about his neck.

◇ ◇

Blackbeard's most important vessel was the *Queen Anne's
Revenge*, a large ship mounting forty guns. At various times he
commanded other vessels that he had taken at sea and thought
too good to sink, burn, or turn back to their owners.

He was at the height of his sea power when he cruised northward from Honduras after adding Bonnet's sloop, the *Revenge*,
to his force. He captured several vessels along the way. Some of
these he sank, after looting them. Others he added to his fleet.

The pirates established a blockade of Charleston harbor,
standing off the bar for a week and capturing the harbor's pilot
boat and every incoming ship. There was an outbound ship, too,
commanded by one Robert Clark, bound for London with mixed
cargo and some passengers. Among the passengers taken was
Samuel Wragg, member of the Council of the Province.

Blackbeard's surgeon had reported a shortage of medicines
and bandages. So the swaggering pirate, who was now slightly
intoxicated with his power and importance, sent ashore a party
in charge of Richards, commanding the *Revenge*, to demand a

full case of medical and surgical supplies from the authorities of Charleston.

Richards took several of his own men and one of the captured passengers, who is known to history simply as a Mr. Marks. Strangely enough, it is not known that Mr. Marks has any descendants in Charleston to-day, or any tombstones in the ancient Charleston churchyards bearing his name. He was simply a Mr. Marks who won brief notoriety because he was compelled to deliver a message from the pirate chief to Governor Johnson of the Province of South Carolina. The message was, in effect:

"Blackbeard is just off the bar with an overwhelming force. He has many Charlestonians as prisoners. Fill a large ship's medicine chest with all things needful, and the prisoners will be released. Refuse or delay, and the prisoners will be murdered, beginning with Councilman Wragg."

The Governor put the ultimatum up to the Council in special session, and both Governor and Council were shocked and humiliated that a notorious pirate should be able to deliver such a demand so insolently at the seat of a government.

But the relatives of the prisoners aboard Blackbeard's ships carried the day. The Province of South Carolina would accede to the pirate's demands. The medicines, bandages and instruments were bought in Charleston at the expense of the government, and turned over to the pirates.

Marks and the shore party had been given by Teach two days in which to make the trip and return with the medicines. The Charlestonians aboard the *Queen Anne's Revenge* were informed that, if the boat did not return with the chest of medicines by the second sunset, they were to prepare for death.

When the second sunset arrived, there was no boat in sight. Blackbeard was in a temper. Just as the sun was dipping to the horizon he had all prisoners summoned on deck. He stormed up and down in front of the frightened company of helpless men, women, and children. He cursed Charleston and its people, and swung his mighty cutlass menacingly. He called out Samuel Wragg. He informed that worthy that he had better enjoy the fine sunset, as it was the next to the last thing he would ever enjoy, the last being the experience of losing his head right where he stood.

Wragg was not a bad advocate. In this emergency he pleaded a hopeless cause before a somewhat prejudiced judge, who was also, by appointment of the court, executioner. Advocate Wragg represented to Judge Captain Blackbeard Teach that the authorities in the city were not crazy, and would not be permitted to cause the deaths of so many citizens merely for lack of a few hundred pounds' worth of drugs and bandages. There had been some mishap, and if the Court please, it was not beyond the bounds of the probable that Captain Richards or some of his men had become slightly intoxicated, or even bewitched by some fair Charleston damsels, thereby and thus delaying the return of the medicines by some few hours.

Blackbeard pondered. He liked the humor of this lawyer who could plead so well in such annoying circumstances. He granted a stay of sentence.

It was as Wragg had suspected. While the Governor and Council were conferring and shopping for balsams and bandages, Richards and his merry men were striding up Meeting Street, taking both sides and the middle of that thoroughfare. They were met with hostile stares at first, but presently the traditional hospitality of the Charleston people was aroused by the genial and swaggering manner of the strange guests. The pirates spent their gold freely, and had plenty of it to spend. They drank enormous quantities of rum, and bought rum for whomsoever would partake. They sang pirate songs for the delectation of the children in the streets, and delighted the young women who had been saving all their thrill capacity for the day when real pirates, with gold ear-rings and red silk sashes, should chuck them under the chin and call them beautiful.

So Richards and his men were in no condition to get back to the *Queen Anne's Revenge* by the second sundown. Marks led the citizens' movement to find ways and means to have the agreement and Blackbeard's orders kept to the letter, and it was he who went out in a rowboat to carry to Blackbeard the news that the shore party was unavoidably detained "by some slight mishap" in the town.

When this message reached the pirate flagship, it was dawn, and Blackbeard was summoning all the prisoners on deck a second time to receive notice that they must die at once. Samuel Wragg was spared the necessity for making another plea by arrival of the message from shore.

Eventually the slightly sobered shore party of pirates arrived with a handsome box of medicines, and Blackbeard made good his promise. He sent all the prisoners ashore, but not until he had robbed them of all their money, jewelry and desirable items of clothing. Samuel Wragg's eloquence did not avail to save the six thousand dollars he had in his money belt.

◇ ◇

Captain Teach felt the shore a-calling. For, while he was a great villain and a picturesque pirate afloat, he was quite a personage ashore too. He was a different person, quite, when he had shed the mantle of sea authority. On land, he was a ladies' man. He always shaved off his fearsome whiskers as soon as he had come ashore, and donned respectability as one might put on a garment for a festival. Thenceforward, as long as his residence ashore lasted, Captain Teach was a Don Juan, courting the women assiduously, astounding the countryside by his generosity and lavish spending, and delighting polite companies with his witty tales of the sea.

Usually Captain Teach stayed ashore on one of these long leaves for several months. Always he married while ashore. It was said by his detractors, at the close of his career, that he had actually been married sixteen times. I do not think this charge can be proved by the scanty records now extant, but it is certain that the gay Captain was a great one for marrying. The mortality rate among his wives was comparable to that prevailing among Chicago racketeers.

When Blackbeard reached Topsail Inlet, North Carolina, as heretofore related, he abandoned his piratical career for a while, and permitted Bonnet to sail away with the *Revenge* on his own account.

While Bonnet was wasting valuable time looking for Captain Teach, that he might show him how good a pirate he had become under the teaching of the master, the redoubtable Terror of the Seas was transforming himself into a Beau Brummel landsman in and about the town of Bath.

But first Captain Teach made friends with the reigning politicians, as all wise pirates have ever done. Charles Eden was Governor of North Carolina, with headquarters at Bath, and Tobias Knight, a finished politician, was the Governor's secretary. Blackbeard approached the Governor through the secretary, and very soon an *entente cordiale* was established all around. Blackbeard became a Prominent Citizen of the community, and Governor Eden and Secretary Knight became very prosperous.

After an understanding had been reached, Blackbeard and twenty of his rogues went before the Governor and formally renounced piracy, whereupon they were handed His Majesty's Most Gracious Pardon for all past crimes, and were certified to all and sundry as good and worthy citizens.

Blackbeard at once began the erection of a suitable home for himself at Plum Point. The site chosen was ideal. It was conveniently distant from the town of Bath. It was isolated, and close enough to deep water to permit the anchoring of a pirate ship close to the land that constituted Blackbeard's front yard. The house, constructed of hand-made bricks, was large and gloomy. Its shuttered windows looked out toward the sea. Its great cellars were well stocked with wines and rum. Its broad verandas were covered by cowl-like roofs that shut out the sun and the gaze of the curious.

When the house was finished, Blackbeard, who was now Captain Teach, the wealthy mariner, dressed up more luridly than ever, and went a-courting. He had had no wife since the beginning of his long cruise that had ended at Topsail Inlet.

The Captain's fancy picked Prudence Lutrelle, a girl of sixteen, only daughter of Marie Lutrelle, widow of a small planter.

◇ ◇

And this is the story of Captain Teach and his last love affair, as told by the oldsters of Bath.

The wealthy Captain called at the humble home of the Widow Lutrelle with a fine swagger, all dressed in red and blue silk, and carrying a sword. He paid his compliments to the widow, while with great coolness and deliberation he appraised the pretty daughter.

Prudence was dark and fragile, and her deep brown eyes were wells of innocence. From the first, she disliked the haughty Captain.

Teach made half a dozen calls. Finally he proposed marriage, addressing the mother while looking at the daughter.

Marie Lutrelle plainly considered this a good match, but she asked the Captain to call later for his answer.

Prudence sat on a low stool beside her mother on the evening appointed for the Captain's coming. She was pale and she could not keep back the tears.

"I am afraid of him, Mother," said the frightened girl. Her mother felt the trembling of the child's frail body as Prudence looked up into the older woman's eyes, a very picture of helplessness. "I have heard much about his piracies and his many wives that have all disappeared. Why should I have aught to do with this man?"

"You are young and full of notions, girl," said the stout Marie. "You are afraid of a husband, and that is the measure of your worry. This day next year you will laugh at yourself. Here is a fine man, this captain, and could he be a friend of the governor's if he were a pirate?"

"I know naught of that, Mother. You have heard the talk and that Governor Eden and Knight, his secretary, do share the loot that this same captain brings in from sea. I fear I shall laugh but little if I become his wife. And, Mother, why should I marry now? I want to wait for—yes, Mother, for love!"

"You are full of notions, I tell you——"

A loud knocking at the door and in stepped Captain Teach, arrayed in his finest, and beside him the Governor of North Carolina himself. Mrs. Lutrelle was in a frenzy of excitement and embarrassment because of the presence of these mighty men in her humble home. She poured wine and the great ones talked loudly.

"So here's the bride you'll be taking with you, my Captain!" shouted the Governor, catching Prudence by the shoulders and holding her up to examine her by the light of the candles on the mantel, "Oho, a right pretty morsel, by my faith! Luck will go with you this time, Captain!"

Prudence was frightened. She tore herself from the Governor's grasp and started for the door. Captain Teach crossed the room in three strides, intercepted her, folded her in his arms and, despite her struggles, kissed her upon the mouth.

The impetuous lover was angry because of the resistance, but the Governor was in great good humor. He roared with laughter, and while Teach still held the fighting maid he stepped to the front door and called in two pages who attended him.

Then there was a marriage. The pages were witnesses. The Governor read the service from a prayer book drawn from an inside pocket.

Prudence wept, but said nothing. The Governor repeated the responses she was supposed to make, and she did not resist, for she saw that resistance was useless.

Marie Lutrelle was worried by the highhanded manner of the marrying, but she was afraid to lift her voice in protest lest there be no marriage at all. And to have a daughter married to a wealthy man by the Governor himself was something in Marie's life.

"You understand, Madam," said the Governor after the brief ceremony, "there is need for haste. The Captain sails upon a long cruise in the morning. Everything is shipshape aboard the *Revenge* and it needed only this one knot to be tied. Now we all go to the Captain's house, for the wedding supper and the guests are waiting."

There was a brief assurance by Captain Teach that everything necessary to his bride's comfort already had been provided. Conveyances were waiting outside. The Governor was conversing loudly with the mother.

Prudence, still white and trembling, stepped into her bedroom to get her wraps. The bridegroom followed her. Immediately there was a sound of struggle, a muffled oath, an overturning chair. The captain emerged smiling, but with blood outlining a long scratch across his left cheek.

"Stormy voyage ahead, Governor!" said the pirate chief. "The jade is wild. I think I have tamed wilder." He spoke in even tones and did not cease to smile, but in his eyes there was fire.

There was a great wedding feast that night in the long banquet room of Captain Teach's new mansion by the sea. Governor Eden was there, at Captain Teach's right hand, and Tobias Knight was on the Governor's right. The place at the foot of the long table was occupied by the white-faced little bride, whose excited mother was beside her, too bewildered to eat. Seventy guests, including Blackbeard's officers for the cruise that was about to begin, drank copious toasts to the bride and bridegroom, and cried loud and tipsy good wishes for the voyage.

Basilica Hands did not sit down. He was not going upon this voyage. His crippled knee was bothering him, and probably would keep him a landlubber the rest of his life, he explained to friends. He wandered disconsolately about the great house, drinking ever and anon a great draught of rum, and occasionally peering through a half-opened door upon the gay wedding feast.

Blackbeard was in good form. He seldom slept on one of these noisy· nights preceding the beginning of a new voyage, or on the eve of a good battle. To-night he was gloriously drunk. He shouted, sang, and exhorted his guests to greater feats of hilarious drinking. He totally ignored the existence of his shrinking bride.

It was nearly daylight when six seamen carried in a great iron chest and heaved it upon the center of the table. Now Blackbeard rose, strode to the center and raised the heavy iron lid. The wedding cake was inside. Otherwise the chest was empty.

"Bride ahoy!" shouted the master of the feast, smashing a bottle of wine on the upraised lid, "This is the bride's chest and it's coming back full of treasure! The greatest treasure that's ever filled a sea chest! Sink me forty fathoms if not!"

There was a roar of appreciation from the crowd as Blackbeard continued:

"What comes home in that chest is not for you, Governor! It's the bride's chest! Pipe up, Mrs. Blackbeard! Fair weather, is it? Hoist a signal to your captain!"

The pale girl sat as if unhearing, or as if hypnotized into silence and immobility.

Captain Teach jumped upon the table and, making a megaphone of his hands, roared: "Mate ahoy! Up anchors! Set sail! To sea we go!"

The guests were struck dumb by the raging of the Terror of the Sea. The gigantic pirate, roaring great sea-curses upon and against everybody, smashed dishes right and left, felled guests with unreasoning blows, and shouted orders to his officers.

While the guests were making the best of their way out of the banquet hall, sailors were busy aboard the *Queen Anne's Revenge,* a few paces from the veranda, carrying out orders for immediate departure. In the midst of the confusion, six men picked up the sea-chest and carried it aboard. Blackbeard himself, roaring a bloody pirate chantey, strode to the end of the room, tucked the little bride under one arm as though she had been a bag of meal, and went aboard the *Revenge,* just as the sails were being spread for the new voyage.

It was a great cruise and a hard one, members of the crew reported to their friends when the *Queen Anne's Revenge* cast anchor at Bath Town thirteen months later. Forty prizes had been taken, looted and burned, with never a hand from any one of them spared. Blackbeard had been himself at his worst. The *Revenge* returned well laden with silver and gold.

The bride? Little was spoken of her by the men unless they were pressed for details. The first day out she had been imprisoned in irons in a little cabin beside the Captain's. Through many months she lay shackled to her bed through storm and calm and battle. She had never come on deck.

After the first month's discipline Blackbeard had visited her.

He came away with a bad knife cut which reached from his left shoulder to a point just over his heart. Prudence had remained shackled from that time on until the day before making port at Bath Town.

Certain members of the crew had been detailed at the beginning of the voyage to carry food to the pale prisoner and to minister to her wants under the Captain's supervision. They were told to cease their ministrations on the last day out of home port. Blackbeard again visited his wife and she was not seen any more by any of the crew.

The first night in port the *Revenge* was anchored off the end of Plum Point. Toward midnight, a working party with shovels went ashore, headed by Blackbeard, grim and silent, and carrying the great iron chest. Six men bore the weight of the big box and found it heavy going.

They dug a pit by the light of lanterns and buried the chest. Blackbeard stood by. They laid a floor of bricks, plentifully mortared, set the heavy chest upon the floor and built up a brick wall around the sides and ends, finishing all with a vaulted roof of bricks and mortar. Then they shoveled in the soil, and nothing at all was said as the party returned at dawn to the vessel.

Every one of those six men of the burial party disappeared during the first week of the *Revenge's* stay in the home port. Blackbeard was known to have killed two of them with his own hands with no apparent provocation. But he was immune from arrest, for he had not forgotten Governor Eden on the occasion of this homecoming.

◇ ◇

The division of spoils by Blackbeard after this last voyage became notorious scandal in North Carolina. It was known that Eden and Knight had received, over and above such gold as the pirate was willing to disgorge for them, most of a cargo of rum and sugar brought in by Blackbeard aboard a French vessel that he had taken.

Knight, who was collector of the port of Bath, sat as Vice Admiralty Judge upon this prize, and condemned her as lawfully taken, although Great Britain and France were at peace. Knight formally declared the vessel to be Spanish. Then he and the Governor divided the cargo between them, and Blackbeard took the captured vessel out into the river and burned her to the water's edge and sank her bottom, so as to destroy the evidence.

Meantime, Blackbeard, according to a witness who survived these events for many years, was burying boxes and cases of treasure at various places along Pamlico Sound.

But the evil-doers were over-reaching themselves.

The planters of North Carolina, outraged by the scandalous behavior of the pirates and politicians, sent a delegation to complain to Governor Spotswood, of Virginia, known as an honorable and law-enforcing officer of the Crown. Governor William Keith of Pennsylvania already had issued a warrant for Blackbeard's arrest, hoping to catch him upon one of his visits to Philadelphia, where he had mercantile connections.

Governor Spotswood was indignant when he learned the story of corruption and piracy from the planters of North Carolina. He took the matter before the assembly, and the following proclamation was issued:

By his Majesty's Lieutenant Governor, and Commander in Chief, of the Colony and Dominion of Virginia,

A PROCLAMATION

Publishing the Rewards given for apprehending, or killing Pyrates. *Whereas,* by an Act of Assembly, made at a Session of Assembly, begun at the Capital in Williamsburgh, the eleventh Day of November, in the fifth Year of his Majesty's Reign, entitled, An Act to encourage the apprehending & destroying of Pyrates: It is, amongst other Things enacted, that all and every Person, or Persons, who, from & after the fourteenth Day of November, in the Year of our Lord one thousand seven hundred & eighteen, & before the fourteenth Day of November, which shall be in the Year of our Lord one thousand seven hundred & nineteen, shall take any Pyrate, or Pyrates, on the Sea or Land, or in case of Resistance, shall kill any such Pyrate, or Pyrates, between the Degrees of thirty four, and thirty nine, of Northern Latitude, and within one hundred Leagues of the Continent of Virginia, or within the Provinces of Virginia, or North-Carolina, upon the Conviction, or making due Proof of the killing of all, and every such Pyrate, and Pyrates, before the Governor & Council, shall be entitled to have, & receive out of the publick Money, in the Hands of the Treasurer of this Colony, the several Rewards following; that is to say, for Edward Teach, commonly called Captain Teach, or Black-Beard, one hundred Pounds, for every other Commander of a Pyrate Ship, Sloop, or Vessel, forty Pounds, for every Lieutenant, Master, or Quarter-Master, Boatswain, or Carpenter, twenty Pounds; for every other inferior Officer, fifteen Pounds, and for every private Man taken on Board such Ship, Sloop, or Vessel, ten Pounds; and that for every Pyrate, which shall be taken by any Ship, Sloop, or Vessel, belonging to this Colony, or North-Carolina, within the Time aforesaid, in any Place whatsoever, the like Rewards shall be paid according to the Quality and Condition of such Pyrates. Wherefore, for the Encouragement of all such Persons as shall be willing to serve his Majesty, and their Country, in so just & honourable an Undertaking, as the suppressing a Sort of People, who may be truly called Enemies to Mankind: I have thought fit, with the Advice· & Consent of his Majesty's Council, to issue this Proclamation, hereby declaring, the said rewards shall be punctually & justly paid, in current money of Virginia, according to the directions of the said Act. And, I do order & appoint this Proclamation, to be published by the Sheriffs, at their respective County-Houses, & by all Ministers & Readers, in the several Churches & Chappels, throughout this Colony.

Given at our Council Chamber at Williams, this 24th. Day of November, 1718, in the fifth Year of his Majesty's Reign.

GOD SAVE THE KING.

A. Spotswood

The Governor consulted with the captains of two of His Majesty's men of war that lay in the James River, but it was known that these deep-draught vessels could not be used in an attack upon Blackbeard in his retreats along the North Carolina coast, for the pirate used vessels of light draught and kept well inside the little islands and shoals that made navigation dangerous for larger vessels.

It was agreed that Governor Spotswood should hire two small sloops, and the navy would man them. Captain Brand and Lieu-

tenant Maynard were given the commands. They were told to go
and get Blackbeard, dead or alive, and to take such other measures for the restoration of law and order in the neighboring
colony of North Carolina as might seem good in the premises.

No cannon were mounted aboard the sloops, because of the
weight such armament would add, and the increased draught that
would result. The Virginians would carry small arms only, although they knew that Blackbeard was supplied with cannon.

The commanders of the sloops were confident that their
trained men could beat the pirates in hand-to-hand conflict, if
once they could get aboard the pirate vessels.

On the evening of Nov. 21, 1718, the punitive expedition
stood off Ocracoke Inlet, where, confidential information said,
Blackbeard was preparing to set sail on a minor expedition.

The confidential information, which proved correct in every
detail, was supplied, we have every reason to believe, by no less
a pirate than Basilica Hands himself. Captain Teach did himself
no great favor when he fired that pistol ball through his worthy
servant's knee!

Teach had warning that the Virginians were coming up the
river on the morning of November 22. Either he did not take
the warning seriously, or he thought little of the prowess of the
boys who were seeking him. He spent that last night in uproarious
revelry. He drank himself into a state of hilarious helplessness.
Of course, most of his men drank heavily too.

The battle, next morning, was as bloody an affair as even a
pirate of Blackbeard's proclivities might wish for.

There was some shouting of defiance between Lieutenant
Maynard and Blackbeard, whose sloop ran aground after giving
Maynard two broadsides that sadly racked the Virginians and
covered their deck with dead and dying. Brand's vessel was out
of the battle most of the time, on account of winds and shoals.

Maynard's men plied their oars in an effort to come aboard the
pirate. The Virginians were exposed to wicked cannon fire, and
were able to reply with small arms only. But they were waiting
for the boarding.

As they came close aboard, Maynard ordered all his men to lie low, some on the deck and some below, only himself and the helmsman appearing in upright postures. The pirates threw bottles of explosives upon the attacking sloop, and then, led by Blackbeard himself, jumped to the smoking deck. They had saved the Virginians the trouble of boarding! Blackbeard, as usual, took the offensive.

This time, as the giant charged down the deck, he met no yielding line of merchantmen, women, children and common sailors. He met, in fact, Lieutenant Maynard in person. Maynard was calm and collected. He was also quite determined. And he was no amateur with the pistol and cutlass.

Blackbeard roared and came at the Lieutenant as if to eat him up. He was met by a pistol ball from Maynard's left-hand weapon, squarely in the chest. As the monster paused ever so little upon receiving this surprise, Maynard dodged his cutlass and inflicted a deep gash across the pirate's body.

The fight was on, and gave promise of developing into something really interesting. The two crews were fairly well matched in numbers, but the King's men had all the better of the battle.

Maynard was handling the long-armed Terror very well, but it must be confessed that he had a little help from his men occasionally. Blackbeard was fair game for any passing naval man who could spare a shot or a sword-thrust from his own engagements.

Maynard suffered the loss of his cutlass at a critical moment. The giant struck it out of the Lieutenant's hand with a great slash, and then, although almost blinded with blood which streamed from a wound in his head, he advanced to finish his gallant foe.

Maynard jumped backward, drew a pistol, and cocked it.

But he would never have had time to fire that pistol, had not one of his men seen his plight, and, leaping to Blackbeard's side, slit the giant's throat from ear to ear.

Blackbeard fell dying to the deck. His body bore five pistol balls and twenty cuts and stab wounds.

The battle was over. The surviving men of Blackbeard's boarding party jumped overboard and begged for quarter. This favor was granted. The pirates remaining aboard Blackbeard's vessel were rounded up and ironed. Counting losses, Maynard found he had lost twelve men killed, while twenty-two were wounded. The Lieutenant himself escaped with a slash across the knuckles.

Blackbeard's head was severed and stuck up on the bowsprit of the victorious ship.

Search of the pirate vessel disclosed correspondence and papers indubitably implicating Governor Eden and Secretary Knight as accomplices of the pirate. Maynard, under his instructions to do what was necessary in the premises, sailed to Bath, where the sight of Blackbeard's head must have struck the Governor and Collector of the Port with chills. In fact, Knight took to his bed that night, and died some weeks later. It was fright that killed him, the doctors said, although meantime he had been whitewashed by a board of inquiry.

Maynard sent a shore party to search the premises of the Governor and Knight, and recovered the cargo stolen from the French boat.

Basilica Hands also went aboard Maynard's vessel at Bath, and delivered evidence against Knight and Eden. Hands was taken back as a prisoner, but turned King's evidence against the other pirates at the trials that followed in Virginia. There were fifteen prisoners. All were hanged except Hands, who was released for the assistance he had given the prosecution, and one Sam Odell who, although badly wounded in the fight, proved that he had been forced by Blackbeard to join his crew only the night before the battle, while the orgy was in progress on the pirate's ship.

Hands lived many years in London, a cripple and a beggar. Much of the substance of the preceding narrative, and much that is known of Blackbeard, was gleaned from the conversations of Basilica Hands in London taverns during those drab days toward the close of this unfortunate pirate's life. So I do not say that all the story is true in detail. I hazard the opinion that it is about as true as the histories of pirates are ever likely to be.

◇ ◇

But what was in the treasure chest that the three strangers took from Plum Point at Christmas, in 1928?

I challenge the finders to tell the world!

VII. *The Loot of Lima*

L IMA is one of the younger towns of Peru. It was founded
in 1535 by Francisco Pizarro, Spanish conquistador. He
called it City of the Kings, and, on the same day on which
he laid out the town, he laid the cornerstone of the great Cathedral of Lima.

Pizarro had completed the conquest of Peru. He had learned
something of the almost inexhaustible wealth of the country, and
had taken for himself, his followers, and the King of Spain quan-

tities of gold and silver and precious stones theretofore un-
dreamed of by the most avaricious of Spanish adventurers.

From the time of the founding of the new city Lima became
the center toward which the treasure of Peru gravitated. Therefore, when we speak to-day of the treasure and the loot of Lima,
we include the vast hoards of wealth taken from the rich earth
of the area which includes the present countries of Peru and
Ecuador.

That mountainous region probably had produced more treasure of gold, silver and precious stones than any other area of ten
times the size. When Pizarro and his little band of mail-clad
Spanish cavaliers began their butchery of the ancient civilization of the Incas, gold was so common that it was everywhere
employed architecturally. No one knows how long the Peruvians
had been taking gold and silver and gems out of the mountains,
but it seems probable that the washing of gold dust and nuggets
from the beds of streams had been going on for a thousand years.
The treasures in the temples of the sun-god were of hoary antiq-
uity before the first Spaniard set foot upon American soil.

The Peruvians valued the precious metals for their pure,
radiant beauty. They devoted these shining metals freely to the
service of the sun-god, because gold and silver so gloriously reflected the rays that the life-giving diety sent to earth. But the
Peruvians could not understand the Spanish gold-hunger.

Indeed, it is hard for anyone to understand the lust for gold.
I do not refer to the desire of civilized beings to accumulate bank
accounts which give a certain security in the world. That is easily
understandable.

But the actual physical aspect of gold in large quantities is
very disturbing to human psychology. Few indeed are they who
can maintain a sane and sober attitude toward their fellows when
there is a large pile of gold within sight. True tales of the finding
of hidden treasure are never altogether pleasant. When the treasure is sighted, someone in the party is sure to lose control of
himself. Somebody goes crazy, or somebody kills somebody else.

We hear a great deal about the gold madness of the Spaniards
in Peru. It was, indeed, disgraceful. It was enough to confirm

the Peruvians in their long-established belief that their civilization was quite superior to any other in the world. But the Spaniards were Europeans, accustomed to view gold as we ordinary Americans view it; as something to strive for, to bleed for, to do battle for. The Peruvians regarded it as beautiful metal with which to adorn temples, homes and public buildings, and to make into personal ornaments. They were astonished at the gold-madness of the Spaniards. But I do not think that the average American of the Twentieth Century should be too much mystified by it. He has seen enough of money-madness to be able to understand something of the fever that burned up the common sense of the Spanish invaders when they saw tons and tons of silver and yellow gold going to waste in an idolatrous land.

In the town of Caxamalca, Pizarro and his little band of invaders treacherously attacked the unarmed Peruvians who had come at the invitation of the Spaniard to pay a ceremonial visit. The Inca, Atahualpa, ruler of Peru, was taken prisoner, and hundreds of his followers slain. Atahualpa was held as a hostage for the good behavior of the Peruvian people. He was confined, usually in chains, in a native palace, but was permitted to have his regular attendants and the company of his counsellors. The Spanish soldiers, meantime, were out looting temples and stealing gold wherever they could find it. They brought in the precious metal on horseback, or forced Peruvians to haul it in for them, and dumped it in the plaza in the center of the town. There the gold piled up, under guard of Spanish soldiers. The Spaniards were amazed by the plentifulness of the yellow metal. But already the natives, observing the rapacity of the invaders, had begun to hide their gold away in caverns, or bury it near their homes.

Atahualpa sent for Pizarro. He said he had noticed the Spaniards valued gold highly, and seemed to want much of it. He stood in a room twenty-two feet long and sixteen feet wide.

"If you will set me free I will have gold brought to you," he said. "We have plenty of it. I will cover the floor of this room with gold and golden utensils. And you will give me my freedom. Will you do that?"

THERE'S BLOOD ON THE GOLD

211

Pizarro looked at his companions as if to say: "The Inca is just boasting!"

Atahualpa misinterpreted the pause. He thought Pizarro was not satisfied with such an offer. So he stood by the wall and reached up with his right hand.

"I will fill this room with gold up to here," he said, "for my liberty. Is it a bargain?"

It was. The Spaniards painted a line around the room at the height indicated by the Inca. Then Atahualpa sent out for the gold. Bearers began bringing in gold dust, nuggets, ornaments, plates, utensils, and piling them up on the floor of that large room. As soon as the word went out, workers began packing gold upon the backs of llamas, and trudging along the mountain roads toward Caxamalca.

When the room was almost full, the Spaniards became impatient. They wanted the gold melted down and distributed among them right away. They were becoming quite unreasonable, and almost insane, at sight of so much gold. When the furore became dangerously intense, Pizarro trumped up charges against the ruler of the Peruvians, condemned him to death, and took him out and had him strangled. The Spaniards melted down the gold, set aside the King's share, and divided up the rest.

The news of the treacherous murder of the Inca spread rapidly throughout Peru. The kingdom of the Incas quickly disintegrated, but the natives began to hoard their gold in safe places.

Raiding the temples at Cuzco and other important towns, the Spaniards obtained another pile of gold, equal to that gathered by the Inca, but the real treasure of the Incas, according to reliable chroniclers, was hidden, and no white person was told of the locations of the secret depositaries.

◇ ◇

The story of Peru in the days of Pizarro is a succession of tales of yellow gold and gleaming jewels. The recital of these tales would serve no other purpose in this narrative than to establish the picture of an incredibly rich region in the mind of the reader. I shall assume that the story of Atahualpa's treasure at least suggests the marvelous resources of the Peru of Pizarro's time, and shall go forward rapidly to modern times.

Between the founding of Lima in 1535 and the war for Peruvian independence in 1820 lies a period of nearly three centuries, during which the wealth of Peru was the motivating factor in the lives of millions of men, and the inspiration for some of the most daring and bloody deeds in the history of the human race.

This was the gold that, like Helen's face, launched a thousand ships. From the accumulated hoards of the Incas and from mines worked by Indian slaves under Spanish masters, the treasure of the richest land upon the globe flowed toward Lima. A powerful and cultured race from distant Spain had come to the empire of the Incas, and had gained mastery. This race seemed interested in one commodity—treasure. Descendants of the royal families of the ancient Peruvian empire toiled night and day up the steep mountain trails and down the steep canyon walls beside their heavily burdened llamas, taking the gold and silver to the golden capital of Treasureland—Lima, the light of the New World. Father and son and grandson grew up, grew old, died and passed on their menial tasks. Under the whip of the foreign master, a once proud race labored brutishly to gather and refine and take to Lima the treasures of those inexhaustible mines.

At Lima the Cathedral grew under the hands of the toiling stone masons, and at length was finished—a gem of Spanish cathedral architecture that still stands to speak to the world traveler of days that have gone, and having gone, seem too dazzling to have been real. Never was a house of worship more magnificently arrayed. Lima lived by handling treasure, and plenty of the treasure lodged in the dazzling capital of the New World as it moved through the clearing house. The churches got their share, and the most overwhelming portion went to the Cathedral of Lima.

There were chalices of pure gold, thickly studded with gems of great size and rare brilliance. Some day those amazing chalices will be brought forth to the light of a modern day, as were those

of the Cathedral of Panama so recently, and they will take the
breath away from astonished beholders who have thought themselves sophisticated in the ways of wealth. For Panama was but
a way-station of the Treasure Trail that led over the mountains
from Peru to Spain's ocean ports. Lima was the capital of the
source of all this wealth.

Vestments worn by the priests who served at the golden altars
of Lima are said to have been covered with jewels. The crosses
and sacred monograms of the numerous chasubles worn by the
celebrants of daily masses in the Cathedral are recorded as having been outlined in double rows of diamonds and rubies, emer-
alds and sapphires, extending from the neck to the hem and
across the shoulders, back and front. The copes that lay upon
the shoulders of the bishop at solemn pontifical services were,
according to tales told by treasure experts, so thickly encrusted
with gold leaf and jewels that they were as stiff as boards and
much too heavy to be borne long by aged shoulders. Reverent
congregations knelt in that dim old Cathedral while processions
passed down the aisles, headed by acolytes bearing crosses that
glittered in the candle-light with jewels sufficient to ransom any
king from any bondage imaginable.

The mint was in Lima too, and still stands, although few
buildings in the Lima of to-day were built before the earthquake
of October 28, 1746. In the mint you may see the interesting old
implements with which the Spaniards cut and cast and trimmed
the pieces of eight and doubloons that, when sent forth in shiploads, whetted the appetites of Spain's powerful enemies, and
brought down upon the colonial ports of the New World the ravaging fleets of Drake and Hawkins, Cavendish, Davis, Sawkins,
Sharp, Morgan and all the other freebooters, pirates and corsairs
who took such a terrible toll of the treasure that flowed through
Lima, bound for the coasts of Spain.

Because it is eight and a half miles inland from its port,
Callao, Lima was fairly safe from seafaring plunderers. Part of
the outgoing cargoes of coin and bullion went down to Callao on
the backs of asses, and ventured out to sea to round Cape Horn.
For many years the greater portion of the treasure went in pack

trains up the coast from Lima to Panama, and across the Isthmus to Nombre de Dios or Porto Bello. From the time the precious cargoes left the gates of Lima, they were in peril. Spain had her fingers upon the world's greatest treasure sources, but she was on the defensive against robbers as long as she possessed such wealth. Only since she has lost all her western colonies and has receded to a position of peaceful poverty, has Spain been permitted to take her ease under her beneficent palms and watch the more progressive nations as they spill their oceans of blood in constantly recurring wars over trade routes and commercial preferments.

◇ ◇

Cocos Island, a possession of the republic of Costa Rica, lies in latitude 5° 32′ 57″ N., longitude 88° 02′ 10″ W.

The island is about four hundred miles off the coast of Costa Rica, in the Pacific Ocean, and about the same distance northeast of the Galapagos group. It is about four and a half miles wide at the widest point, and is covered by a very heavy jungle growth. There are two inlets from which landings on the island can be made from boats. One is called Wafer Bay, after Lionel Wafer, surgeon buccaneer, who knew the island well, and probably helped to bury treasure there. The other inlet is called Chatham Bay, and is not a safe anchorage for a vessel in rough weather.

The island is rocky and rough. While the ground slopes down to sea-level along the narrow beaches at the two inlets, it rises rapidly, and in the center of the island it reaches a height of three thousand feet. The undergrowth is so dense and the boulders and precipitous hills so numerous that treasure-hunters who frequent Cocos usually confine their digging to a small area near the beach. The climate, needless to say, is oppressive. Few North Americans or Europeans can stand the hard labor of digging on Cocos Island for more than a few hours at a time, or for a longer term than a week or two. These are among the reasons why treasure is not found on Cocos, although the island is seldom free from treasure hunters for more than a few weeks at a time, especially during the more favorable season of the year.

Cocos is one of those isolated tropical islands providing an obvious place for the hiding of treasure by pirates and buccaneers. The number of separate and distinct treasures buried there probably never will be known. But the two most famous treasures of Cocos Island may be classed as part of the loot of Lima. One is associated with the name of Edward Davis, buccaneer. I will sketch the story of this treasure before proceeding to consider the second hoard.

This Edward Davis pursued a profitable piratical career from 1683 to 1702. He was associated with Captain John Cooke as quartermaster when Cooke was pirating in the West Indies, in African waters, and later in the Pacific. It was in February, 1684, that Cooke and his company, in the *Batchelor's Delight*, rounded Cape Horn and stood northward for the island of Juan Fernandez. There was a notable company of about seventy men aboard, all well schooled in pirating. William Dampier and Dr. Lionel Wafer were the writing members of the company who made the voyage famous. Writing pirates were almost as popular in those days as are writing aviators, explorers and baseball players today, and both Dampier and Wafer achieved great glory with the publication of their journals of this and following expeditions. Captain Cowley was aboard also, and kept a journal which afterwards was published. Cowley explains one of the misfortunes of the expedition very effectively. It was when the *Batchelor's Delight* was just about to round Cape Horn.

"We were choosing valentines and discoursing on the Intrigues of Women," writes Cowley, "when there arose a prodigious storm." He tells how the storm drove the vessel far south, many miles off its course, and perhaps farther south than any Europeans had ever been up to that time. To brace the men against the wild blasts out of the frozen south, the Captain ordered plenty of brandy served, and the sailors found to their great comfort that plenty of brandy in that weather, when they were continuously exposed for many hours at a time, meant three quarts per man per twenty-four hours! It is recorded that no man showed any signs of intoxication.

Cowley writes in his journal that "we concluded the discoursing of Women at sea was very unlucky, and occasioned the storm." He did not know, perhaps, that other mariners, who did not chance to be discoursing of women, had also suffered severely in Cape Horn weather.

Bearing northward, the *Batchelor's Delight* made Juan Fernandez, and later the Galapagos Islands, made notable in our own time by a very large book written by William Beebe after a stay of a few weeks in the little archipelago. Cowley devoted himself to the re-naming of all the islands of the group. He had a passion for giving names to places and things. He traveled much about the world and saw strange places, and he always gave every place a new name, regardless of what earlier visitors may have done. He named the islands of the Galapagos group after his powerful friends in England, and after prominent politicians of the hour, possibly in the belief that he might need some friends at court if ever he returned to England with his piratical record behind him.

On the way to Cocos Island from the Galapagos, the *Batchelor's Delight* stopped at Drake's Island, also called the Isle of Plate. It is a little island, still known by both names. Drake stopped here, a century before the visit of the *Batchelor's Delight*, and divided up the loot he had taken along the Pacific coast. After each of the forty-five men in the *Golden Hind* had been amply satisfied and the treasure reserved for Drake and the shareholders at home, including Queen Elizabeth, had been stowed away in the hold, it was found that the vessel was dangerously low in the water, and Drake, to make the passage of the Pacific possible, decided to jettison part of the cargo. With great éclat, fully conscious of the fact that they were doing an unprecedented thing, the men of the *Golden Hind* began dumping bars of pure silver into the sea. They continued dumping until the ship was considered safe, and went on their way hilariously.

The crew of the *Batchelor's Delight* spent some time fishing for the treasure that Drake's men had thrown overboard a century earlier, but without much luck.

Sailing for New Spain, in the hope of carrying off some of the treasure intended for Lima or making its way from that port, the *Batchelor's Delight* changed captains. Cooke died, and Ed Davis was elected to the chief command of the expedition.

Under Davis, the enterprise prospered. Davis was a quiet, capable captain, and knew how to win and hold the confidence of his men. He did not hold with that school of piracy, well exemplified by L'Olonnois the Cruel, and in later years by Blackbeard, which depended upon cruelty and terrorism for all important achievements. It is doubtful that Davis ever considered himself a pirate or a criminal. He was a man of intelligence, and he had made for himself a philosophy which suited his needs. He saw nothing reprehensible in robbing Spaniards. Had he not seen many of his countrymen honored and knighted for such activities? Davis put a patriotic and a religious complexion upon his labors, and his men would follow him anywhere.

For a time, Captain John Eaton in the *Nicholas* sailed in company with the *Batchelor's Delight*, but he separated from Davis, taking Cowley with him, and sailed across the Pacific. He had mutiny and many other troubles before he reached home.

Captain Swan, in the *Cygnet*, also joined the *Batchelor's Delight*, and rendered some valuable service in encounters with the Spaniards. There was another Swan in the expedition, who won a place in the annals of the buccaneers by his heroic death. This Swan was an old man, and the heat of the tropics overcame him on a land march. He sat down beside the road, refusing to allow anyone to help him or stay by him, and, at the age of eighty-four he died fighting, for the Spaniards overtook him, and he, by firing at them while he was unable to rise to his feet, compelled them to shoot him.

Davis and his men foraged up and down the coast, their force sometimes being augmented by parties of several hundred French and English buccaneers. They took the town of Leon, and got rich booty out of it.

When the *Batchelor's Delight* was well furnished with gold and silver, Davis sailed away with his own little company, permitting the other groups of adventurers to go their several ways. Davis headed for Cocos Island, that lone and friendly outpost which had made a favorable impression upon his memory, and there careened his ship, buried his treasure, and gave his men a rest ashore.

Sailing again up the coast, Davis led an attack upon the town of Guayaquil, and brought out enough loot to make his ship heavy and the hearts of his men light. A few cargoes bound to and from Lima were taken, and when the *Batchelor's Delight* cast anchor at Juan Fernandez again, there was a division of spoils in which each man is said to have received twenty thousand dollars.

Davis is believed to have made one more visit to Cocos Island to put away his winnings before sailing around the Horn and heading up for Jamaica. Here he "surrendered to his Majesty's mercy," accepting amnesty offered to all pirates by King James the Second. He went over to Virginia, where he settled down to a life of ease, probably awaiting a good chance to make a voyage to Cocos Island to recover his treasure. He started out, in 1702, in a small vessel called the *Blessing*, pirated along the coast as far as Porto Bello, where he made a fruitless attack, and disappeared from the world of men. His end is shrouded in mystery.

◇ ◇

There were other buccaneers who stopped at Cocos Island to give their men an occasional holiday, and some of them are said to have buried treasure there.

But for the next grand treasure deposit we must go forward to the year 1820. Lima was then a city with as many years behind her as New York City has to-day—approximately three centuries of existence. She was the seat of Spanish power in the Western world, and the capital of wealth and culture. There probably was more gold and silver within her walls than had ever been gathered together in any colonial city in the history of the world.

But the end of her colonial history was approaching rapidly. Simon Bolivar, the Liberator, was carrying the banner of revolt against Spain throughout the Spanish states of South America. Already he had led the people of Venezuela and Colombia to independence, and the effect of his spectacular progress was a deep stirring of revolt throughout the rich colonial possessions of Spain in the Western world.

The grandees and the Governor and the clergy of Lima were perturbed. Wealthy families took their cash and their treasures of gold and silver plate, family shrines and candlesticks and carried them to the fort which protected the town. The military authorities gave receipts for gold and silver totalling thirty million dollars in value, all belonging to private families of Lima.

As the unrest of the people increased, and rumors of the approach of Bolivar became more and more circumstantial in their details, some of this treasure was taken out of the fortress and shipped away on vessels that happened to be in the harbor of Callao. Some families carried their treasures into the interior and hid them in mountain caves, and there some of these treasures lie to-day. Others sent their gold and silver by pack animals up the coast, hoping to find safety for their fortunes in the young republics already established under Bolivar, rather than risk their possessions in a country that was expected to be the scene of desperate fighting and unlimited looting during a long period of chaotic revolutionary activities.

The treasure of the Cathedral and the State treasure remained as symbols of confidence in the established order just as long as their guardians felt that they could afford to take the risk necessarily involved. For risk there would be when the revolutionists began to loot the city.

The day of emergency came, hot and wild and fraught with panic. Lord Dundonald, commanding the fleet of the neighboring state of Chile, came up by sea and demanded that one-third of the treasure in the fort be delivered to him so that he might pay his mutinous crews. In consideration of the peaceful delivery of this third of the fort's treasure, Dundonald promised to permit the Protector, General San Martin, to march out of Lima with the other two-thirds.

Dundonald later seized the Protector's private yacht, and found it ballasted with pieces of eight and ingots of solid gold.

But San Martin's men got away with much of the treasure in the fort. Whither they carried it, no one now living can tell. What they carried away is part of the untraced loot of Lima. Many families and corporations managed to charter small vessels in an effort to escape with their treasures to Spain or to some peaceful colonies. Some of them won through, but many fell victims to the pirates who were roving the seas for just such luscious prizes.

The treasure of the Cathedral has been estimated to be worth sixty million dollars in modern American money. What the value of the State treasure was, we cannot estimate with any pretense to historical accuracy.

When the situation in Lima was thought to be no longer tolerable, the Governor and the clergy began to look about for means of transporting the treasure to some safe place. The only ship in the harbor that looked at all safe was the *Mary Dear,* which flew the ensign of Great Britain and was commanded by a Captain Thompson, or Thomson, a Scotchman.

Was his real name Thompson? Was he a legitimate trader, as he represented himself to be? What of his past?

These questions, pertinent though they be, must remain unanswered. The authorities of Lima thought Captain Thompson possessed an honest countenance. He had credentials and ship's papers that looked well enough. He was waiting at Callao for a cargo.

Very well, he should have a cargo. He agreed to undertake to carry the treasure presently to be stowed aboard the *Mary Dear* to any port decided upon by the Honorable Government of His Most Catholic Majesty and the Reverend Clergy of the Cathedral. The decision would be made and announced to Captain Thompson after the *Mary Dear* should be out upon the high sea.

There followed some hectic days of transporting the treasure from the city to the port, and stowing it aboard the *Mary Dear.* Among the items in the cargo were two life-size statues of the Blessed Virgin Mary holding the Divine Child, each cast of pure gold, according to records which have survived. Also, there were 273 jeweled swords, and candlesticks of gigantic proportions.

At length, the *Mary Dear* weighed and stood for the open sea.

The dignified authorities went into conference. But their decision, although they considered it important enough, no doubt, was never rendered. Captain Thompson had seen the cargo of gold, and he had admitted some of his men to the sight of the gleaming mass. And while the dignitaries deliberated, they were massacred. Their bodies were tossed over-side, and Captain Thompson gave orders to steer a course for Cocos Island.

Having put away the loot of Lima in a cave, Thompson held a conference with his men. It was decided that all were now pirates, liable to capture and hanging by any nation. There might be some international unpleasantness over the disappearance of the great treasure of Lima. It would not do for the possessors of this great plunder to take it to market in any city in the world just yet. Here was a stake for old age and a patrimony for one's children. It would be possible for the company to return to Cocos and extract gold and silver coins from time to time, but the great treasure must wait there in the secret cave for some years, or until the search for the loot of Lima should be abandoned by Spanish and Peruvian authorities.

Meantime they would go pirating and add to their present wealth. So the Captain and crew of the *Mary Dear* joined up with Captain Benito Bonito, a notorious scoundrel who was then scouring the seas and striking terror into the hearts of honest seafaring folk.

Stories vary as to what happened to the united piratical companies of Bonito and Thompson. One tale has it thus. The British frigate *Espiegle* overhauled the pirates in the *Mary Dear*, and hanged or shot all of them except Thompson and one other. These were permitted to live when they promised to lead the English officers to the hiding place of the treasure of Lima. The frigate made sail for Cocos, where the two pirates escaped into the interior of the island. This would not be a difficult feat, if the pirates were not kept in irons. The Englishmen had to sail away without any clue to the treasure, and Thompson and his companion lived on the island, close to their treasure trove, yet unable to enjoy the fruits of their plundering.

In fact, the two castaways nearly starved before they were taken off by a whaler, and Thompson's companion died aboard the rescuing vessel of a fever contracted on the island.

Another story has the shipload of pirates captured by Spanish authorities and hanged—all but one—in Cuba, after some of the loot had been hidden on the island of Trinidad, off the coast of Brazil, in the Atlantic Ocean.

It is possible for both stories to be true. There is no evidence that Bonito shipped on the *Mary Dear*. In fact, there is reason to believe that he had his own ship, and that he and Thompson pirated in company and in partnership, without abandoning either his ship or the *Mary Dear*. It is possible that Thompson and his men may have been taken by the *Espiegle,* while Bonito escaped with his ship and crew, only to be captured later by the Spaniards.

Bonito is said to have had aboard his ship some of the treasure from the Lima Cathedral, including two great golden candle-sticks, and to have buried all this loot on Trinidad. This is not beyond possibility. It is not improbable that Bonito may have compelled Thompson to share with him the Lima loot before the partnership arrangement was made. In fact the association of Thompson with Bonito may have grown out of Bonito's surprising the men of the *Mary Dear* at the task of hiding their loot on Cocos Island.

Thompson somehow reached civilization, after his lonely sojourn on Cocos Island, but his days of pirating were over. He was a sea captain in a small way, but whether he actually sailed a ship or merely lived on what he had been able to bring away from Cocos Island and maintained the air of a retired sea captain, is not in the record.

In 1844, a resident of Newfoundland named Keating met a mysterious sea captain while on a voyage across the Atlantic in a sailing vessel. Keating liked the stranger, and the two spent many hours together on the long and monotonous trip. The stranger was Thompson. He told Keating something about the treasure of Cocos Island. He told enough to make the Newfoundland man's eyes bulge. He said that if ever he could get a vessel in which to go down there, he could make the fortune of every man concerned, and have plenty left for his own old age.

Keating invited Captain Thompson to be his guest while some effort should be made to fit out an expedition. The owner of a small vessel was approached. When the treasure tale had been whispered in his ear, with many injunctions against repeating it, he consented to furnish the ship, provided a certain mariner of his acquaintance, Captain Bogue (sometimes spelled Boag), should be chief in command and should represent the ship's owner. This was agreed to, and it seemed that there would be some very wealthy Newfoundlanders within a few weeks.

But Thompson, the hardy old pirate, died while the ship was being fitted out. In Keating's care he left a map of Cocos Island, with a cross marking the spot where the treasure lies. This map, and one or two copies thereof, exist to-day. Maps that purport to be exact copies or improved versions are not difficult to find. Whoever owns a private yacht can get a copy after a little search and the expenditure of some money.

Keating and Bogue went on the voyage to Cocos Island, as soon as old Captain Thompson had been decently buried. They went ashore with their map, and they found the place marked by the cross.

Now, unfortunately for most seekers after the Lima treasure, the chart and accompanying instructions, as they exist to-day, are just the least little bit uncertain and indefinite. A creek is indicated, emptying into a little inlet, and the directions say that the seeker is to walk to the high-water mark in the creek, take forty paces in a certain direction, and then a few paces in another direction, which would bring the treasure-seeker to the top of a big rock. Looking closely at the surface of this rock, one would find a hole about big enough to contain a man's thumb. Insert a bar of iron into this hole in the rock, and turn and pry with the bar, and the rock will swing upon a central axis. There before you will stand the doorway into the cave of the treasure.

Bogue and Keating found the rock, found the hole in the rock, followed directions explicitly, and their eyes beheld the dazzling treasure of Lima.

The two men were touched a little with gold-madness. They decided to say nothing to the crew about having found the loot. It was much too good a thing to share with any common sailors, and one couldn't tell what common sailors might want if ever their eyes should rest upon this hoard.

Some sort of scheme was devised for fooling the crew by pretending failure and sailing back to Newfoundland with only a few pocketfuls of gold; enough to outfit another small ship, but not too much to hide about the persons of the two principals. The fortunate two planned to make another trip, all by themselves, and take away the treasure. Gold madness works that way. The greater the abundance of gold, the more determined is the finder to have it all for himself. The more plentiful the loot, the greater the greed and selfishness it inspires.

Bogue and Keating went back to the ship that evening and told the men they had had no success thus far in locating the treasure. But the men were not so easily fooled. They could tell by the gleam in the eyes of the finders that the search had been successful. They noted the excitement and suppressed elation of Keating and Bogue.

The men rose in mutiny and threatened to kill the two principals unless the crew were cut in on the treasure right away. In the middle of the night, to save their lives, Keating and Bogue promised to lead the men to the treasure cave early in the morning, and to share the loot with them.

But they didn't intend to keep their promise. Toward morning they slipped over the side into the ship's longboat, and quietly put off to the shore. I can only suspect what mad scheme they had afoot between them.

To me it seems probable that they foresaw that they would not be able to keep the men away from the treasure cave if the expedition were to run its regular course, and so planned to do a few hours' work concealing as much of the treasure as possible in some place not to be disclosed to the crew. This would constitute their own share, over and above what they would be able to get through agreement with the crew, and they could return for it on another voyage.

Possibly the two entertained some vain scheme of hiding in the interior and living there until the crew should sail away homeward, and later somehow getting off with the treasure. In any case, you may be sure that Keating and Bogue spent a hectic night.

They put off for the ship in their boat next morning. They had their pockets full of gold, and as much of the precious metal was stowed about their persons as they could carry. What did they intend? It is impossible to say.

The boat overturned. Bogue was drowned. The weight of the gold about him pulled him down. Keating managed to get back upon the overturned boat, and was carried far out to sea. A Spanish ship picked him up, after days of drifting, and landed him in Costa Rica, whence he made his way back to Newfoundland, moneyless.

That's one version of what happened at Cocos Island after the Keating expedition arrived. It is the version Keating told most of the time. Another version has been pieced together out of what Keating told when close to death, and out of something he didn't tell.

According to this version of the story, which seems the more probable, the two men went ashore in the boat with only one plan: to hide on the island until the crew should depart, and later wait for a whaler to take them off with as much gold as they could conveniently carry with them without giving away their secret.

But Keating had a scheme of his own, whereby he might not be obliged to share the treasure with anybody. Gold madness was consuming his decency altogether. Perhaps Bogue had schemes too. But Keating managed to get Bogue inside the treasure cave and then swung the great stone door to from without. Then Keating went up into the center of the island to see what he could find to subsist upon until the next whaling vessel showed up.

Several months later the expected whaler came along and took Keating off. According to one story, he arrived in Newfoundland, not penniless, but with approximately fifteen thousand dollars' worth of old gold about him. He evidently had gone back to the cave, where Bogue had starved to death. But what he saw on that visit must have affected him deeply. In all negotiations looking toward a return trip to Cocos Island to get the treasure, Keating specified that he was not to be required to enter the cave.

Fifteen years after looking upon the maddening loot of Lima, Keating was near beggary in his home town. A master mariner named Nicholas Fitzgerald took pity on him and supplied him with comforts and food, keeping him out of an almshouse.

It was early in the eighteen seventies that Keating died, leaving his chart of Cocos Island, with accompanying notes, to Fitzgerald. This seaman never attempted the voyage to Cocos, but when he was near death he sent the chart and directions to Commodore Curzon-Howe, a well-known English officer, who had saved Fitzgerald from drowning when Curzon-Howe was in command of the British naval fleet in Newfoundland waters. It seems to be an ancient tradition of treasure and the sea that one gives one's map or chart of the treasure trove in payment of a debt of gratitude. In point of fact, seamen have a fine code of honorable gratitude toward those who save lives or extend hospitality.

Fitzgerald's letter, in which he offered to disclose the secret of Cocos Island to Curzon-Howe is:

> *Harbor Grace, Newfoundland,*
> *September 10, 1894.*

To the Honble. Commodore Curzon-Howe.
Dear Sir,

I presume to address you in what may appear to be a very strange and romantic subject.

I believe there is a treasure lying concealed in the Cocos Island, Pacific Ocean, believe that I am the only person who knows the secret where it lies.

Now as you are occasionally on duty in the Pacific and as a warship is the most suitable means of carrying out such a project, I thought that it would be to my advantage to write to you and explain the facts of the matter to you.

How I came to the knowledge of this: in 1868 fortune had thrown me as a shipwreck sailor from a sealing vessel on the shores of Codroy village on the west side of Newfoundland, and there I met the owner of another schooner that had been lost in the ice at the same time that we were. This man's name was Keating, a native of this country, and generally known at least by the old inhabitants of St. John's as the man who was on two occasions fitted out with vessel and crew to bring the treasure that still remains hidden, in a very secure way, at Cocos Island.

When I met Keating in 1868 he was in great distress. I had the power to assist him, which I did, bringing him to my lodgings and my own bed, caring for him in his sickness. In return for acts of help on my part he entrusted to me the secret of where the treasure lies hidden at the Cocos Island. We drew up an agreement, one of the conditions being that I should go with him for the treasure, another condition was that I should enter the cave alone as he had pledged himself never again to enter it (I attribute that to fear of something).

However, the agreement was not carried out because I, having a family to see to and believing that Captain Boag, the only man who had the secret from Keating at the time, had mysteriously disappeared in his company while at the Cocos Island, I thought I would be running grave risk of my life to go single-handed with him. This disappearance of Boag was unsatisfactorily explained to me by him.

Therefore, I believe that I alone possess the secret of where the treasure lies hidden at Cocos Island. I am the only person who can find it or show how it may be found.

The condition that I will disclose the secret is this:

That you will send me an agreement signed by you, sir, that if you or any person acting for you, or any way on account of his information, get the treasure you will hand over to me one-twentieth part of the gross value of what is in the cave. The treasure comprises gold coin, silver coin, gold images of the Madonna, life-size church images.

If you desire any further information on this matter I shall be only too happy to supply it you or any question you may be pleased to put.

Yours respectfully,
NICH. FITZGERALD

I do not know how many of the treasure-seekers who have gone to Cocos have had the advantage of seeing and handling the Thompson-Keating-Fitzgerald-Curzon-Howe map and instructions. Several, certainly, have had these documents or purported copies of them.

◇ ◇

Keating's young widow was interested in an expedition that never made land on Cocos, due to mutiny in the crew. A strange, bewhiskered creature named Gissler went to the island to find the treasure, and refused to leave. He called himself Governor of Cocos Island, and when treasure-hunters came his way, he graciously gave them permission to dig. The story of Gissler and his queer life on this solitary island would make a very interesting book in itself. When his authority was flouted by some of the less imaginative of the modern treasure-hunters, he was deeply hurt, and set out at once for Costa Rica, to obtain a commission as governor. He was picked up, destitute, by Lord Fitzwilliam, an Englishman who was on his way to Cocos, and taken before the Costa Rican authorities, who were persuaded to issue to Gissler such papers, bearing big, red seals, as might be most impressive when displayed to treasure-seekers. Maybe the papers were notary public commissions, or maybe they were addresses of welcome, properly inscribed, but they made Gissler happy. Most of the visitors to Cocos who saw the papers during the twenty years following were duly impressed, and promised to buy the old man a new suit of clothes out of the proceeds of their winnings in the mysterious treasure cavern.

Captain Shrapnel (which sounds like a Dickens name for a fictitious character, but isn't) was in command of the British warship *Haughty,* which happened to be in the neighborhood of Cocos in 1896. The Captain had romantic imagination in him, despite strict naval training, and he landed a party of gobs with plenty of gunpowder and dynamite. The rocks near the inlets were blasted extravagantly in hope of uncovering some of the Lima loot, but the search was unsuccessful.

Returning to England, the Captain was rebuked by the Admiralty for indulging in such an unofficial undertaking as treasure-seeking. Captain Shrapnel thereupon obtained leave, and in 1903 sailed with an expedition of his own, aboard a little vessel called the *Lytton*. The story of this expedition is told quite fully in "On the Track of a Treasure," written by Hervey de Montmorency, who was a member of the party and kept a journal of the proceedings.

On this trip, Captain Shrapnel had a chart with a cross marking the treasure-trove. I presume it purported to be a true copy of Thompson's famous map. Several weeks were spent in blasting suspicious-looking rocks. When the period of the *Lytton's* lease was about to expire, Captain Shrapnel told his company that he had lost hope of finding the treasure. He blamed the destructive blasting done by previous visitors, as well as the effects of tropical storms, for changing the face of the landscape so as to obliterate all charted traces of the treasure cave. The party paid its respects to Governor Gissler before leaving, and was informed by this dignitary that he had indeed found part of the treasure. It was a Spanish doubloon, dated 1788, and bearing the image and inscription of King Charles the Third of Spain. Perhaps it had been dropped by some wandering pirate, probably visiting Cocos in the hope of finding some of the treasure buried there long before his time. Or was it one of the coins from the treasure cavern, extracted by the greedy Keating, and accidentally dropped by him when he was hastening to the shore to hail the whaler that was to take him back to civilization?

I wear as a watch fob a doubloon bearing the date 1788 and the image and inscription of Charles the Third of Spain. I bought it in London. I often wonder whether it is the coin that represented Governor Gissler's share of the loot of Lima in 1903. Poor Gissler would have been glad enough to sell the coin for a fair premium to some English treasure-hunter, bound back to London after a disappointing attempt to obtain the treasure in the cave.

Lord Fitzwilliam's party, in 1904, fought with a treasure-seeking party headed by Arnold Gray, also from England. Both parties interpreted the charts they possessed so as to lead them to the same spot, and both began dynamiting the same rocky mound. It proved an exciting arrangement, but more conducive to broken heads than to finding gold.

◇ ◇

Captain Malcolm Campbell, the noted British automobile racer and sportsman, is one of the modern Cocos adventurers who has gone into the enterprise of finding the loot of Lima, properly equipped. He came into possession of the Thompson map and accompanying directional notes in 1925, and talked the matter over with his friend, K. Lee Guinness, who owned a fine private yacht, the *Adventuress,* and was willing to take a hand in the romantic venture. Another Guinness, Claude Robert, had gone out to Cocos on a similar treasure hunt in 1904.

I have a letter from Captain Campbell, dated March 24, 1930, in which the redoubtable adventurer gives me some of the details of his attempt to get the treasure out of Captain Thompson's glittering cave. I quote from the account he sent me, which was published in The Sunday Express, London, October 6, 1929:

This boat, the Adventuress, was a very tight and handy little Diesel yacht of some 250 tons, with a crew of a dozen and a company of five sportsmen—Lee Guinness, Admiral A., two other friends and myself. Admiral A. was to sail to Jamaica in a liner and join us there.

We took picks, spades, crowbars, rifles and revolvers and sailed from Southampton with no reporters or photographers to announce our mission.

Weeks later, weeks of quiet sailing on a sea of tropic blue under a sun of torrid heat, we saw land, a dim, hovering cloud on the horizon, a cloud no bigger than a man's hand—Cocos, the pirates' isle.

I shall never forget my feelings as we sailed round the bluff into full view of Wafer Bay.

We were all on deck and we expected to see, lying inshore, a ship, and on shore a busy encampment with boats going to and fro and excavators at work—for we had heard that two other expeditions were also on the way.

We knew that if others were there it might mean a fight. When you are 400 miles from an inhabited coast, with £12,000,000 in sight, law and the twentieth century take a back seat.

Imagine then our feelings. Round the cape glided the yacht, and the bay opened up—empty!

Slowly we rounded the next headland and slowly Chatham Bay opened up, a great lonely bay with a white, gull-haunted strand where the palm trees stood down to the tide-line—empty!

We anchored a mile off shore, as the bay was full of terribly dangerous reefs and rocks. Admiral A., two men and I went ashore in a dinghy.

I shall never forget my feelings as we landed.

We were on a shore which had been trodden by the feet of Incas, buccaneers, pirates and treasure seekers for the past 500 years, yet a shore so remote and forbidding that no man remained to live on it.

The dinghy was followed right into the surf by sharks ten or twelve feet long, some of the most vicious brutes I have ever seen.

High-water mark was rimmed by great boulders which made it impossible to beach a boat on the top of the tide, and the vegetation was so dense that one had to hack one's way through with a bush-knife.

We searched at once for the creek and found it, a rippling little stream of clear water, which splashed over the shingle into the sea.

I could scarcely contain my excitement when I proceeded to high-water mark at the bottom of the creek, and with compass in hand stepped out forty paces. Having done this with some difficulty, due to the large boulders with which the beach is strewn, and the thick undergrowth which runs right down to the beach, I stopped and turned north, but the only bare rock I could see was some little distance out at sea, a huge table top, still partly covered by the surf.

I retraced my steps, wondering whether high-water mark meant further up the creek, and tried again, but I got entangled with undergrowth, and at the end of my paces could see no bare rocks of any description. By this time the rest of our party had landed, and we held a consultation.

We worked our way inland, but could find no rocks or boulders that could possibly apply to our clue. So we split up into two parties, one walking along the beach to the north-east, and the other to the north-west to ascertain whether there were any further creeks on this side of the island.

I could not keep my eyes off the huge, bare rock which stood out at sea, and although the rest of the party said that this could not possibly be the rock, I decided to investigate the spot, as, if the clue was to be relied upon, this rock stood on the exact bearings.

I plodded wearily off to the rock while my friends proceeded to investigate both sides of the bay.

It was very hot, and the sun beat mercilessly down. I got within twenty-five yards of the rock, and then the tide turned, coming in very

fast, well over my knees. With the tide came the sharks, so I decided
to investigate this rock the next day. Two other large rocks lay in a
direct line nearer the beach, and I investigated both, but on neither
of them could I find a hole or see any crack where an opening could
possibly be hidden.

By the time I had got back to the creek the other two parties
returned, and reported that there were no other creeks, and they therefore somewhat hurriedly came to the conclusion that either the clue
was a wash-out or else it referred to Wafer Bay, and not to Chatham
Bay.

I was convinced that Chatham Bay was the spot, so when the
others decided to return to the ship for lunch I made up my mind to
stay on the island and watch the tide, to ascertain exactly high-water
mark, as I thought the sea might possibly go some little distance up
the creek, which would obviously mean that the forty paces would take
us further inland.

One man volunteered to stay with me, and the others departed
for the ship.

The tide rose and we found that we were only four feet out in our
original calculations. So we tried to penetrate inland and climb a coni-
cal hill which dominates the bay so as to get a panoramic view of the
whole and perhaps locate the rock among the undergrowth.

Campbell is a strong, sturdy Scot, capable of hard labor under a hot sun. He and the few men who were willing to work
along with him put more honest labor into the search for the
Lima treasure than has been invested by many a party that has
gone to Cocos and reported, after digging a little in the clearing
near the shore, that there is no treasure there. They toiled up
the high hill, only to find that it did not give them the view of
the island that they had expected to get from its summit. They
toiled up many another rocky hill, cutting their way with heavy
knives and axes through the undergrowth. They worked back
from Wafer Bay as well as from Chatham Bay, digging and
blasting wherever there appeared a suspicious-looking rock.

Far inland the Campbell party found a great excavation, 20
feet wide and 12 feet deep, with two similar excavations near it.
These were evidences that some other expedition had had in it
men who were not afraid of hard work and honest digging.

Beside a stream that has been diverted by a landslip, Campbell found a series of big boulders, under one of which he still believes the treasure of Lima lies hidden. He and his men searched these rocks for the keyhole into which the iron bar was to be inserted to open the door of the cave, but they could not find it. They found great cracks in the rocks, and realized that the keyhole may have been obliterated by the cracking of the stone since Keating closed the door upon his unfortunate companion.

They blasted and pried and rolled away the stones that were shattered by the blasts, but did not find the cave.

Says Campbell:

When we reached the beach Lee Guinness came ashore with a dinghy, and said that the weather was breaking, and the yacht would never weather a storm off a coast so dangerous as that of Cocos—which was sense.

We struck camp and rowed back to the yacht, defeated on what I believe was the verge of success.

Next morning the Adventuress weighed anchor, and Cocos dropped behind us into the blue, still guarding its treasures.

I wonder if I shall ever again see that green, enigmatic isle, climb the great round hill and descend by the ancient stone path in the cliff side to that mysterious ledge which still holds its secret.

As I write this there comes to me news that Campbell is planning another expedition to Cocos Island, to complete that bit of work he was engaged in when it became necessary to return to England. With all my heart, I wish him success!

◇ ◇

That portion of the loot of Lima which found its way to Trinidad is not without its following among those who like to go down to the sea to hunt treasure islands.

The treasure Trinidad is not the Trinidad which is so well known to the asphalt trade. It is not the Trinidad that has the famous lake of pitch and the Port of Spain, beloved of tourists.

The Trinidad on which the treasure is buried is out of the

track of steamers. It is uninhabited, and, most of the time is uninhabitable. It is a mysterious island, lacking in the charm of many rivers, springs, lakes, and murmuring waterfalls possessed by Cocos Island. If you are out for vacation rather than for the treasure itself, go to Cocos. If you believe in the treasure that went to Trinidad and want hard work under discouraging conditions, go to Trinidad. The desert and lonely island of Trinidad lies in latitude 20° 30′ south, and longitude 29° 22′ west, about seven hundred miles off the coast of Brazil. It belongs to Brazil, together with the neighboring little islet of Martin Vas. But it is so far away from Brazil and everything else that the treasure-seeker need not be afraid of being interfered with by any local authority. About the only way to get to Trinidad is by providing your own yacht, since you cannot depend upon even the occasional whaler to land you or pick you up, as you can in going to Cocos Island. You can hire a small vessel to take you out from Rio Grande do Sul, in southern Brazil, if you have the money and the time requisite to a search for such a vessel. But all treasure-seekers in remote places should have their own yachts, manned by their own countrymen, and not overmanned at that. Mutiny on a treasure hunt is too disastrous to be courted. And the hardships faced at Trinidad are enough to drive to mutiny any but the most faithful and interested workers.

Trinidad is about five miles long and not more than three miles wide at the widest point. There are two very contradictory descriptions of the island found among documents referring to it. Some captains who have put in there for water have described it as a lovely island, covered with green trees and thick jungle, and inhabited by many birds. Others have described it as a desert waste, forbidding in its bleak bareness, supporting hardly any vegetation, and inhabited by flocks of filthy seafowl and multitudes of gigantic land crabs.

The reason for the variation in description is that some sea captains have found the island during a period of recuperation from volcanic disturbances, while others have visited it after it had been laid waste by floods of lava. During the period covered by the memory of men now living Trinidad has been a desert waste.

There are high mountain peaks, deep ravines, and steep brown hills. The landscape is unstable. Storms disturb it. An explorer who makes his way over its surface afoot is in grave danger of causing a landslip of major proportions merely by placing his weight upon some unstable promontory.

The land crabs along the shore are so big and so unafraid of man that they are an almost insurmountable nuisance to any party that wants to dig for treasure in comparative peace and quiet. These crabs will nibble voraciously at the feet of sleepers unless someone stays awake to drive them off, and they are so numerous that the one who stands guard has to work hard to kill them as fast as they present themselves.

Many expeditions have gone to seek the treasure of Trinidad. It is a fully documented treasure, like that of Cocos Island, and the papers describing its location specify that the two great candlesticks of solid gold that stood before the high altar in Lima Cathedral are included in the hoard.

Few of the treasure-seekers are able to land. The forbidding coast of Trinidad is surrounded by coral shoals, and the breakers from the open ocean crash thunderously upon these shoals, directly in the openings to the bays. Landing is in itself a perilous enterprise, and to land sufficient stores to support a digging party for a month or two is an undertaking for experts in this kind of work.

The most notable expedition to Trinidad was that headed by E. F. Knight, a London journalist, in his own yacht, *Alerte*, in 1889. He wrote the story of his adventure very fully in a book now out of print, "The Cruise of the *Alerte*," published in 1890 in London by Longmans, Green & Co. This book is now difficult to obtain, and is not to be confused with another book of the same name, describing an entirely different kind of cruise on another vessel by other persons. There is no copy of Knight's "The Cruise of the *Alerte*" in the Congressional Library, or in the New York Public Library.

Knight was a correspondent of the London Times. After his

Trinidad adventure he returned to his journalistic work, and lived to lose an arm in the Boer War. Even after that, he went on many an exciting cruise, but his treasure hunt at Trinidad was the high spot of his romantic career.

He first visited Trinidad in 1881, when cruising in his yacht *Falcon*. He could not forget the lonely desert island. Returning to England, he came into possession of documents relating to the treasure of Trinidad. He investigated, with true reportorial thoroughness, to verify his information at such sources as remained available.

Sailing with a small company of gentlemen adventurers and a few laborers, Knight reached Trinidad, managed a landing, followed by many more landings, so that he was able to establish a good working camp, with spades, shovels and picks, wheelbarrows to carry away the earth removed by the workers, and food enough to last several weeks. It was necessary to keep part of the crew aboard the *Alerte* while the others worked ashore, and it was found best to keep the yacht out on the open sea, slowly cruising to and fro, so as to keep her off the coral reefs, during most of the three months the treasure hunt lasted on the island.

Knight and his associates did a workmanlike job. They located the point that seemed to be indicated by their chart as the opening of the ravine that should lead directly to the cave in which the treasure reposed. Then they spent nearly all of their three months shoveling a landslip out of the ravine.

The impression the men received was that they had moved but an insignificant part of the landscape in those weeks of backbreaking toil, and that it was almost hopeless with such labor and such tools to try to uncover a treasure that might have been buried under thousands of tons of the lava dust that constituted most of the soil of the island.

There comes an end to the most persistent of treasure hunts. The plucky company managed to get off the island, and sailed back to England without the great tall candles from the sanctuary of the Cathedral of Lima.

Modern steam shovels might do a more effective job. But

even for them the task of nosing through those mountains of lava soil would be a discouraging one.

The treasure-seeker should place a big black cross on the Island of Trinidad—and possibly go elsewhere to find treasure easily.

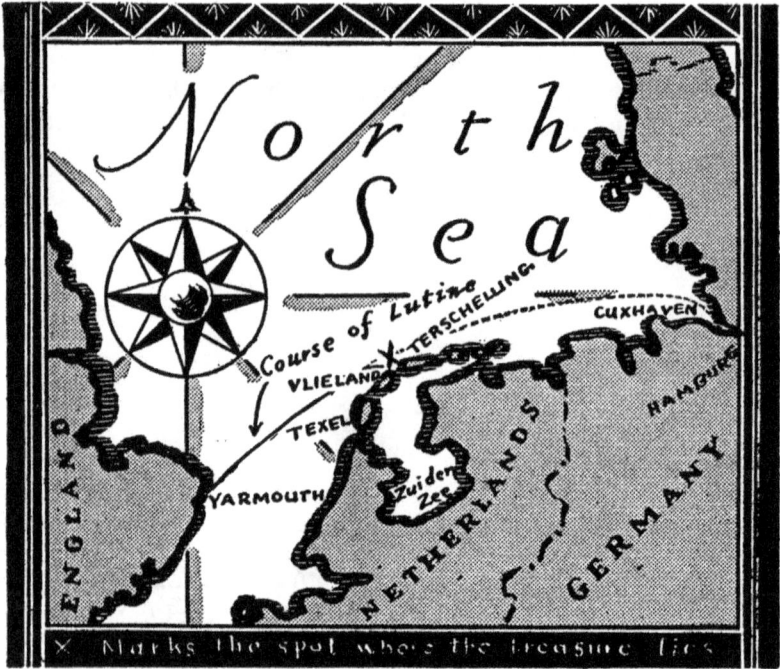

X Marks the spot where the treasure lies

VIII. *The Golden Cargo of the "Lutine"*

H IS Britannic Majesty's man-of-war *Lutine,* laden with a cargo of gold and silver bars and coins, sailed from Yarmouth, England, bound for Hamburg, Germany, on the morning of Wednesday, October 9, 1799. That same night, having gone far off her course, she struck on a sand-bank between the islands of Vlieland and Terschelling, off the coast of Holland, and went to pieces.

She lies there to-day, with most of her cargo intact, about

seventy feet below the surface of the water. She is covered with a heavy blanket of sand and silt.

Submarine engineers estimate the job of salvage thus: It will be necessary to remove thirty thousand cubic yards of sand before getting at the treasure. Then the gold and silver bullion will have to be brought to the surface, and all must be accomplished between storms. The water in which the wreck lies is subject to frequent and violent storms, each of which stirs up and moves the sand and silt.

Whoever would recover the treasure of the *Lutine* must do so by special arrangement with the firm of Lloyd's, London, for the wreck is the property of that concern. Lloyd's has, technically speaking, kept a watchman "on the wreck" since 1799, with only such interruptions as are incident to wars and strained diplomatic relations.

The amount of unrecovered treasure in the *Lutine* wreck is not known to a penny, but it is conservatively estimated at somewhere in the neighborhood of five million dollars. Indications are favorable for ultimate recovery of an amount greater than that, rather than less.

Certainly, no one who contemplates treasure-seeking on a large scale can afford to pass up the *Lutine*. The exact location is in Vlie Stroom, or Fly Roads, near the Texel, Holland. The exact bearings of the wreck are 53° 21′ N. latitude; 5° 3′ E. longitude, and there are poles and monuments on the nearest shores, from which the wreck can be located. Lloyd's possesses records and maps that will make the job of locating the treasure quite simple.

Much treasure has been recovered from the wreck of the *Lutine*, and pieces of the wreck have been brought up by various salvage operations.

I have before me as I write a complete collection of records relating to the *Lutine*, her cargo, and the salvage operations. It is a unique book, known among hunters of treasure as "The Lutine Bible." Bible, I take it, is here used in its original sense, meaning Book. This is the Lutine Book, of which there is in existence only the one copy. It is ten inches long by six and one-half inches wide, and a little more than an inch thick. The covers are made of boards, carefully carved by hand. The wood is dark oak, and once was part of the rudder of the *Lutine*. Inlaid in the center of the front cover is a circular piece of copper, taken from the sheathing of the ship's hull. The backbone of the book is of stout leather, and bears the single word "Lutine." A label inside the cover says the binding was done by A. Land, Voorstraat, Harlingen, Holland.

The title page is printed: "The Wreck of H. M. S. Lutine." No more. Seventy-five pages of the book are written, the other sixty-eight pages are blank.

The book was prepared, over a period of many years, by clerks and researchers in the offices of Lloyd's. It is still incomplete, because the salvage of the *Lutine* has not been finished. The sixty-eight blank pages remain to be filled.

The handwriting throughout the book is a fine, painstaking, legible chirography, and there are several maps, charts and scale drawings, carefully done as permanent records of a valuable property.

◇ ◇

The *Lutine* was a frigate in the British navy, taken from the French in 1793. It was customary in the British navy in those days to add a captured warship to the navy register without change of name. Of course, this frigate was *La Lutine* in the French navy, and *The Lutine* in the British navy. She was a 900-ton vessel, 143 feet long, 38 feet in beam, and twelve feet deep. She carried 32 guns.

The French Royalists at Toulon, in 1793, were in panic. The Republicans were making a great demonstration, and appeared to be sweeping the country. The Royalists were such devoted patriots that they turned over most of the French naval fleet at Toulon to the British under Admiral Lord Hood. *La Lutine* was one of the prizes thus easily gained by the British navy.

The British navy used the frigate *Lutine* as a tender at Woolwich for a time, and in 1795 overhauled her, resheathed her hull with copper, and put in a new deck. She then did duty in the North Sea, and October, 1799, finds her at anchor in Yarmouth Roads, under command of Captain Lancelot Skynner, a young man who had attained his rank only four years previously, and was at this time engaged to be married to a well-to-do London merchant's daughter.

Merchants and the navy were in closer contact in 1799 than they are to-day. The British navy was looked upon as the protector of England, to be sure, but more especially as the protector of the trade whereby the merchants of London lived and thrived. The navy was frankly considered by the powerful merchants as a sort of publicly supported armed subsidiary of the banks and mercantile houses of the English metropolis.

So it is not surprising to learn that in October, 1799, when the merchants of London needed a ship to perform an important and somewhat risky service for them, they called upon the Royal Navy for a well-armed and fast-sailing vessel.

There was a money panic in Hamburg. Several banks had failed, and great mercantile establishments that were correspondents and customers of London houses were tottering. The merchants and bankers of London decided to rush to the rescue of the merchants and bankers of Hamburg. It was determined in conferences in London that a shipload of English gold and silver should be sent to Hamburg to stop the panic. Such aid, appearing with much flourishing of trumpets at the crucial moment, should restore public confidence and halt the catastrophic panic.

The Bank of England is known to have participated in the aid that was forwarded to Hamburg, and the powerful Lombard Street house of Goldsmid was heavily interested in the venture. The influence of these interests was such that the Admiralty was constrained to grant the use of the frigate *Lutine* for the service of the merchants in this emergency. There was a war on, as usual, involving France, Holland and England, and any large shipment of specie would be in danger of capture if not protected by guns.

So the treasure was duly set aside, collected, piled into heavily guarded vans, and hauled to Yarmouth, where the *Lutine* waited. And the *Lutine's* captain, we may well surmise, was pacing his deck in true naval style, thinking of nothing but the fair daughter of the London merchant, to whom he was soon to be married. Perhaps the prospective father-in-law was one of the owners of the treasure that Captain Skynner was now taking under his care. A prospective son-in-law of one of the proprietors of the treasure would not be overlooked as a suitable captain upon whom to place so great a responsibility.

But before the *Lutine* raised her sails, the precious cargo was insured with Lloyd's. The Lloyd's policy was for a sum approximately equal to $4,500,000. Additional insurance was taken out in Hamburg for $800,000. The *Lutine* cargo is said to have included £147,000 in British Government money, uninsured. This would bring the total value of the cargo to well over six million dollars. However, there is evidence that not all of this cargo was placed aboard the *Lutine*. Some of the money is said to have come to hand too late for this shipment, and was sent over by packet later.

Admiral Duncan, who had taken over the *Lutine* from the French Royalists in the first place, was still in charge of the frigate's destiny at the time of the fateful voyage. It was he who gave permission for her use as a merchant packet. He wrote to the Admiralty under date of October 9, 1799:

The Merchants interested in making remittance to the Continent for the support of their credit, having made application to me for a King's ship to carry over a considerable sum of money, on account of there being no Paquet for that purpose, I complied with their request, and ordered "LA LUTINE" to Cuxhaven with the same, directing Captain Skynner immediately after doing so, to take in charge under his protection, the Hudson's Bay Ships, and see them in safety to the Nore.

The *Lutine* deviated from her course that night, and there always has been some mystery or supposed mystery about this deviation. A direct course from Yarmouth to Hamburg would not have taken the vessel near Fly Roads, or Vlie Roads, as the place is called by the Dutch. The only reason for this deviation that seems at all probable is that the Captain decided to seek shelter in the Texel Roads, or thereabout, from a heavy storm. It is known that there was a storm, but it is considered strange by mariners that a ship captain should have run toward those dangerous shoals for shelter, instead of riding out the storm on the open sea. By running for shelter, Captain Skynner courted disaster.

It is possible that the frigate may have been driven off her course by the storm, despite the Captain's intention to keep out to sea and on his course. But reports of the storm that night which have come down to us do not indicate that it was so violent as to force a good mariner so far off his course.

The possibility that some person or persons on the *Lutine* may have steered for the shoals deliberately, perhaps during a mutiny, for the purpose of wrecking the ship and in the confusion getting away with some of the rich plunder, has never been mentioned in any account of the wreck I have ever seen. It seems a remote possibility, but not unworthy of consideration.

In the height of the storm, the ship struck on the lonely coast. According to the best information now obtainable, only two persons escaped alive from the wreck, and both of these died before they were able to shed any light upon the reason for the fatal deviation from the vessel's course to Hamburg.

There were some interesting items in the newspapers, following receipt in England of news of the disaster. In these accounts there are many errors of fact, and much guessing about the extent of the treasure and the purpose for which it was shipped.

Lloyd's Evening Post, October 21, 1799, says:

It is with great concern that we have to state that advices were on Saturday 19th, received at the Admiralty, brought in by Captain Portlock of H.M. Ship "Arrow," of the loss of the "Lutine" frigate, Captain Skynner. This ship sailed from Yarmouth Roads on the morning of the 9th inst for Hamburgh, having on board the sum of £140,000 in Specie,

The wind being at N.N.W., a heavy gale; "La Lutine" was driven towards the Vlieland on the coast of Holland, and a strong lee tide setting in during the night, she went ashore, notwithstanding the exertions of the officers and crew, and went to pieces before the morning. All who were on board perished, except two men who were picked up. A nephew of Messrs. Goldsmid who was going over from the respectable house of his uncles, for the relief of the Hamburgh Merchants in consequence of the late failures, is, we are sorry to find, among the number of those who are lost.

The *London Chronicle,* October 22, 1799, copies the *Post* account, and adds:

To this account so full of calamity, it is added that the "Lutine" was to have proceeded to Hamburgh with money to check the commercial failures at that place. It is even said that one house in the city, whose active and generous benevolence has created more than common interest with the Public, had sent one hundred and fifty thousand pounds, and that the whole sum which thus went to the bottom, amounted to half a million, of which £200,000 had been insured.

Bell's Weekly Messenger, October 20, 1799, says:

It is with extreme concern that we have to notice the loss of the "Lutine" frigate—Captain Skynner. She foundered on Borkum reef, and every person on board was lost but a Notary. The "Lutine" was bound for Hamburgh, and had on board a quantity of Dollars amounting to £140,000 the property of Messrs. Goldsmid who had remitted it for the purpose of taking up their own Bills in that City. The loss of so large a sum in Specie which would have been a salutary supply in preventing any further Commercial embarrassments at Hamburgh, must be severely felt. Measures as we understand, are taking by both the East India and the Bank Directors, with a view of assisting the Merchants, whom the present shock is likely to affect in a sensible manner.

The *Naval Chronicle* for the year 1799, says:

We learn from good authority that there was over £600,000 in Specie on board the "Lutine," which had been shipped by individual merchants in this country, for the relief of different Commercial Houses in Hamburgh. There were also several Merchants on board.

The *London Times,* October 26, 1799, says:

According to letters from the Helder, it appears that the "Lutine" was lost late at night to the Northward of the Fly Island, having been imperceptibly drawn too near the Island, by the Strong currents which set in to the Rivers Weser and Elbe.

The *Norwich Mercury,* October 26, 1799, contains this account:

There is little doubt of the "Lutine" frigate being lost, but it is not yet known if she has gone to the bottom, or how many of the crew have been saved. She was going at a great rate, when she missed stays, and struck on the reef near Texel. Her masts went overboard, and with them a person who is reported to have been taken up by the "Isis." The wreck has not been seen since or heard of, and Admiral Duncan has sent out a Cutter to ascertain her loss. On board the frigate were 40 passengers, including the Duke de Montmorenci, who was going out to join the Duchess at Altona. The intelligence respecting the "Lutine" says that she was lost on the outer bank of the Fly Island passage, on the night of the 9th inst. in a heavy gale at N.N.W. The "Lutine" on the same morning sailed from Yarmouth Roads with several passengers, and 140,000 guineas for the Texel, but a strong lee tide rendered every effort of Captain Skynner to avoid the threatened danger, unavailable, and it was altogether impossible during the night to receive any assistance either from the "Arrow," or the shore, from which several Schouts were in readiness to go to her.

When the dawn broke "La Lutine" was in vain looked for, she had gone to pieces, and all on board, except two men, who were picked up, were lost. One man has since died from the fatigue he had encountered.

Lloyd's sent representatives to the scene of the wreck as soon as news of the disaster reached London, and the very day after confirmation of the loss sent a packet boat to Hamburg with a cargo of gold and silver equal in value to the insured treasure that was lost. It was hoped that some of the sunken bullion might be recovered by prompt efforts at salvage. However, the agents of the financial house found that nothing could be done without divers and equipment for a serious salvage undertaking.

The house of Lloyd's has always been diligent in guarding and preserving all of its rights in the *Lutine* treasure. The wreck has never been "abandoned," since an abandoned wreck, under international maritime law, becomes the property of the salvor. From time to time, during the days and years following the loss of the *Lutine*, Lloyd's agents collected evidence concerning the disaster, and made every possible effort to learn where the fault lay, if there was a fault behind the disaster.

Jan Folkerts Visser, a pensioned Dutch pilot, was interviewed in 1857, and his deposition was recorded thus:

That he was twenty years of age at the date of the occurrence. He saw several rockets from the Vlieland banks, which were answered by several English men of war which were lying at the time in the Vlie Roads. An armed sloop came to Vlieland to fetch a Pilot boat to give assistance to the crew of an English Man of War in distress on the Vlieland Banks. That the bodies of the Commander and two officers of the "Lutine" were picked up, and they were recognised by Captain Portlock, Commander of the British Man of War "Wolverine" then lying in the roads of Vlieland.

Their Epualettes and buttons were cut off by Captain Portlock and they were buried in the West corner of the Churchyard of Vlieland, against the Church, in the piece of ground, opposite the general Poor-house. That besides the bodies, they picked up a piece of wreckage upon which was a man still showing signs of life. They had much difficulty in getting him aboard, as the said man did everything to prevent them. They took him to the Roads at Vlieland to get medical assistance from the English men of War. When they arrived a Doctor came on board, under whose treatment the man regained his senses. He then heard that the man was a clerk of the "Lutine." The next day he saw this man walk about the Deck of the "Wolverine" several times. He himself often took fresh water to the "Wolverine."

On the little island of Sylt, in the church of Westerland, there is a tablet bearing this inscription:

Sacred to the Memory of
Daniel Weinholt
Second son of John Weinholt Esqre.
of Great St. Helen's in the city of London Merchant, who was
lost to the inexpressible grief of a mother, a brother, and a
sister, in H.B.M. Frigate "Lutine" off the coast of Holland,
on the night of the 9th Oct. 1799
Having drifted on the shore of Sylt
He was discovered by
Herrn Stroendvdgt Deckker
to whom the family owe a debt of gratitude for his great attention, and for his careful preservation of the property found
upon the body—which was interred in Westerland Churchyard
on the 11th Nov. 1799.

This Daniel Weinholt sailed upon the ill-fated *Lutine* in
charge of a shipment of £40,000 in gold bars, the property of
his father's London firm, a house trading in indigo and other
Indian goods. The elder Weinholt lost his money, as well as his
son, since this particular shipment was uninsured, the Weinholts
considering the premium too high.

◇ ◇

Salvaging the *Lutine* treasure was a matter of immediate
interest to the fishermen of the Zuyder Zee. A veritable gold
mine had been dumped in their front yard. The fishermen were
not slow in rallying around the wreck.

The wreckage lay at first only about twenty feet under
water at low tide. Later the hulk seems to have slipped off a
sandy shelf into deeper water. Not a few of the inhabitants of
the small islands in the vicinity of the wreck dived from their
fishing boats and went home with enough gold to keep the household going through many a rainy day.

England was at war with Holland at the time of the disaster.
Wars were not very efficient in those days, however. They were
carried on in a casual, almost lackadasical manner, stopping now

and then for lack of enthusiasm, and beginning again for no particular reason that anybody seemed to know about.

The war was not serious enough to keep agents of Lloyd's away from the wreck in Holland waters during the weeks immediately following the disaster, but it served as a good excuse for seizure of the wreck by the Dutch government as a prize of war, as soon as government circles became aware of the richness of the cargo.

For a short time, after the wreck of the *Lutine*, the war between Great Britain on the one hand and France and Holland on the other hand was called off. For some reason, altogether unconnected with the *Lutine*, the nations decided to quit fighting. But before Lloyd's could make any arrangement for systematic salvage work, the war was declared on again, and the treasure was taken over by the Dutch government.

In 1800 and 1801 operations on the site of the wreck were carried on by an official of the Dutch government called the Strandvonderij. We would call him the Royal Wrecker or the Official Receiver of Wrecks.

The Salvage work was very simple in its mechanics. The workmen stood on a large raft anchored above the wreckage, and with long poles fished for the gold and silver prizes. Three kinds of tools were used on the ends of the long poles. One of these tools worked almost exactly like a pair of ice tongs, with the two handles connected by chains. Another was a mechanical hook quite similar to the tool used by grocers in taking packages down from the high shelves. One jaw of this tool was fixed; the other could be opened and closed by the operator. The third device in this simple fishing enterprise was a net made of iron chains, arranged dipper fashion on a circular ring held at the end of a pole.

The stern of the *Lutine* had been broken open by the force of her grounding, and the gold and silver bars were spilling out as the wreck was moved by tides and storms. The salvors let down their tongs and hooks and grasped many of these bars. Some they brought to the surface, but these fishermen told heartbreaking tales of the big bars that got away. The iron nets were used for gathering up the piles of coins that were spilled out of broken kegs, boxes and casks.

The government official in charge had to render a strict accounting of every day's takings. When it was decided to abandon the work, owing to the settling of the wreck into deeper water, the recovered treasure reported consisted of 58 gold bars, 35 silver bars, some gold and silver French and Spanish coins, four English guineas and two half guineas. The valuation of the recovered treasure was a little less than $300,000.

The wreck was covered by a heavy blanket of sand after a few severe storms, and even the fishermen gave over their spasmodic efforts to recover more gold and silver bars. A war was occupying all the spare time of the Dutch officials. When Napoleon was sent away to Elba in 1814 and Europe again took thought of peaceful pursuits, the King of the Netherlands received a proposal from his Wreck Receiver, Heer Pierre Eschauzier, looking toward a serious effort to salvage the treasure of the *Lutine* by means of divers. Eschauzier, who was of French extraction, had done much figuring as to the amount of treasure that might be got out of the wreck in a successful salvage effort. He had studied the lists of gold and silver bars already recovered. Each bar had its identifying letters and numbers. In some cases the letters represented the name of the firm that had shipped the bullion, and the numbers may have run in series, say from 1 upward, a new series of numbers being identified with each set of letters. Assuming this to be the case, the magistrate of the wrecks made up lists of the missing numbers in each series, and figured up the value of the unreclaimed treasure. The King of Holland was much impressed, and in 1814 he assigned the sum of 300 guilders for work to be performed in finding the wreck. The wreck was located, but was found to be badly buried in sand.

In digging about in the vicinity of the wreck, the workers brought up chunks of iron rust, mixed with gunpowder and sand, which had caked into hard masses. In these chunks they found seventeen coins.

After retiring from his government position, Heer Eschauzier

formed a company called Onderneming up het Wrak van der
Lutine, which organization is usually referred to, for the sake
of brevity, as the Decretal Salvors. This company on September
14, 1821, received a royal concession to loot the *Lutine*, provided it paid over one-half of the salvage to the crown. Lloyd's
of London seriously objected to this bartering of its rights by
the Dutch government, but the objections had to go through
the slow process of governmental review and consideration, and
the Decretal Salvors meantime went ahead with efforts to get
at the treasure.

When about $25,000 had been spent in fruitless efforts and
seven years had passed, the claim of Lloyd's was recognized by
a royal decree of the King of Holland. The decree, however,
merely gave to Lloyd's that half of the treasure which had been
reserved to the crown in the contract between the Dutch government and the Salvors. It did not invalidate the contract.

In 1828 a salvage company, acting for Lloyd's, did some
diving on the wreck, but recovered nothing. In 1837 Heer
Pierre Eschauzier died, and his son, Heer Brandt Eschauzier,
succeeded to his interest in the salvage.

A drifting buoy chanced to pass over the wreck in 1856, and
the chain, dragging over the golden hoard, became fast. When
hauled up, the chain brought with it a gold coin in a mass of
rust, gunpowder and sand. The hunt was on immediately. The
peculiar combination of rust, gunpowder and sand at the site of
the *Lutine* wreck has, from very early times, been the chief
identifying mark, and because these masses so often have contained coins, the finding of this substance always starts excitement in the Terschelling neighborhood.

In 1857, the salvage work was renewed with much spirit.
It was done by the Decretal Salvors, and Lloyd's coöperated.
In July the stern of the frigate was found at a depth of 36 feet.
So enthusiastic did the workers now become that an engineer
was employed to superintend the work, diving suits were ob-
tained from England, and a diving bell was tried out. Some
money was brought up with tongs in August. In October, a
Dutch fisherman named Koding decided that the treasure was

as much his as anybody's, providing he could get at it. He appeared on the site of the wreck with an outfit of tongs, and paid no attention to the warnings and orders issued by the Salvors. He was so persistent and elusive that a company of marines was finally called out to compel him to desist.

In 1858, a diver in the employ of Decretal Salvors picked up a bar of silver, and during the months that followed many gold and silver bars were recovered. But another storm drifted sand over the treasure trove, and the findings in 1859 and 1860 were few. The total treasure recovered in this attempt comprised 41 bars of gold and 64 bars of silver, as well as a considerable number of coins. The total value of this salvage was about $220,000.

During the operations of 1859 the ship's bell, rudder and rudder chain were recovered and turned over to Lloyd's. From the rudder a chair and table were made, and from remaining scraps the binding of the "Lutine Bible" was lovingly fashioned by some good workman. The chair and table are in the offices of Lloyd's in the Royal Exchange, London, and on the table reposes the *Lutine's* bell.

On the table a silver plate carries this inscription:

H.B.M. Ship La Lutine.
32 Gun Frigate
Commanded by Captain Lancelot Skynner, R.N.
Sailed from Yarmouth Roads
On the morning of the 9th October, 1799, with a large amount
of specie on board,
And was wrecked off the Island of Vlieland the same night,
When all on board were lost except one man.
 The rudder of which this table was made and the rudder chain and the bell which the table supports, were recovered from the wreck of the ill-fated vessel, in the year 1859, together with a part of the specie, which is now in custody of The Committee for managing the affairs of Lloyd's.

The bell has been used at various times to sound the note announcing the loss of a vessel at sea. Shipowners and persons interested in shipping and salvage frequent the big room in which the bell is mounted, looking for news and gossip of the seven seas. When a missing ship is posted as lost, the *Lutine's* bell is struck with a hammer and the announcement of the loss is made to the assembled company.

The treasure recovered in 1859 was nearly all found near the rudder. It was decided to raise this part of the ship, both for its sentimental value, and as a possible means of uncovering more bars. The rudder was 26 feet high, four feet broad at the bottom, and eight inches thick.

About this time Lloyd's obtained an act of the British Parliament, officially constituting the Corporation of Lloyd's the sole owners and heirs of the *Lutine* wreck and contents. This was done as a precaution against other possible claimants in England, and did not, of course, affect the claims of the Dutch company.

In 1886, a Hollander, Ter Meulen of Bodergraven, who had been studying the tides and currents near Terschelling for more than a quarter of a century, always with an ambition to recover the treasure of the *Lutine*, undertook a salvage campaign. He entered into a contract with the Decretal Salvors and Lloyd's of London for a percentage of the profits.

Meulen employed steam dredges on the wreck for the first time. He expended much time and effort in locating the wreck, and when he found it he discovered to his dismay that the steam dredges seemed incapable of bringing gold and silver bars to the surface. During three years of intermittent operations, he recovered gold and silver coins to the value of about $3,500.

In 1907, Simon Lake, American submarine engineer and inventor, became interested in the *Lutine*. He took over a salvage contract with Lloyd's that had only two years to run.

Lake already had built a submarine cargo recovery apparatus that had proved quite successful in operations in Long Island Sound, within a radius of thirty or forty miles of the inventor's submarine boat factory at Bridgeport, Connecticut. He purposed to apply the same principles and similar, although larger, apparatus, to the recovery of the *Lutine* treasure.

Simon Lake is one of the most interesting of American inventors. He read Jules Verne's "Twenty Thousand Leagues Under the Sea" when he was a small boy, and has been working on submarine inventions ever since. He has built submarine boats for many navies, and, unfortunately for the peaceful business of salvaging treasure, wars and rumors of wars have kept him busy during most of his lifetime. When governments have given him time for peaceful pursuits, he has always turned toward the fascinating problem of the wealth of Davy Jones's locker.

As soon as Lake had his contract for the *Lutine* salvage in hand, he went to work to construct his recovery apparatus.

He built a steel tube, 95 feet long, and susceptible of extension. The general plan of the apparatus may be described in nontechnical terms, somewhat thus: The steel tube is designed to be connected with a surface vessel at one end, and with a specially designed steel submarine working chamber at the other end. The surface vessel takes up her position over the wreck, and the tube is let down so that it slants at a convenient angle, the submarine working chamber resting on the ocean floor or on the wreck itself, depending upon the nature of the operation in hand.

Operators descend to the working chamber by walking down a ladder through the tube. Without diving suits they may look through the glass ports, operate searchlights, and examine the wreck in detail. Without changing clothes, also, they may direct the operations of cranes and dredging apparatus mounted on another surface vessel, above the wreck.

The submarine working chamber is fitted with an air-lock. By introducing into the chamber sufficient air pressure to keep out the sea, the workers may open a sea door and reach out with tools. Thus it would be possible for men in ordinary clothing to pick up bars of gold and silver by reaching out through the sea door with tongs, if the bars were close enough to the chamber. Also, the workers may put on diving clothes in the chamber and step out on the ocean floor or on the wreck and work, returning to the protection of the submarine working chamber at will.

Lake completed his apparatus for salvaging the *Lutine* treasure, tested it in the English channel, and then dismantled it. He was called back to America by business. Before arrangements for surface craft could be made, the contract period had advanced so far that it was deemed impossible to get the *Lutine* treasure uncovered and lifted before the expiration date. Apparently, two years was too short a period within which to expect a successful carrying through of such an enterprise, from beginning to end.

The apparatus was stored in a warehouse at Brightlingsea. As this is written, it has lain there unused for more than twenty years. The world war kept Simon Lake so busy with the building of submarines that he had no time to devote to treasure-hunting. Since the war, several salvors have tried to make arrangements to use the Lake apparatus on the wreck of the *Lutine* or on the Tobermory galleon, but Lake, always busy on the American side of the water, has refused to grant permission for the use of his salvage machinery except under his own supervision.

Lake's contract for the *Lutine* job had been taken over from an English firm that had worked on the wreck with suction dredges from 1896 to about 1907. The dredges uncovered the wreck, and a barrier of sandbags was constructed all around the *Lutine,* to keep sand from drifting in. This barrier was effective until it was completely swept away by a storm.

After expiration of this contract, a new company was formed in England, called the National Salvage Association. This concern spent nearly half a million dollars. It operated a powerful suction dredge from a steamer, the *Lyons,* leased for the enterprise. When the wreck had been almost cleared, a storm wiped the company out by covering the *Lutine* and her treasure under many tons of sand.

Another salvage operation, begun in 1912, was ended by the war. Operations since that time are briefly summed up in the following letter, which I have received in answer to an inquiry addressed to Lloyd's:

Dear Sir,

"LUTINE"

I beg to acknowledge the receipt of your letter of the 17th instant, and in reply to inform you that the salvage operations on the site of the wreck of the above vessel, which you state were begun about 1912, were suspended owing to the War.

There have been one or two further attempts at salvage operations since the War, but so far as I am aware none of these operations have been successful in recovering any specie.

Yours faithfully,
W. A. S. BOXFORTH
Clerk to the Committee.

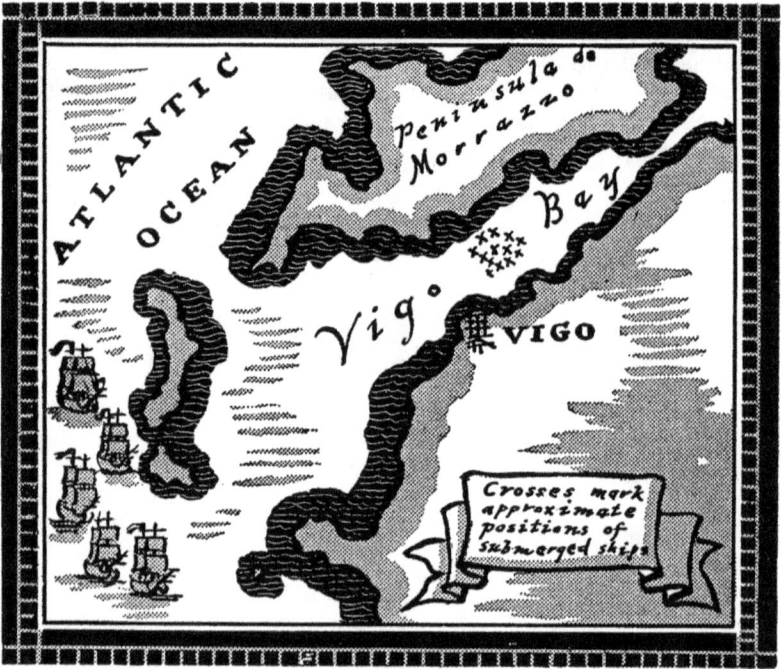

IX. *Down Under the Sea*

VIGO is a city of about 55,000 people, in the province of Pontevedra, Spain. It is only fifteen miles north of the boundary of Portugal. Although it is almost exactly due east of New York City, and closer to New York than any other city in Europe, it is seldom visited by American tourists. Certain passenger liners of the Spanish Royal Mail Line sail directly from New York to Vigo about once a month, taking eight days to make the trip. The one I sailed on in 1929 carried two English-speaking Americans besides myself. The rest of the passengers were Spaniards, Spanish-Americans, Cubans and Mexicans. Stewards and crew, almost without exception, spoke only Spanish. In the city of Vigo I heard no English spoken.

Vigo is a grand old city, redolent of romance and history and high emprise. It rises in dignified terraces from the Bay to the majestic mountains. Its streets are narrow, and the gay Spanish boys and girls, in their picturesque costumes, saunter down the middle of the streets in the evening, singing, playing the guitar, making love, and looking off to sea with dreamy and incurious eyes.

It is not much different here to-day from the scenes one might have beheld in these streets in October, 1702, when a most incredible chapter in the history of golden argosies was being enacted.

The ship on which I sailed to Vigo lay at anchor just outside the inner harbor for a whole day and a night, waiting for the fog to lift. Vigo Bay is a glorious sight from sea or land, with its ageless rocky islands and the frame of austere mountains rising beyond. There is room in the Bay for hundreds of ships, but the entrance is dangerous and beset with rocks and shoals. In a fog, it is best to cast anchor and wait. Fortunately, the Spaniards are not much averse to waiting. They are a patient people, improving each shining hour of the afternoon in restful siestas, and venturing forth to sing and trade and gently urge their oxen through the streets when the hours are less shining and more inspiring.

As we rode at anchor in the outer Bay, I was thinking of a fleet that rode there, 227 years earlier, waiting also for the fog to lift. That was on Sunday, October 11, 1702, and Sir George Rook, Vice-Admiral of England, was pacing the deck of his noble flagship, the *Royal Sovereign*, impatient of the fog blanket that made it impossible for him to proceed.

Sir George (whose name is sometimes spelled Rooke) was 52 years old, and, although he was not at all sure of it on that momentous Sunday afternoon, he stood then at the turning point of his life. He had been in the navy since boyhood. He had been knighted in 1692 for burning six French ships at Barfleur. He took a seat in Parliament in 1698, and retained his seat while at sea. He was deep in politics, and had many enemies at home. There were politicians aplenty who were watching for Sir George to slip ever so little.

And Sir George had just slipped. He had been sent out from England, sailing from Spithead on June 19, 1702, to make a descent upon the Spanish port of Cadiz. The richest Spanish treasure fleet of all time was reported to be about to make port at Cadiz. Sir George was given a fleet of thirty sail, nearly half of which were contributed by the Dutch. He was expected to capture and destroy the town and port of Cadiz, establish an English naval base there for the prosecution of the rest of the war, and be ready to take the Spanish treasure fleet when it should arrive.

The particular war which happened to be on the calendar at this time was the War of the Spanish Succession. Europe had almost settled down to peace after the signing of the Treaty of Ryswick, in 1697, and Rook was not the only great sea hero who had gone into politics as a career, believing that there might be no further opportunities for winning glory at the cannon's mouth.

But the King of Spain died in 1700, leaving the Empire in his will to Philip, Duke of Anjou, grandson of King Louis XIV of France. England wouldn't stand for such a will. France was her hereditary enemy, and England had thought that the Treaty of Ryswick had secured her against any further growth of the power of France for a century or two at least. And here, with the ink hardly dry upon the treaty, the King of Spain dies and leaves a whole empire to the French King's grandson!

King William of England died soon after the news of this will brought home to him the dismal fact that England had France and Spain to whip all over again. He was succeeded by Queen Anne, and in 1702 the war was on.

Sir George stepped down from his Parliament seat and sailed forth to destroy Cadiz.

His Grace, the Duke of Ormond, sailing aboard the *Rane-laugh,* in Rook's fleet, had command of the soldiers who were

IN DAVY JONES'S LOCKER

taken along to reduce Cadiz to the status of a British outpost.
By the time the fleet reached Cadiz it had been joined by many
smaller contingents, both English and Dutch, and consisted of
203 vessels—a veritable armada!

Three months after the sailing of Sir George and his fleet
from Spithead, nothing had been accomplished at Cadiz beyond
the landing of the Duke of Ormond's army, some marching and
countermarching, the loss of a goodly number of Englishmen,
and the reëmbarking of the army. On the nineteenth of September, exactly three months from the date of sailing, the English
fleet was not there, but a goodly Spanish army was in control of
Cadiz. The expedition was a failure, and Sir George headed for
home, with ruin staring him in the face. How his political enemies
would pounce upon him when the news came into London!

Meantime, Sir Cloudsley Shovel had been dispatched to sea
with twenty-seven ships to intercept, if possible, the Spanish plate
fleet, which advices to London had reported as headed for Cadiz.
It was realized that the fleet might suspect that an English fleet
would be waiting for it at Cadiz, and might thereupon change its
course. Shovel was to take care of this contingency.

The fleet of treasure-ships had indeed learned that a war was
on between Spain and England and that a British fleet had been
sent to Cadiz.

There were seventeen Spanish treasure ships, all loaded down
with gold and silver in coins and great ingots. This treasure had
been accumulating at Porto Bello and Carthagena during three
years. It had always been the custom to remove the treasure of
America to Spain once a year, but for three years the Spaniards
had been a little uncertain about political conditions affecting the
sovereignty and the general stability of the nation. It had been
thought best to let the treasure accumulate in America, rather
than deliver it at home, where the King might be French or
Spanish or even English by the time the treasure fleet should
arrive.

Don Manuel de Velasco was now upon the sea, Cadiz-bound,
with the greatest bulk of gold and silver ever shipped from one
port to another. Modern estimates, based upon extensive docu-

ments in Spanish and English archives, set the value of the
treasure carried by the fleet at about $150,000,000.

Near the Azores, the Spanish fleet was met by a French convoy fleet, consisting of twenty-three men-of-war, and informed
that Cadiz was no safe port for Spanish treasure ships. Admiral
Château-Renaud, commanding the French fleet, strongly urged
that the treasure be taken into a French port until the English
should quit the Spanish coast. Admiral Velasco thanked him for
his kind invitation, but insisted that this was, after all, Spanish
treasure, and no small treasure at that. To Spain it should go!
If Cadiz could not be reached at this time, some other Spanish
port must serve until the English should be chased out of Cadiz.
Vigo was picked as a likely port.

Now, when the treasure fleet and its friendly convoy were
safely at anchor in the spacious harbor of Vigo, Admiral Velasco
was informed of the danger that threatened. The English were out
after that treasure. They would search the coast of Spain for it.
They would hardly be likely to pass up Vigo in their search.

Defensive measures were taken. A log boom was stretched
across one of the narrowest parts of the channel leading into the
harbor. A battery of eight brass guns and twenty iron guns was
mounted on the north side of the Bay. On the south side of the
channel a platform was erected, mounting forty guns, half of
them brass. The old stone fort overlooking the harbor entrance
was surrounded by a deep ditch, and ten guns and five hundred
soldiers with small arms were stationed within.

Now began the comedy relief of this majestic Spanish tragedy.
Velasco wanted to get the treasure off the ships and safely stowed
ashore, for he knew that his defences were insufficient to hold
off any determined attack by the English. But it wasn't so easy
to get gold and silver unloaded at Vigo. Cadiz was the officially
appointed port of debarkation for treasure from America, and
the merchants and jobholders of Cadiz were known to be extremely jealous of this royal privilege. They would make trouble
for any admiral who might dare to unload the precious stuff into
the lap of a rival city, such as Vigo.

But this was war time, and Admiral Velasco was not alone

in the belief that Spain must arrange either to unload the treasure or lose it. There are noble mountains just back of Vigo, as I have said. If the treasure could be unloaded and carted into some cave or clearing in these mountains, surrounded by a small military guard, it would be safe.

So messengers were sent hither and yon, and dispatchers burned up the roads in an effort to unwind enough red tape to get that treasure safely ashore. When royal consent was obtained to land the treasure, it was still necessary to bring a customs receiver from Cadiz, overland, to count the money and value the bullion, with proper ceremony. So the treasure fleet lay at anchor with all its freight aboard, after a month of scurrying (if Spanish officials may be said to scurry under any circumstances) to and fro, issuing of orders and stamping of red and yellow wax with handsome seals.

◇ ◇

While the defeated English fleet was making the best of its way toward a home port, and Sir George Rook was contemplating the toppling structure of his naval-political career, a few ships ran short of water, and Captain Hardy, of the *Pembroke,* was detailed to put into Lagos Bay to obtain a supply. It chanced that the Reverend Mr. Beauvoir, chaplain of the *Pembroke,* was a native of one of the Channel Islands, and spoke French as well as he spoke English. He was the only French-speaking member of the landing party, and so fell into conversation with the French Consul at this little port. The Consul, regarding the Channel Islander as almost a Frenchman, talked freely. In fact he boasted. He told of the mighty fleet that the King of France would soon send against the English and Dutch, and very unwisely boasted that a French fleet had successfully convoyed the famous Spanish treasure fleet to the harbor of Vigo, where it now lay at anchor.

When the water party climbed aboard the *Pembroke* that night, the Reverend Mr. Beauvoir made bold to get the Captain out of bed to give him the startling news about the treasure fleet. Captain Hardy immediately weighed anchor and made after the English fleet, which now had some hours the start of him. After some days, he overtook the flagship, went aboard, and delivered his news to the pleasantly astonished Sir George. A council of flag officers was called at once, aboard the *Royal Sovereign*, and it was decided to stand for Vigo.

During that Sunday afternoon and night, while waiting for clear visibility, Sir George Rook did not spend all his time pacing the deck. He called conferences and councils of his officers. He learned that nobody in the fleet knew much about the depth of the channel ahead, but it was thought that the water was shallow. The *Royal Sovereign* was the biggest ship in the Royal Navy at that time, 3,953 tons, 330 guns, 850 men, drawing 22 feet of water. It was adjudged impossible to get such a giant into the inner harbor without pilotage, so Sir George transferred his flag to the *Somerset*. Admiral Hopson was transferred out of the great Prince George into the lighter draught *Torbay*, and was given the place of honor and danger—leading the van. It is worth noting that Midshipman Edward Vernon, destined to become one of the most noted admirals in the British navy, received his baptism of fire aboard the *Torbay* in the Battle of Vigo Bay.

Fifteen English and ten Dutch vessels were selected for the attack. Instructions were to destroy or capture the men-of-war and to capture the Spanish treasure galleons as nearly intact as possible.

Next morning, a landing was made on the outer beach by the soldiers under the Duke of Ormond. There were 9,663 English officers and men, and 3,924 Dutch soldiers in the landing party. These forces advanced and captured the fort that was surrounded by a ditch.

Then the fog lifted, as fogs eventually do if given time, and Sir George Rook gave the order to advance. He left the line-of-battle ships *Association* and *Barfleur* to shell the forts on both sides of the channel. Hopson in the *Torbay* crowded on all sail in a stiff breeze, and struck the boom head-on, breaking it beautifully. He then headed directly into the broadsides of several French vessels that were drawn up across and on both sides of the channel, inside the boom.

There is a rare chronicle of the battle which I shall quote

regarding some of the details. It was published soon after the return of the British fleet, to vindicate Admiral Rook against his political enemies. I found the only copy I have ever heard of in London recently, and it is before me as I write. The title page reads:

AN

IMPARTIAL ACCOUNT

Of all the

Material Transactions

OF THE

GRAND FLEET

AND

LAND FORCES

From their first setting out from Spithead, June the 29th, till his Grace
the Duke of Ormond's Arrival at Deal, November the 7th. 1702.
In which is included a particular Relation of the Expedition at Cadiz,
and the Glorious Victory at Vigo.
By an OFFICER *that was present in those* ACTIONS.

LONDON:

Printed for R. Gibson in Middle-Row in Holborn, and sold by J. Nutt
near Stationers-Hall. 1703.

From this chronicler, who was present and evidently had the assistance or coöperation of Rook in preparing his account, I take this excerpt:

October the 11th, In the Afternoon we came to an Anchor against Vigo, which fired several Shot at us, but with no effect. Also a Council of War was called on Board the Admiral, for all Flag and General Land-Officers, where 'twas agreed, to send in 25 Sail, but first to Land our Infantry, to facilitate the Ships passing the Boom, which was cross their Harbour; also on each side was a Battery to defend it, and their Ships were in a Line within the same at Rodendella: So this Day about 10 in the Morning, we Landed in a Sandy Bay about 2 Leag. from Vigo, and march'd towards their Battery and Fort on the Starboard side going into Rodendella, which we Attack'd, and met with a vigorous

Opposition, but our Men so boldly pressing forward, made themselves
Masters of the Battery and Trenches, and the Enemy to retreat, al-
tho' they had at least 20000 in and near this place, yet durst not engage
us, because they saw the Resolution of our Forces. We had no sooner
took the Platform, on which were 38 Cannon, but the detach'd Ships,
which were drawn up in a Line of Battel, began to sail, Admiral Hopson, with undaunted Courage, leading the Van, and forc'd the Boom
with his Ship; at the same time the Association, Captain Bucknam
laid his Broadside against the Battery on the other side the Harbour
(in which were 17 guns) so that for a considerable time, the firing of
great and small Shot, on both sides, was so terrible, that I want words
to relate it; besides the dismal aspect of many Ships on Fire, which
our Enemy put in Flames and then left them. Some they Sunk, and
others we Took; and our Grenadiers drawing up against a Fort they
had of 12 Guns, and saluting them with their Grenadoes, they surrender'd, and became Prisoners of War, and in it were above 200
French and Spaniards, and amongst them several Men of Note, as the
Vice-Admiral of the French Fleet, with several Captains of their Ships,
and the Lieutenant-General of the Spanish Flota, but all the private
Men were dismiss'd in few Days. Admiral Hopson's Ship was clapt on
Board by a French Fireship, and had been burnt, had not the latter
fortunately Blown up, yet the former received much damage by it,
and lost in the Action, being kill'd and drown'd, upwards of 100 Men,
the other Ships loss being inconsiderable, and our loss on shoar was
two Officers kill'd, and four wounded, and about 40 private Men kill'd,
and as many wounded; our Enemies loss was not inferiour to ours; and
amongst theirs, the Governour of the Fort was Kill'd. This Glorious
Victory was obtain'd in about 2 Hours time.

It will be observed that the date of arrival of the English fleet
at Vigo was October 11. The writer neglects to note the advent of
another day, the twelfth, when he says, "So this day about ten
in the morning." The battle, then, was on October 12, 1702. For
some reason that I have been unable to discover, many modern
historians give the date as October 22 or 23.

When the Spaniards saw the noses of the English ships push-
ing through the harbor entrance, they decided to disregard red
tape, at whatever risk, and unload the treasure. There is diversity
of testimony on this point, but it seems probable that the aroused

custodians of the port did succeed in getting ashore a very little of the gold. There wasn't much time in which to do any workman-like job of cargo handling. Two hours after the British and Dutch guns began to boom, the treasure ships were all afire and scuttled. Admiral Rook succeeded in saving one big galleon, the *Tauro*, which he took back with him to London. Her cargo of gold and silver amounted to one million dollars. It was sent to the British Royal Mint. All the gold coins minted from this cargo in 1703 were stamped with the word VIGO, in commemoration of the victory.

Five galleons in all were captured, but four of these must have been unimportant vessels, possibly not belonging to the treasure fleet at all. Three Spanish men-of-war were sunk, the *Jesus Maria Joseph, La Buffoona, La Capitana de Assogos*. They carried a total of 178 guns.

These treasure galleons went to the bottom of Vigo Bay, and there they lie to this day:

Santo Christo de Mariacaia, Santo Christo de Buen Viaje, Santa Cruz, Nostredam de Mercy, Santa Domingo, Le Trinidad, Nuestra Señora de Mercedes, St. Juan de Baptista, Philippo Quinto, Jalashe del General, La Sacra Familia, Santa Susanna, and another *Santa Cruz.*

I give the list as set down officially by the English. It may contain some errors, especially as to spelling.

Eighteen French ships were sunk or captured. They carried a total of 5,810 men and 998 guns.

Our unidentified eyewitness adds this quaint paragraph to his account of the battle:

So the same Night we marched about three Miles farther, where we lay on our Arms all Night, tho' very wet, etc. and the Ships, and Galleons on Fire, saluted us with several Shot; when burnt down to the lower Tier, and when they blew up, 'twas (tho' dismal) unexpressible fine; the next morning we march'd to Rodendello, from whence the Inhabitants were fled, yet great Bodies drew together on the Mountains, but finding us in so good a posture to receive them, they would not attack us; also about this place we took many Prisoners, etc. but had none taken and kill'd of ours.

Under the head of "Damage Sustain'd," he says:

Torbay had her Fore-topmast shot by the Board, and most of her
Sails burnt and scorch'd; the Foreyard burnt to a Cole; the Larboard,
Shrouds fore and aft, burnt at the dead Eyes; and several Ports blew
off the Hinges; and her Larboard Side scorch'd, and had 115 Men
kill'd and drowned, and 9 wounded; so Admiral Hopson went, and
hoisted his Flag on board the Monmouth.
Association had her Main-mast shot, and two Men kill'd.
Kent had her Fore-mast shot, and Boatswain wounded.
Barfleur had her Main-mast shot, two Men kill'd, and two wounded.
Mary had her Boultsprit shot.

That shipload of gold and silver saved Sir George Rook's face,
his reputation, his Parliament seat, and his career. There was
loud rejoicing throughout the land, punctuated by shrill jeers
concerning Cadiz, emitted by Rook's implacable enemies. But
Queen Anne, having regard to the gallant conduct of the Englishmen at Vigo, made Rook her Privy Councillor. He was re-
elected to his seat in Parliament in 1705. But the favor of the
Queen could not stave off an investigation of the Cadiz fiasco by
the House of Lords, where there were many politicians opposed
to Rook. To escape the humiliation that might follow explanations before this investigating committee, Rook retired to private
life, and soon ended his days on his farm in Kent.

Admiral Hopson, the real hero of Vigo, who drove his ship,
Torbay, to certain destruction, broke the boom and faced the
withering fire of the French broadsides, was knighted by Queen
Anne, and given a pension of five hundred pounds a year.

Admiral Shovel, who came up with his fleet after the battle
had been won, was left behind with a large force to consolidate
the position won, and to try to recover some of the lost treasure.
Divers were sent down at once. But the Spaniards, taking refuge
in the hills overlooking the harbor, took pot shots at the divers
and the surface crews assisting in the salvage work, and the
job had to be abandoned.

◇ ◇

There have been few years, since 1702, when salvage of the treasure on the bottom of Vigo Bay has not been attempted or at least planned.

Salvage by the aid of submarine boats was foreseen by Jules Verne in his "Twenty Thousand Leagues Under the Sea." Captain Nemo, hero of that remarkable piece of fiction, went to Vigo Bay in his submarine boat, *Nautilus*. These two paragraphs from the story, containing, by the way, the persistent error in date, describe the imaginary salvage:

For half a mile around the Nautilus, the waters seemed bathed in electric light. The sandy bottom was clean and bright. Some of the ship's crew in their diving dresses were clearing away half rotten barrels and empty cases from the midst of the blackened wrecks. From these cases and from these barrels escaped ingots of gold and silver, cascades of piastres and jewels. The sand was heaped up with them. Laden with their precious booty the men returned to the Nautilus, disposed of their burden, and went back to this inexhaustible fishery of gold and silver.

I understood now. This was the scene of the battle of the 22d of October, 1702. Here on this very spot the galleons laden for the Spanish Government had sunk. Here Captain Nemo came, according to his wants, to pack up those millions with which he burdened the Nautilus. It was for him and him alone America had given up her precious metals. He was heir direct, without any one to share, in those treasures torn from the Incas and from the other victims of Cortez.

Actual salvage of the sunken galleons has not proved so easy. The work was undertaken by the Spanish government immediately after the departure of the hostile fleet. It was soon turned over to a private company, but the job was thought to be so easy, and the treasure was obviously so great, that the government retained 95 percent of the prospective recovered treasure to itself.

Since that time, the amount demanded by the Spanish government has decreased from year to year, and from century to century. For fifty years divers worked intermittently, but almost no treasure was recovered. A French contractor succeeded in locating a wreck, fastening chains and cables around it, and towing it to very shallow water in 1728. It turned out to be one of the sunken French warships, and the only salvage consisted of guns which were just old enough to be a little out of date, and not nearly old enough to have value as antiques.

The next recoveries consisted of some silver bars and plates, brought up by William Evans, an English salvor, who worked with a diving bell. In 1825, a Scotchman is said to have succeeded in bringing up some of the treasure, the amount of which was never known to the Spanish authorities, because of the cleverness of this salvor in eluding inspectors. I suspect the canny Scot must have scuttled off with his gold while the Spanish inspectors were enjoying their siestas.

An American salvage company was organized in Philadelphia in 1822 to recover the Vigo treasure, and obtained a royal concession. There was some sort of internal strife in this International Submarine Company, and it was succeeded, about fifty years later, by the Vigo Bay Treasure Company, headed by a Doctor Palen, said to have been a brother-in-law of Jay Gould, and Charles F. Pike, both of Philadelphia. This company succeeded in hooking a galleon and bringing her to the surface, under the watchful eyes of a whole warship filled with Spanish supervisors and inspectors. It turned out that this galleon was not one of the treasure-carriers, but was loaded with mahogany. Despite the fact that the mahogany had been under water for a couple of centuries, it was in prime condition, and in the open market brought enough money to defray the expenses of the expedition. But the Spanish government would not renew the Americans' concession.

In 1904 a royal concession for the Vigo Bay treasure salvage was awarded to the Pino Company, Limited, of Genoa, Italy. This concern, which proposed to use some weird and wonderful salvage devices invented by D. Jose Pino, went to work energetically to plow the field. A world-wide campaign of publicity and stock-selling was put on, and some of the rosiest pictures of easy money that have ever been drawn were presented to possible investors of large and small means. Many Americans and Canadians bought stock.

Since 1904, the royal concessions covering the treasure salvage have been renewed from time to time in the names of various successors of the original Pino Company. One of these companies is at work in Vigo Bay at the time of this writing.

The Pino companies have brought up many brass guns, some of which eventually found their way to a New York antique shop, and were sold for good prices. Some ingots have been recovered also. But the entire operation since 1904 could hardly be called a success.

Under date of December 26, 1929, Walter H. McKinney, American Consul at Vigo, writes me:

> The Italian company, "Sociedad Internacional Pino," which at present holds the concession for the recovery of the treasure, has been engaged during the past two years in diving and salvaging operations in the region in which the treasure is supposed to exist, and according to reports reaching me several of the hulks have been definitely located, but nothing has been heard of the recovery of any of the treasure. I regret that I cannot give you any further information in the matter.

Mr. McKinney made a report to the State Department in November, 1927, from which I take the following extracts:

REPUTED EXISTENCE OF SUNKEN TREASURE IN VIGO HARBOR

The action of the Spanish Government in recently awarding to an Italian company a concession for the search and recovery of a number of treasure-laden Spanish Galleons which are supposed to be somewhere at the bottom of Vigo harbor has revived a considerable amount of interest both locally and in other parts of the world in this rather romantic story of the sea.

The belief that these waters cover a fortune of fabulous value has been prevalent for more than two centuries. The recovery of the treasure by the submarine of Captain Nemo is an episode in Jules Verne's romance "Twenty Thousand Leagues under the Sea." Macaulay mentions in his essay of the Wars of the Spanish Succession the naval action in which the fleet was destroyed. . . .

Various attempts have been made during the past hundred years to salvage the treasure. A number of the hulks are said to have been located, and some wood, ancient cannons, and other objects of some interest but little value have been brought to the surface, but as far as the writer has been able to ascertain no gold or silver has been recovered.

From time to time various American salvaging and wrecking concerns have expressed some amount of interest in the possibility of obtaining permission to undertake recovery of the treasure. The awarding of the concession by the Spanish Government would seem to have precluded any such possibility for the time being at least.

It is the writer's opinion, however, and this opinion is based on the idea held locally by the authorities and men who are in a position to know something of the legend, that there is no foundation for the belief in the existence of the treasure. The hulks of the ships are doubtless lying deep in the silt of the upper end of Vigo harbor, and are probably recoverable with adequate equipment, but legend in Vigo states that all of the treasure had been removed from the ships some days before the English succeeded in penetrating the harbor barrier and burning the fleet.

The translated text of the Royal Order granting the concession is as follows:

As result of the request presented by D. Jose Reicevich, a subject of Italy, in the name of the "Society International Pino" soliciting that the said company be authorized to raise the galleons sunk in the Bay of Vigo in the year 1702, and in the same conditions which by the Royal Order of August 24, 1907 was conceded to D. Jose Pino, His Majesty the King (q.D.g.) in accord with the recommendation of this Direction General, Captain General of the Department of Ferrol, and Assessor General of this Ministry has granted the said petition, subject to the condition that the work does not interfere with the normal navigation of the waters of the said bay and that the passage of the Channel of Rande will not be obstructed, duly subject to the conditions imposed by the Royal Order of December 20, 1907 awarded to the said Senor Pino and with the following additions; 1st., and in every case compliance will be made with the regulations already made or which may be made to effect the protection of the national artistic patrimony; and 2nd., the concessionaires will be subject to all the Spanish fiscal legislation, and to the laws relative to industrial accidents and the others regulating the rights of the laborers.

It seems that the American Consul is not a bull on the treasure story. But he speaks officially, with all the restraint considered becoming to the official commercial representative of the United States of America. He cites local tradition as authority for the belief that the treasure was removed before the ships were sunk. Any real treasure-hunter would prefer some more substantial ground upon which to base so conservative an opinion concerning a rather heavily documented treasure. Or, if local tradition is to be accepted, I would be curious to see a detailed report of the tradition, where found, how extensive, and whether persisting among the ignorant or among the well-informed.

Water in the upper Bay is shown on U. S. Hydrographic Office charts to be from 60 to 72 feet deep, with a mud bottom, in the area generally believed to contain the wrecked galleons.

◇ ◇

The British sloop of war *Braak,* under mainsail and reefed topsail, was just about to cast anchor a mile from the lightship in Old Kiln Roads, off Cape Henlopen, Delaware, at four o'clock on the afternoon of Friday, May 25, 1798. A boat was alongside, to take Captain James Drew ashore to Lewes.

A sudden squall caught the sloop in a terrific swirl, and there happened one of those sudden tragedies that darkened so many days in the romantic Age of Sail. The sloop was instantly overset, and she filled and went to the bottom like a hulk of lead.

The unfortunate vessel took with her to the bottom her Captain and thirty-eight officers and men.

At Lewes you may see to-day a modest monument bearing this time-worn inscription:

HERE REST THE REMAINS OF
CAPTAIN JAMES DREW,
WHO COMMANDED HIS BRITANNIC MAJESTY'S SLOOP OF WAR
"DE BRAAK,"
In which he lost his life when she foundered at the Capes
of Delaware, the 10th June, 1798.
He was beloved for his virtues, and admired for his bravery.
His affectionate relict has erected this monument to perpetuate
his
MEMORY.

The date given on the monument is incorrect. It is probable that many months elapsed between the date of the disaster and the carving of the inscription. Newspapers of the period and official records fix the date unmistakably as May 25, 1798.

The *Braak* was built in Holland for the Dutch navy in 1787, and was the *De Braak* while in that navy. She was captured by the French, and later taken by the British. She was built of oak and teakwood. The Dutch, and later the British, built many warships of teakwood because of the lightness and strength of this material, which was imported from the Dutch East Indies.

Captain Drew took command of the *Braak* for Great Britain on June 3, 1797. Although the fatal catastrophe cut short the career of Captain and ship within one year from that day, and ships did not travel as fast in those days as they do to-day, the *Braak* saw plenty of exciting service under Captain Drew's command.

The crew consisted of 86 men, and the armament of sixteen brass carronades. The *Braak* was assigned to duty in Caribbean waters, where Spanish prizes might make pleasant picking.

One day in the spring of 1798 the *Braak*, setting out in chase of a Spanish vessel, outsailed her squadron and found herself in foul weather, all alone. Thenceforward she played a lone hand in her own isolated war against the ships of Spain.

Her first prize was a Spanish ship laden with gold and silver bars. The crew worked long and hard transferring the cargo, and then the galleon was sent on her way. The next notable prize was the Spanish ship *St. Francis Xavier*, captured by the *Braak* off the Delaware capes. Her gold and silver cargo was transferred to the sloop, and a small prize crew took the *St. Francis Xavier* to Halifax for sale.

There were 213 prisoners aboard a small Spanish prize which accompanied the *Braak* to her fatal anchorage off Cape Henlopen. These Spaniards, who had been accumulating since the first capture made by the *Braak* in the Caribbean, testified that the English ship had taken in all five rich galleons, and had transferred all treasure to her own holds.

According to some accounts published about the time of the

wreck, the *Braak* was carrying, besides the gold and silver she had taken, about seventy tons of copper, taken out of her last prize. This copper had been transferred hurriedly, just before making for port, and probably had not been well stowed. Much of it was piled upon the deck, and possibly a list developed from the unequal distribution of this cargo. Thus, when the sudden squall caught her, the *Braak* turned over quickly and sank immediately.

The spot where the ship went down is said to have shown a depth of 84 feet of water.

For some time after she sank, according to some of the old inhabitants of Lewes, the tops of the masts of the *Braak* showed above water. If this is true, the ship must have righted as she went down, and settled on her bottom.

The British government in due time received official reports that the lost sloop of war had carried £80,000 from Jamaica, which was officially entrusted to her Captain for transportation to England, and a cargo of loot estimated to exceed ten million dollars in value. Ships and divers were sent to salvage the treasure. The frigate *Assistance* spent fifty-two days at the site of the wreck, accomplishing practically nothing. The frigate *Resolute*, towing a dismasted hulk, went to the scene the following summer, and tried by very primitive means to raise the *Braak*. Lines around the empty hulk were fastened by divers to the hull of the wrecked sloop. The hulk would be pulled low in the water by these lines at low tide, in the belief that high tide, raising the empty ship on the surface, would raise the treasure ship off the bottom, so that she might be towed into shallow water. Of course, the lines snapped or the fastenings pulled loose when high tide came. The treasure ship was much too heavy to be moved in this manner.

That fall the wreck was definitely abandoned by the British government.

Several expeditions were fitted out to salvage the treasure of the *Braak* during the years immediately following her loss. But an era of feverish activity began in 1880, and lasted for about twelve years. The International Submarine Company of New Haven, Connecticut, entered into a contract with the United States Treasury Department for recovery of the gold and silver. It turned the actual salvage work over to a subsidiary, the Ocean Wrecking Company. A prospectus was issued, as is customary in such cases, and stock was sold.

The Ocean Wrecking Company had difficulty in locating the *Braak*. The trouble was that so many wrecks were found that it was almost impossible to identify the treasure ship. Eight wrecks were located so close together, and so close to the bearings given for the *Braak*, that any one of them might have been the wreck containing the treasure. This is a difficulty experienced in almost any such salvage effort. The ocean floor is so thickly strewn with wrecks, ancient and modern, that all too often valuable time and effort are given to salvaging worthless hulks in search of gold.

Grapnels brought up bits of timber from some of the wrecks, and timbers from one wreck were identified as teakwood. This settled the identification to the satisfaction of the salvors.

Suction dredges were used on the wreck, but it has been demonstrated over and over again that suction dredges cannot bring any large pieces of gold to the surface. The gold is too heavy.

Up to 1893, salvage efforts were carried on off Cape Henlopen fairly continuously. For several seasons Captain Jeff Townsend of Somers Point, N. J., worked over the wreck with his steamer, *Tamasee*. He brought up a large iron chain, identified by old-timers as closely resembling the hand-forged chains used by the first British salvage vessels sent to raise the *Braak*. This probably was one of the chains that broke with the rising tide, proving to the British naval men that the *Braak* was too heavy to lift.

It is safe to say that all of the gold and silver carried by the *Braak* is still down there in the mud, not more than 90 feet deep, and probably somewhat closer than that to the surface. The treasure can be located, with the aid of old records and a little sweeping, diving and testing.

No searcher for submarine treasure should neglect to place a big cross mark on the map off Cape Henlopen.

◇ ◇

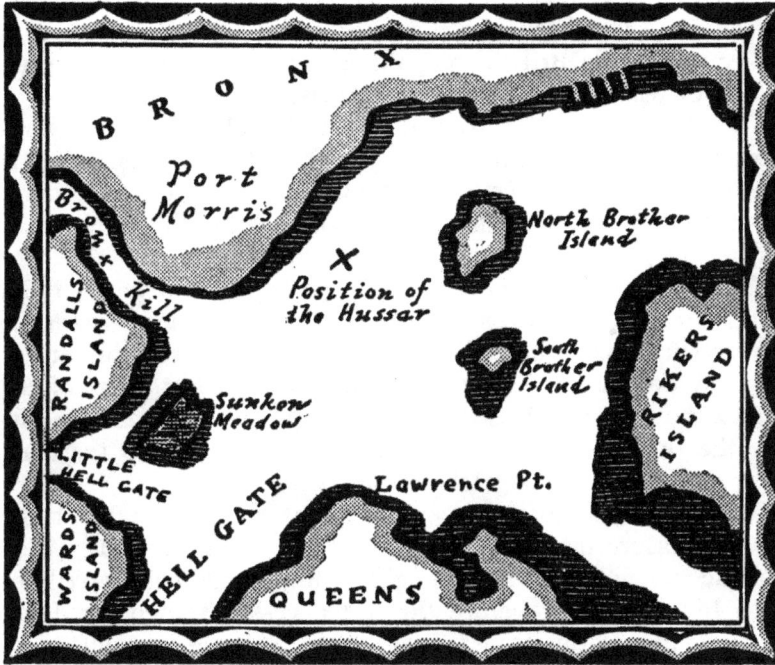

While many treasures take the treasure-fancier on long voyages to remote islands and terrible climates, the *Hussar* is a city-broke treasure-ship, lying more or less quietly in the heart of New York City. She is a domesticated Golconda, upon which the romantic diver may work during union hours and spend his evenings among the white lights of Broadway.

Interest in the *Hussar* was revived in the spring of 1930, when Simon Lake began preparations to clear up the mystery of her treasure for all time. Lake proposed to use a treasure recovery plant similar to the one described in a previous chapter which he built to salvage the treasure of the *Lutine*.

The *Hussar* was a new frigate in the British navy in 1780. She mounted twenty-eight guns, and sailed from England, according to tradition that is fairly well supported by official records, with money to pay the British troops that were just about to give up the job of whipping the American rebels.

The treasure carried by the *Hussar* is believed by treasure-seekers to have been approximately four million dollars. There is a heavy shadow of uncertainty about it, however, due to reports and denials and all the official secrecy that naturally would have guarded such a sum of money at the time of sailing.

The *Hussar* anchored at New York on September 13, 1780. Soon thereafter she cleared for her destination, somewhere on the Connecticut coast, where she was to land her treasure in care of the army paymaster. It is said by some of the historians of the *Hussar* that her destination was Newport, Rhode Island. Whatever the port headed for, the *Hussar* was routed up the East River and out into Long Island Sound.

One of the points of uncertainty that makes search for the *Hussar* treasure interesting is whether the frigate *Mercury*, also carrying money for the British fighting forces, had transferred her cargo to the *Hussar* before the latter vessel headed for Long Island Sound. If this transfer was made, as some chroniclers assert it was, the *Hussar* treasure may be much greater than four million dollars.

The passage between the East River and Long Island Sound includes Hell Gate, noted in song and story as one of the most dangerous traps for shipping that sailors have had to contend with. Millions of dollars have been spent in blasting rocks out of Hell Gate since the days of the *Hussar*, and some work had been done before she attempted the fatal passage.

The passage through the Gate is crooked and fringed by rocks and shoals. Worst of all, there are swirls and eddies caused by conflicting tide movements. These whirlpools and undertows vary from day to day and from year to year, because of the varying volumes of water that meet and mix and retreat near and within the terrible Hell Gate.

All of these dangers were thousands of times greater in 1780 than they are to-day, for the engineering that has been expended upon making the passage safe for American naval vessels has been the best and the most persistent that the United States government could command. A United States Navy Yard on the Brooklyn waterfront renders safe passage into the Sound an essential in war and peace for the navy.

During the American Revolution an official report was issued, showing that out of every twenty-five vessels passing through Hell Gate, one was seriously damaged or altogether lost.

The *Hussar* struck Pot Rock, since blown up, and started to fill rapidly. She struggled on for some distance, and went down at a point opposite Port Morris. The exact spot is indicated in many old records. It is a spot passed daily by millions of people in a city that has changed quite noticeably since the gallant *Hussar* laid her treasure on the muddy bottom of the river.

According to a well authenticated tradition (as authenticity standards go among traditions), the Captain of the *Hussar* headed his vessel for shore and succeeded in getting a rope hawser fastened to a tree that stood some little distance back from the water. But the water was about 75 feet deep, and the *Hussar* was much too heavy to be kept above the surface by this cable. The tree came up by the roots, and the vessel went down with a rush of water and the confusion of many voices.

An account published in papers of the period says there were seventy American prisoners in chains in the *Hussar's* hold when she went to the bottom.

Attempts to salvage the treasure of the *Hussar* were made while her masts still showed above the water. During the War of 1812, the British Admiralty office gave out a statement, purporting to have been made by Fletcher Betts, an officer of the *Hussar*, to the effect that there was no treasure aboard the vessel when she went down. Treasure hunters discount this report as having been made by the British Admiralty in war time to keep Americans from salvaging the cargo of the *Hussar*, with the hope in view that in later years the Admiralty might salvage the treasure for England, especially in case of a crushing defeat of the Americans in the war then in progress.

About fifty years after the sinking of the *Hussar* an English expedition, equipped with a diving bell, did make an effort to recover the treasure. The currents of Hell Gate were much too strong and eccentric for the apparatus, and the attempt failed.

This expedition aroused curiosity in America, and some of the survivors of the *Hussar* wreck were questioned at length by persons who had a taste for treasure hunting. Stories of the treasure at the bottom of the East River began to be discussed seriously, and much data relative to the sunken frigate was collected.

Several attempts to locate the wreck were made in succeeding years by divers, but silt brought down by the Harlem river had covered the hull, and the masts had disappeared altogether.

In 1880 Captain George Thomas of Brick Church, N. J., succeeded in getting a concession from the United States Treasury Department, permitting him to salvage the treasure of the *Hussar,* under scrutiny and inspection by government agents, who were to see that the treasury at Washington got its share of the gold and silver.

This Captain Thomas was a character worthy of a permanent place in some good fiction story of treasure seeking. He had been for many years a familiar figure about the wharves and docks of New York. He wore a long whisker, prayed aloud upon the slightest provocation, and peddled contraband snuff among the sailors and longshoremen. He represented himself always as the personal agent of Jehovah, and, when taken to task for crooked conduct, always resorted to loud invocations, addressed directly to Jehovah.

An official report now reposing in the archives of the Treasury Department describes Captain Thomas as a notorious hypocrite and goes into his personal history with official ruthlessness.

Thomas sold stock in a company called Treasure Trove, Inc. He obtained a steamship called the *Chester,* and equipped her with suction dredges. The pumps worked long and loudly, pumping silt from the bottom of the river in an effort to uncover the *Hussar.* Every morning before the pumps were started, the white-whiskered snuff-peddler called the crew and divers on deck and read to them a Scripture lesson, and then launched into a noble prayer for success of the venture.

While the engines were throbbing away in the river, Captain Thomas went out among the country folk of New Jersey and sold them stock on the ground that this treasure-hunt was the Lord's work and that whatever gold and silver were recovered would be devoted to the conversion of the heathen.

Judge Nelson Cross was appointed receiver of the treasure for the United States government. Cross soon was at cross-purposes with the sanctimonious Captain Thomas, and the record of the salvage business is one long story of quarrels, dissensions and recriminations. Cross complained to the Treasury Department frequently of the unreliability and unbusinesslike methods of Thomas.

There is more than a faint suspicion that Judge Cross double-crossed the saintly Thomas, for when he had succeeded in getting Thomas's contract cancelled, Cross appeared as one of the proprietors of a new treasure company, displacing the old. But Cross suffered the fate he had forced upon Thomas, and enemies of his in the Treasury Department had him ousted in favor of one Francis M. Eppley, formerly associated with Thomas in the treasure venture. Meantime, a concession had been awarded to the firm of Bean & Hartwell in 1892, and soon afterward it was cancelled. Politics of a virulent nature had grown up around the *Hussar's* hidden hulk.

When Thomas lost his government concession he went to work on the wrecking job much more vigorously than ever, operating from the deck of an old scow, on which he posted a big sign: "Keep Away—Government Work." The Treasury Department ordered him to desist.

Ever since those days of hectic *Hussar* politics, the Treasury Department has attached one iron-bound condition to its concessions to salvage contractors seeking the treasure of the *Hussar*. The concession must not be used in publicity or in selling stock, and the concessionaire must not go about bragging that he has "a contract from the Government" for the recovery of the treasure. At this writing a concession has been granted for the raising of the treasure, but it is inadvisable to make public the name of the concessionaire in this connection.

It is extremely doubtful whether any concession or contract with the Government is required to authorize one to hunt for such an abandoned treasure as that of the *Hussar*. But a treasure-seeker feels safer when armed with a contract specifying that ten percent of the treasure will be paid to the federal treasury, because he then looks for government protection against other persons who might flock to the wreck and start removing treasure after the wreck had been located and partly raised.

Fred Knowles, who lives at the National Arts Club, New York, has a fine black cane that was made from one of the planks from the hull of the *Hussar*. His father-in-law, H. K. McMurray, marine engineer, acted as technical consultant to one of the salvaging companies of the 90's. When the only salvage that was recovered before the money ran out proved to be a plank of black oak, the thoughtful directors had a cane carved from the relic and presented it to McMurray, who passed it on to his son-in-law.

About 1900 a yacht on the way to a race in Long Island Sound struck a rock and sank off Port Morris. Divers sent down to salvage the yacht brought up an old iron anchor. On it was found this inscription, cast into the metal: "H.M.S. Hussar."

The stern of the old frigate was lifted above water in 1823 by a salvor named Samuel Davis. He had a lifting device that worked on the principle of ice tongs. But when the ancient stern had cleared the water, the cables broke, and the *Hussar* settled back to the bottom of the river.

None of the treasure of the *Hussar* has been recovered by any of the salvage enterprises thus far. Nor has the skeleton of any American patriot in chains been recovered.

There's good romance to be had out of that old hulk at Hell Gate, and there will be a goodly audience looking on and cheering when the *Hussar* or her timbers again see the light of day.

◇ ◇

It should be easy to put the cross mark on the wreck of the steamship *Merida*, of the Ward Line, for no dark mists of history and legend obscure her story. She collided with the *Admiral Far-*

ragut of the United Fruit Line shortly after midnght on May 12, 1911. The position was fifty-five miles east of Cape Charles, Virginia.

There was a heavy fog, and the collision was said to have been unavoidable. The hole in the *Merida's* side was enormous. The water rushed in so that the efforts of the crew to stop the leak with mattresses and cargo were hopeless.

The wireless operator sent out this message: "S. O. S. Need immediate assistance. Floating on forward bulkhead. Send help quick." Scarcely was the message on the air when the steamship, the pride of the Ward Line fleet, turned over on her side and went down quickly.

There were two hundred passengers on the *Merida*. The *Admiral Farragut* lowered boats to take them aboard, and the officers of the stricken ship held pistols on their crew to guarantee the passengers first chance at the boats. Not a life was lost, despite the sudden plunge of the vessel and the thickness of the fog.

The *Merida* was a steamer of six thousand tons. She carried a cargo of Jamaica rum and other merchandise in her holds. In the purser's safes she carried bullion, specie and jewels said to be worth more than four million dollars. Agents of Porfirio Diaz had boarded the ship at Vera Cruz with most of this hoard. They were fleeing from revolutionaries under Francesco Madero. A part of the Mexican state treasure at that time consisted of a collection of rubies of enormous size which once adorned the crown of Maximilian, the unfortunate Emperor of Mexico. The Diaz agents were taking no chances. They loaded the state treasure into bags, carted it to Vera Cruz, and put it on board the first steamer bound for New York. The rubies were part of the loot. So were many bags of gold coins.

The wreck of the *Merida* was lost. Despite latitude and longitude data supplied by the *Farragut* at the time of the disaster, the first salvage operation failed because the wreck could not be located. Captain Charles Williamson had built a steel caisson which was to be sunk beside the wreck. Large steel hooks were to reach out from this caisson and get the money and the rubies. The devices resembled somewhat the ones used with indifferent success in Vigo Bay by the Pinto people.

In 1916 a salvage company was formed in Wall Street to get the treasure of the *Merida*. Percy Rockefeller, Grayson M. P. Murphy, Charles Sabin and Albert H. Wiggin were among the financiers who organized to get the rubies and the state funds of the defunct Mexican government.

George D. Stillson, a former navy man, was the chief promoter of this enterprise, and Admiral Colby M. Chester was quoted as having approved the technical plans. The yacht *J. H. Beckwith* served as a diving base. Two square miles of ocean floor were searched in vain. Twelve divers wandered around on the bottom, finding plenty of wrecks, but not the *Merida*. After a month the search was abandoned.

American millionaires again became interested in this elusive treasure in 1924. Anthony J. Drexel-Biddle, Jr., Roswell C. Tripp, J. Harvey Alexander, Worthington Davis, Franklin Mallory, and W. Howard Drayton 3d formed an expedition, hired two trawlers, and went out to the cold water off Cape Charles. They had Fred Nielsen, a Danish diver who had done sensational work in salvaging the sunken submarine *F-4* in Pearl Harbor, Honolulu.

The summer and fall were spent trawling for the wreck. A wreck was found late in October, but the winter storms were coming on, so it was marked with a buoy, and the expedition went home for the winter. Next summer the buoy was missing, and the work of trawling was resumed. The wreck was found again, two hundred feet below the surface. Nielsen went down, walked around the steamer, which was lying on her side, and made the identification positive. When he came up, a storm was brewing. That storm was a terror, and it was succeeded by many others. The wreck was again lost, and the expedition was abandoned.

Nielsen is the only person who has seen the treasure ship *Merida* since she hit bottom. She has not been located again.

◇ ◇

The *Lusitania* lies in 240 feet of water off Old Head of Kinsale, Ireland. When the salvors are ready for her, she will not be hard to locate. But hundreds of rich cargoes in more shallow and more quiet locations will be salvaged before the *Lusitania* is seriously or successfully tackled.

Nevertheless, the problem of the salvaging of the *Lusitania* has been worked out, so far as it may be worked out with the data at hand, by several competent submarine engineers. The prize may range in value from three or four million dollars to ten or twelve millions, depending upon how much of the ship and cargo can be saved intact. It is possible that the historic liner may be refloated and repaired so as to be made seaworthy after she is raised, and if this can be done, the reward will be much greater than the higher estimate named.

Submarine engineering is advancing so rapidly that there can scarcely be a doubt that the *Lusitania* will be raised or her cargo salvaged eventually. Already a steel ball containing observers and equipped with glass ports for observation and motion picture taking has been built and lowered to depths far greater than that at which the *Lusitania* lies. We may expect late pictures of the famous wreck, taken with the aid of such a device, in the very near future. When the position of the wreck has been studied from pictures, the salvaging of the cargo will not be far in the future.

The *Lusitania* lies in water that is often swept by storms, and the job of the salvage ships would be difficult on account of high waves. Much more valuable cargoes are to be had in less exposed situations, but the historic and sentimental value of the *Lusitania* wreck is such that its salvage will be attempted before its turn comes in the list of wrecks. The war-time controversy as to whether the liner carried contraband, guns, and explosives would be settled definitely and forever. A large consignment of gold and silver would be recovered from her vaults. And if the great ship herself could be made seaworthy, the world would be thrilled and history would be served.

◇ ◇

Of the thousands of vessels sunk by submarines and mines during the World War, the most notable in point of treasure was the British liner *Laurentic*. She was torpedoed off Donegal, Ireland, going to the bottom with thirty million dollars in gold and silver bullion and coins. She lay in 120 feet of water. The Admiralty undertook the salvage operation, as soon as the war was over. The naval salvors finished the job in about eight years. More than sixty lives were lost in the enterprise.

The entire German fighting fleet was sunk in Scapa Flow by simultaneous scuttling of the ships, in accordance with a secret plan among the German officers, at the close of the war. Work on the salvaging of the fleet went on steadily for eleven years, and was altogether successful. This fleet was sunk in water that did not quite cover the mastheads of the larger vessels, but the salvage operation was laborious and expensive. The junk value of the steel ships was enough to show a profit on the enterprise.

Around the British Isles the ships sunk during the World War lie so thickly strewn on the ocean floor that cross marks indicating their positions upon a large wall chart form a closely woven pattern. Comparatively few of these wrecks lie deeper than the *Lusitania*.

The *Elizabethville*, a British vessel sunk off the coast of Africa during the war, carried a cargo of diamonds. Work on the salvage of this cargo has been in progress intermittently for several years. The value of the diamonds is one of the secrets of the war, and will not be disclosed until the cargo has been recovered.

One of the submarine salvage jobs in American waters that deserves a good cross on any treasure map is the wreck of the steamer *Islander*, which lies in 310 feet of water off Taku Inlet, near Douglas Island, Alaska. The *Islander*, carrying five million dollars in gold from the Klondike, struck a rock or an iceberg on the night of August 9, 1901, and went down with her treasure and sixty-five persons, mostly Klondike prospectors who were on their way back to the United States with their winnings.

Lloyd's of London paid two million dollars on the portion of the cargo insured. But the wreck has been abandoned, and now belongs to the salvors.

Besides the gold and silver, there are many barrels and cases of Scotch whiskey that may not have been damaged much by the passing years. Some cases of Scotch and a few packages of miners' personal effects were removed from the wreck during salvage operations in 1928.

The draining of Lake Nemi, in Italy, under orders of Mussolini, was one of the most spectacular treasure-hunting enterprises of the post-war decades. It disclosed relics of the Roman Empire and other relics going far back beyond the first of the Cæsars. It was an expensive undertaking, since the water was pumped out of the lake mechanically.

The greatest operation in lake-draining for finding treasure probably will be the draining of Lake Guatavita, on the top of a volcanic mountain in Colombia. This lake was for hundreds of years the center of religious activities of a pre-Inca cult. A part of the annual ceremonies consisted of throwing gold and other precious objects into the lake, as a sacrifice.

A British syndicate bored a tunnel to drain this lake, under authority of the Colombian government, in 1903. The operation was never completed, because the mud in the lake hardened under the sun's rays into a kind of semi-solid concrete. This unexpected phenomenon so discouraged the treasure-seekers that the job was given over. The lake filled up again, and the recovery of the treasure awaits the enterprise of engineers who are ingenious enough to overcome the difficulty that defeated the Englishmen in 1903.

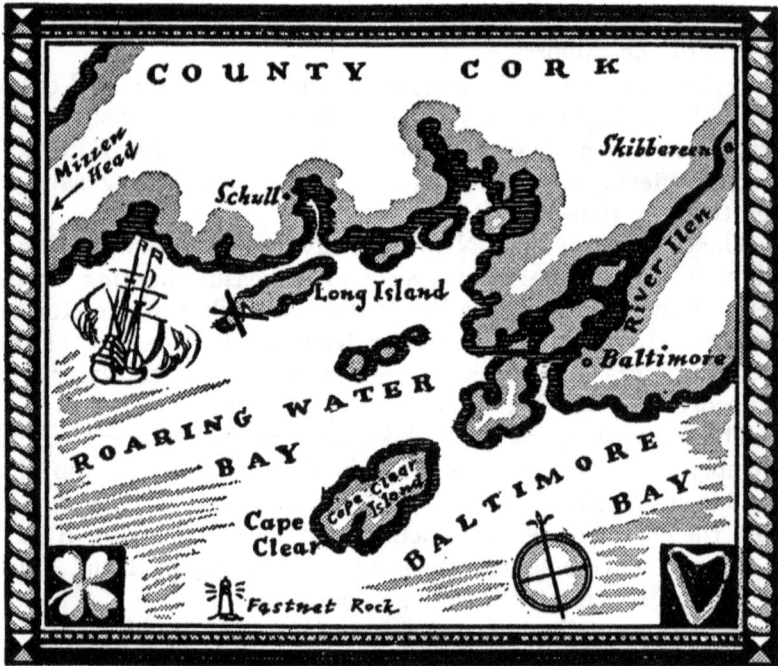

X. *In the Bay of Roaring Water*

R OARING WATER BAY is a beautiful inlet in the extreme
southern point of Ireland. On either side of its broad entrance rise Mizen Head and Cape Clear, southern outposts
of the Emerald Isle. Many of the great ocean liners that make
port in New York and Boston pass within hailing distance of
these two headlands, on their way to and from the harbor of
Cobh, which once was Queenstown.

It is thirteen miles, in a straight line, from Cape Clear to

Mizen Head. Inside the Bay, about twelve miles from the point of Mizen and nine miles from Cape Clear, lying just off the town of Schull, or Skull, is Long Island. From this island Roaring Water Bay takes the name of Long Island Bay in many modern maps.

It is on Long Island that the treasure is buried.

So we come to the family skeleton of the Driscolls and the O'Driscolls. I used to hear it spoken of in whispers by the elders when I was a very small boy, but when I sought details, I was told to go on out and play. To this day I have not found much willingness on the part of the elders to talk about the O'Driscoll hoard on Long Island in Roaring Water Bay, although I have gone to the O'Driscoll country and interviewed many of the aged men and women of the tribe in the hope of getting the truth about this treasure that nobody seems to want.

My father, Florence Driscoll, was born on Long Island. Florence (which is Fineen in the ancestral Gaelic) is a traditional Christian name for the males of the O'Driscoll clan. In the days of its glory, the surname was spelled with the O. It is still so spelled by many branches of the family. But when the castles of the clan were destroyed and the lands about them were apportioned among foreigners, the O'Driscolls who settled on Long Island as fishermen and sailors dropped the O. They felt it was an aristocratic prefix to which they were no longer entitled.

These sailors and fishermen were a long-lived lot. Not many generations intervened between Sir Fineen O'Driscoll, who buried the treasure in 1606, and my father, who died at the early age of eighty-three during the present century. My father's father, who lived all his life on Long Island, in Roaring Water Bay, lived one hundred and four years, and his father lived nearly a century. The story of the treasure has never before been written, but it was handed down by word of mouth, and you can readily see that if my father had it from his grandfather the tale was almost first-hand to him. I know that it was a very personal matter with my father, who never discussed the affair of the treasure with any of his children. But we heard the story just the same.

My father emigrated to America about 1860. He gave up the

sea and went to Kansas where he became a farmer, about as far from the roar of the salt surf as anybody ever got. To the Kansas farm where I was born there came occasionally an Irishman from the "Ould Sod," and then we children would sit about the fire at night and hear tall tales of storms at sea, of shipwreck off Fastnet Rock, and sometimes the talk would drift to the O'Driscoll treasure of Long Island. Then, if the stranger could speak Gaelic, the conversation would be unintelligible to us. But some of the old cronies could neither speak nor understand the Irish language, and it was not always practicable to send us children to bed, so we picked up some tag-ends of the story which later in life interested me so much that I made extensive personal investigations and researches into such angles of the tale as I have been able to obtain any light upon.

Three points about the treasure seemed clear from the first.

It was buried by a son of Fineen O'Driscoll the Rover. This rover, or pirate if you will, was a hero in his own day, but not at all the kind of ancestor one could boast about in Wichita society.

There was blood on the treasure, and it would never be touched by any Driscoll or O'Driscoll, so long as Christian blood should run in our veins.

It was buried under the house in which my father was born.

With so little light, I began to make research into the history of the region known as the O'Driscoll Country, which includes Roaring Water Bay and the adjacent Baltimore Bay, together with the lands washed by those waters.

It is easy to verify the fact that the O'Driscolls were well settled in this territory before the dawn of written history in the West. One of the widely venerated monuments of Ireland is a stone cross on Cape Clear, said to have been carved out of the native rock by Saint Ciaran (or Kieran), a member of the O'Driscoll clan, thirty years before St. Patrick first set foot on Irish soil. The feast day of St. Kieran, March 5, was the great day of the year in the O'Driscoll clan.

The Carew Manuscripts, which are early Irish history sources, contain interesting items indicating that in the year 1413, some years before the birth of Christopher Columbus, the O'Driscolls of Baltimore were already ancient proprietors of a great castle, and were known as fighters, with especial grudges against the merchants of Waterford.

The clan had been going to sea in galleys and carrying on wars of its own for many generations prior to the chieftainship of Fineen, whose son buried the treasure, but it was, I think, this Fineen who put the brand of piracy upon the clan. From his day forward the O'Driscoll arms were surmounted by a cormorant, a bird of prey.

◇ ◇

So I went to the O'Driscoll Country, to Baltimore Bay, to Skibbereen, to Schull, and finally to Long Island.

On Long Island I found the poorest and the hardest-working members of our tribe; sailors and fishermen all, hard-bitten by cruel winds and bowed down by back-breaking labor. On Long Island, inhabited by 145 people, there is a stoop to the shoulders and a look of resigned wistfulness in the tired eyes.

Yes, they knew about Fineen O'Driscoll the Rover. Sure, Florence, the twelve-years-old-boy, could recite his history for me. They had poems about the great Fineen in the school-books. The boy recited:

FINEEN O'DRISCOLL THE ROVER.

An old castle towers o'er the billows
   That thunder by Cleena's green land,
And there dwelt as gallant a rover
   As ever grasped hilt in the hand;
Eight stately towers of the waters
   Lie anchored in Baltimore Bay;
And over their twenty score sailors
   Bold Fineen the Rover holds sway.

     Then O, for Fineen the Rover,
      Fineen O'Driscoll the free,
    As straight as the mast of his galley,
     And strong as a wave of the sea!

The Saxons of Cork and Moyallo,
  They harried his coasts with their bands;
He gave them a taste of his cannon
  And drove them like wolves from his lands;
The men of Clan London brought over
  Their strong fleet to make him a slave;
He met them on Mizen's rough breakers,
  And the sharks crunched their bones 'neath the wave!

      Then O, for Fineen the Rover,
        Fineen O'Driscoll the free,
      With step like the red stag of Beara,
        And voice like the bold sounding sea!

Long time in that strong island castle,
  Or out on the waves with his clan,
He feasted and ventured and conquered,
  But ne'er struck his colours to man.
In a fight 'gainst the foes of his country
  He died as a brave man should die;
And he sleeps 'neath the waters of Cleena,
  Where the waves sing his keen to the sky.

      Then O, for Fineen the Rover,
        Fineen O'Driscoll the free,
      With eye like the osprey's at morning,
        And smile like the sun on the sea!

The Treasure? Fineen O'Driscoll's gold? Arrah now, they couldn't tell me anything about that.

The weather-beaten fishermen smoked their pipes and gazed off to sea. There was something in the depths of their blue eyes, but, like the gold of our pirate ancestor, it was buried, far beyond the reach of strangers from America.

"In our family," I explained, "there is a tradition that the gold was buried where afterward was built the house in which my father was born. Can you show me that house?"

"It was pulled down," answered one.

"When?"

"Oh, a long time ago!"

"How long ago? Ten, thirty, fifty years ago?"

"Faith, it was long ago it was pulled down."

"Can you show me the place where it was?"

"The place where that house was? Indeed, nobody goes there. 'Twould be hard to find, I'm thinking."

I never found the place. I was fully convinced that every man, woman, and child on the Island knows exactly where the spot is, but none would guide me to it.

"There's blood on that gold," a devout old lady of the Island told me. "No good ever came of money with blood on it. What happened to Sir Fineen O'Driscoll, the son of the Rover? What happened to Mary, his daughter? Look at Baltimore Castle, and at the other castles of the O'Driscolls! No, we want none of that gold! It has been buried long, and there leave it, says I. We are poor here, and when the fish are scarce we are sometimes none too well fed, but we'll never need Fineen the Rover's gold, please God!"

This coincided so perfectly with the attitude I had heard my father express toward the treasure of Long Island that I was not especially surprised to hear it. But it was decidedly dampening to my ardor as an investigator to hear this same sentiment expressed over and over again, with no material variation. It was quite evident that the treasure will never be disturbed by these people, no matter how bad the season may be for fishing.

It puzzled me, too, to find old Fineen the Rover so highly honored among the families of the clan, while the treasure that he captured was considered accursed. It is all right to sing the praises of the pirate ancestor, it seems, but all wrong to use any of the gold he got. I asked questions of some of the scholars in the vicinity.

Their testimony was somewhat thus:

"Fineen was a rover, but whether he was a pirate or wasn't a pirate is a matter of opinion. If he confined his depredations to attacks upon the ships of the Algerines and the English, then he was no pirate at all in the eyes of the Irish, just as John Paul Jones is no pirate in the eyes of Americans, although he is always included in any list of famous pirates published in England.

"Now as to this treasure that is said to be buried on Long Island, there is a fine point of honor involved in the decision of the descendants of Fineen to let it lie untouched. Some say the gold was got in fair fight with the Algerines, and others say that, while the fight with the Barbary pirates was fair enough in itself, there is a taint upon the gold nevertheless, and all seem to agree that one of the greatest disasters that ever fell upon the house of O'Driscoll was in some way connected with the curse of Spanish blood upon that gold. This being the case, nobody seems to have any desire to remove the treasure, and the Driscolls of Long Island are not at all thankful to anyone for reminding them of the existence of the accursed hoard."

The story they told me practically begins on the night of the fifth of March, St. Kieran's Day, 1600. A great celebration was held that night at Baltimore Castle, the stronghold of the clan, and Fineen's "head house." Young Fineen, the apple of the old chief's eye, was fifteen years old that day, and on the morrow he was going out with his father on a cruise for the first time. The "eight stately towers of the waters," the O'Driscoll galleys of war, were anchored directly in front of the high walls of Baltimore.

It was on that night that young Fineen met Margaret O'Sullivan, daughter of Daniel O'Sullivan of Skibbereen, an ancient town not far from Schull. There had been much fighting between the O'Sullivans and the O'Driscolls in times past. In fact, there were whole centuries when it took an expert to predict which, if either, of the two clans would survive the fighting. But a peace had been patched up, for both families realized by now that they had some fighting against foreign enemies on their hands that might require a good deal of blood and brawn to carry through. Ever since the meeting of young Fineen and young Margaret there have been many romantic meetings between O'Sullivans and O'Driscolls, and the two clans are now strongly knit together by ties of blood.

Young Fineen and Margaret, the lass from Skibbereen, danced that night to the music of Irish bagpipes, and they fell in love.

Next morning, when the O'Driscoll fleet moved out to sea to

find the Algerines who had been reported cruising off the coast, Fineen the Younger stood upon the deck of his father's flagship and waved madly to a slip of a girl in white who stood in the great doorway of the Castle.

It was two days later that the O'Driscoll chieftain sighted the Algerines. How many corsair vessels were in the fleet we do not know. But they were engaged in a hand-to-hand battle with two large Spanish galleons, off Old Head of Kinsale, almost on the spot where the *Lusitania* afterward sank to rest.

These were two treasure ships that had been cut out of a Spanish plate fleet that had been buffeted by storms and driven somewhat out of its course while carrying gold from the Americas to Spain. The Spaniards were at a terrible disadvantage, and were unable to hold out long against the savage corsairs from Northern Africa.

The corsairs captured the Spaniards by boarding, transferred the gold from the half-sinking galleons to their own vessels, and turned to confront the invincible O'Driscolls, fresh for the fight.

Now, here we come to the question of Fineen's guilt or glory.

Fineen did not reach the scene of the battle until the Spaniards had been disposed of, and the Algerines were in possession of the treasure. According to his friends and supporters, this was due to an unfavorable wind during part of the day and a dead calm during two or three hours. These supporters of Fineen say that he certainly would not have chosen to fight the pirates without help if he could have reached them when they were suffering from the resistance of the Spaniards.

The enemies of O'Driscoll (and some of them were in his service) spread the story that the Irish fleet stood off and on throughout the day, refusing to take part in the combat in time to help the Spaniards. The implication of this story was that Fineen foresaw exactly how the battle, and the one to follow, were to turn out.

Some of Fineen's countrymen took the middle ground, saying that the Lord of Baltimore saw that the Algerines were engaged in a desperate battle, but thought the ships they were attacking were English, and therefore could not take any part in the fight, lest he aid one of his two enemies or encourage them to join forces against him.

Whatever the reason, the Baltimore fleet did not engage the Algerines until the Spanish treasure was aboard the Algerine vessels. Then Fineen attacked the enemy, and the Algerines were shown a kind of fighting they had not yet tasted.

Fineen himself closed with Nudda, chief of the Algerine pirate squadron, on the deck of the latter's flagship, and that fight was never forgotten by any of those who witnessed it and lived to tell the story. It ended when the gigantic Irishman, having knocked the black man's sword out of his hand when parrying a thrust, dropped his own weapon to the deck, rushed upon his enemy, flung his arms about him, pinning the Algerine's arms to his sides, and flung him backward over his shoulder into the sea.

Young Fineen saw plenty of action that day. He had his own share in it, and acquitted himself manfully.

The blacks are said to have outnumbered the Irishmen three to one. But after hours of fighting the O'Driscoll fleet turned homeward with five of the pirate galleys in tow, and sixty Algerine prisoners—the only black pirates left alive—in irons. The treasure was brought to Baltimore.

Among the prisoners taken, there was one small boy about seven years old, a nephew of Nudda. He was known to his own people as Ali Krussa, but he had not been long at Baltimore before he was baptized with the name of Michael.

Most of the prisoners were exchanged during the next two years, for Christian prisoners who were then pulling oars for the heathen. There was a well-organized system of prisoner exchange in operation between the Europeans and the Barbary corsairs, even though the Europeans did consider the pirate states outlaws and enemies of all mankind.

Michael was not exchanged, but was brought up by the O'Driscolls as a Christian, and received the same schooling and much the same treatment as though he were a member of the family.

After the battle off Old Head, the treasure was taken up the

River Ilen to the newly finished O'Driscoll stronghold known as Old Court. I do not know whether the place went by that name when it was new, although that is quite possible, for it may have been constructed upon the site of an older building. Much of the castle still stands. It is a ruin, of course. I have spent pleasant Irish days clambering over its walls, climbing up to its parapets, and searching for Spanish gold at the bottom of the dark donjon keep. Old Court is owned by Sir Eustace Beecher, an English landlord, whose family acquired most of the O'Driscoll ruins in the vicinity of Baltimore and Roaring Water bays from the descendants of Lord Bandon. This English nobleman, I believe, got the properties by some sort of royal grant when the O'Driscolls became too obstreperous in their opposition to English rule in Ireland.

Old Court was built by Fineen the Elder as a home for Fineen the Younger when the latter should marry. The castle had a frontage of 225 feet on the Ilen at tidewater, and was defended by nearly two hundred brass cannon, some of which you may still find imbedded in the mud at the edge of the river. The donjon keep, under a tower that stood back from the water, was twelve by eighteen feet interior dimensions, with walls ten to twelve feet thick, and well below the surface of the ground.

"Here," said Fineen the Rover, "the Spanish treasure will be safe. We do not need it now. There let it lie until it can do us good."

Old Fineen was not one to discuss such matters at length. And he paid no attention whatever to the controversy over the propriety of his tactics off Old Head of Kinsale.

Fineen used some of the Spanish gold to fit out a newer and stronger battle fleet for himself, and two years after the battle off Kinsale he met an English man-of-war, engaged her, and died on the enemy's deck, shouting defiance and wielding his broadsword.

Fineen's followers fought even harder after the death of their chief, for they would not leave his body in the hands of the enemy. They returned to Baltimore with their green flag at half mast, and the body of their honored chieftain lying in state upon the deck where he had fallen.

There was a wake at Baltimore Castle, with keening and candles and tolling of bells.

Fineen the Younger became "The O'Driscoll," head of the clan. He was not the fighter his father had been. He had no ambition to make a name for himself as a sea rover or a thorn in the side of the English monarchy. He wished to live in peace among his people, and to give some time to study. He was a bookish young man, and he hoped to compile a creditable history of the O'Driscoll Country.

He applied himself assiduously to courtship of the black-haired, blue-eyed beauty, Margaret O'Sullivan of Skibbereen.

Margaret was not unmindful of the very obvious attractions possessed by the head.of the O'Driscoll clan. But she stood pat on this ultimatum:

"Fineen, boy, we'll never be married so long as there's an ounce of that Spanish loot in Old Court. There's blood on that gold, and it's only throuble and a curse it'll be after bringing upon us if we make use of it."

"But, Margaret asthore, I'm building a great abbey on Sherkin Island, and I expect to pay for it with that same gold, and turn it over to the Franciscan monks. I can't give the money back to the people it was taken from, for they're all dead and I know nothing of their heirs, and I don't even know who owned the treasure."

"Ah, my poor Fineen, it's fooling yourself you are! I don't know whose gold it is either, but I know it's none of ours. Come, now, my fine lad, we'll bury the cursed gold together, and that same day we'll be wedded. What do you say, Fineen?"

"Aye," said Fineen. For he, like his father, knew when to stop talking.

And so it chanced that on a bright June morning, when Fineen, chief of the Clan O'Driscoll, was in his twenty-first year, and Margaret, the blue-eyed belle of Skibbereen, was just turned eighteen, the two of them dropped down the River Ilen from Old Court in a sloop manned by five trustworthy sailors.

Long Island was chosen as the final resting place of the treasure, because it was owned by the O'Driscolls, and was a lonely place, close enough to the church where it had been arranged to have the marriage. Margaret had at first insisted that the gold be thrown into the sea, but Fineen had talked her out of this notion by representing that some day the rightful heirs might come asking for their gold, and no one could produce it out of the bed of the sea.

So they buried it there near the seaward end of Long Island, facing Roaring Water Bay, the five sailors doing the digging and lowering the heavy freight into the deep hole. Rocks were plentiful thereabout, and a pile of them was made, pyramid-shaped, just over the place where the gold lay.

The marriage of Fineen and Margaret took place in the church at Schull. The couple set up housekeeping in the great head house of the clan, at Baltimore, and there they flourished, reared a family, and faced the world as they found it in that troubled time.

◇ ◇

One of the disturbing factors in the life of Baltimore was Krussa, the black boy.

Krussa was a silent youth, and he grew into a silent man. Although he spoke with the musical brogue of the people among whom he lived, his heart was elsewhere.

The Algerine boy was never fully civilized by the gentle people of Baltimore. He was quarrelsome and moody. He was cruel to dumb animals. He was a servant, but a privileged one. He worked when he wanted to work, and he was taught out of the same books that the O'Driscoll children studied.

Now Krussa was something forward in his attitude toward Mary, the little daughter of Fineen the Younger. When, at the age of twenty-six, the black fellow was rebuked somewhat roughly by Fineen O'Driscoll for a bit of familiarity toward the daughter of the house, who was then but twelve, the Algerine spoke up and asked whether he were not, after all, a Christian, and entitled to marry Mary if he should make up his mind to do so.

At this, Fineen O'Driscoll, a great, long-armed, loosejointed man, closely resembling his noted father, let out a roar that could be heard across the water on Sherkin Island, and gave the impudent servant a cuff on each side of his head that sent him rolling down the stone stairs at the rear of Castle Baltimore.

Ali Krussa, who was called Michael, did not forget. Two years later he disappeared, and with him went a large rowboat with a jury mast and sail.

◇ ◇

So we come to June, 1631, a time of dark days, troubled winds, and, the old folk said, much mysterious wailing, as of lost souls in the night.

Fineen has become Sir Fineen O'Driscoll, lord of many lordships, but a sad man withal. The O'Driscoll fortunes are in shadow. There have been bad crops throughout the region of Carberry, and the French have been getting all the fish by working outside the harbor. Extensive repairs to some of the castles have cost great sums. The coffers of Baltimore are depleted.

Throughout the day on the nineteenth of June, Sir Fineen O'Driscoll had been pacing the halls of his great castle, staring moodily out to sea, and irritably rejecting advances made by members of his household.

Money must be had for Mary's wedding festivities. The wedding was set for the following Saturday, and the prospective bridegroom was young Jerry O'Donovan, from Ballydehob. The head of the O'Driscoll thought well of Jerry. Mary thought—well, what Mary thought was eloquently expressed by her deep, dark eyes.

Sir Fineen O'Driscoll had talked long and earnestly with his wife about the situation. He had suggested and strongly urged the obvious remedy: resurrection of the old O'Driscoll treasure from its berth on Long Island, where it had been buried on that other wedding day.

Margaret O'Driscoll, wife of Sir Fineen, was not open to conviction on this matter.

"Fineen, my boy," she said, "there's blood on that gold. We buried it once, and buried it must remain. We couldn't start our child out in the world with the gold that has the curse of Spanish blood on it."

" 'Tis old woman's talk, Margaret," said Sir Fineen, a heavy frown upon his brow, and a dogged look in his blue eyes that are overshadowed by bushy, graying eyebrows, "Why should we be in need of money, and a shipload of gold lying under that pile of rocks over there, wasting away?"

"Don't talk to me, Fineen," says she, "That gold will be there on Judgment Day, when the Old Nick comes to claim his share of the earth, and 'tis misfortune you'll bring upon this house if ever you touch an ounce of it."

So night came on, and the great, stooped form of Fineen, his troubles full upon him, stood large against the rising moon, down by the waterside. The Lord of Baltimore, all alone shoved off a rowboat, and alone he rowed and sailed around the point of Long Island. Alone he landed, and at midnight struck his spade into the soil.

At dawn the new hole beneath the deserted stone mound was closed, and the tired, worn form of the chief of the O'Driscoll once more bent to the oars before raising the little sail to catch the morning breeze. There was a cowhide bag in the bottom of the boat, and the bag was heavy.

The sun was shedding his golden glory over the green hills of Ireland when Sir Fineen O'Driscoll put into the cove at the head of which stood Baltimore Castle. But castle it was no longer. A long black wall loomed at the waterside and smoke still poured from the interior that had been so quietly homelike a few hours before. One tower yet stood, crazily jagged against the blue sky. This was ruin.

The Algerines had come to Baltimore. While the master of the castle had delved for just a shovelful of the treasure that had been taken from Nudda by his fighting father, the black men had surprised the castle of the O'Driscoll. A Dungarven fisherman named Hackett had been bribed to pilot the galleys of the heathen up the dangerous bay, and Ali Krussa, no longer Michael of Baltimore, had come back to claim his revenge.

Surprise had been complete. The castle was sacked and the homes of the townsfolk in the shadow of the castle had been overrun and looted. Retainers and warders had arisen with sleep in their eyes, to meet the invader's scimitar and death. And the Lord of the Castle was nowhere to be found!

Margaret O'Driscoll had been allowed to live, probably because she wanted to die. She was there on the pier when the sun came up, wringing her hands, praying, and waiting for the return of her husband.

But Mary, the colleen of Baltimore, she of the black hair and the mysterious blue eyes, that was to be the bride of young Jerry O'Donovan next Saturday, was not there. She had been carried to the Algerine flagship in the arms of black Ali Krussa.

Once aboard the corsair, Mary had drawn a dagger from her gloating captor's belt, and quickly stabbed him through the heart. Then she had leaped overboard, and had been seen no more.

When Sir Fineen O'Driscoll had heard this much of the story from the lips of his broken-hearted wife, he walked silently to the water's edge, and tossed from his boat into the water the cowhide bag that weighed so heavily.

As the bag of gold sank to the bottom of Baltimore Bay, the sorrowing woman on the pier thought she saw a body, with long black tresses floating, sink alongside of it. Doubtless the illusion was caused by shadows that always lurk in deep water.

Baltimore Castle stands to-day as it stood that morning, three hundred years ago, except that the jagged walls and dark tower have been covered by that gentle ivy that always helps the Irish to forget, while it forces them to remember.

As to the treasure on Long Island, I could find no trace of it, and the fishermen are silent as they gaze far off to sea.

Postscript

As this book goes to press, divers are demonstrating that the harvest time for sunken treasure is at hand.

They are working on the wreck of the liner *Egypt* at a depth of nearly 400 feet, and already have brought up the Captain's safe and other goodly loot.

The *Egypt*, Peninsular and Oriental steamship, was sunk in collision with the French steamer *Seine*, off Cape Finisterre, near Brest, France, in 1922. She carried gold and silver bullion having a present value of between five million and eight million dollars.

An Italian salvage corporation, using the salvage ship *Artiglio* and diving equipment never heretofore used in practical deep-sea salvage work, found the wreck early in September, 1930, and within forty-eight hours was bringing up parts of the liner's machinery and dynamiting a way to the strong room where the bullion rests. Ironically enough, one of the first items recovered from the wreck was the key to this treasure vault.

If these Italians can work successfully at a depth of four hundred feet, salvaging of thousands of wrecks, including that of the *Lusitania*, becomes a simple contracting job. There should be no further serious obstacles to the recovery of all the gold in Vigo Bay, Tobermory Bay, and the Zuyder Zee. The sea is just beginning to give up its treasure.

And, as this last page of DOUBLOONS goes to the printer, I am urged to join three friends in a gold-shoveling enterprise. They wouldn't call it treasure-hunting, for they know exactly where the ten million dollars' worth of gold lies, under scarcely twenty feet of water, off the coast of Venezuela. My three friends are a former newspaper editor, a diamond mining engineer, and a financial man. A fourth member of the party, Venezuelan, says he helped put the gold where it lies, during a revolution early in the century. He gets seventy per cent of the recovered loot; the Americans divide the rest. It sounds tempting, but I bid them all good-by and *bon voyage*.

Simon Lake, busy with the designing and building of a submarine boat for the Wilkins polar under-the-ice expedition, has postponed salvage of the *Hussar* until 1931.

It would seem that the nineteen-thirties are to be the great years for reclaiming the treasure that the sea has taken from man.

In October, 1930, the government of Ecuador was called upon to furnish troops to guard a great treasure in a cave, discovered by Julio Torres, lawyer and treasure-hunter. This was believed to be the treasure of Atahualpa, last of the Inca chieftains.

Señor Torres has devoted years to a determined effort to find this treasure, hidden by the subjects of Atahualpa after their leader was put to death by Pizarro. He followed the directions left by Juan Valverde, who is said to have lived extravagantly, early in the nineteenth century, from the sale of gold taken from the treasure cave.

There have been many legends about the Atahualpa treasure. The most persistent of these tells how Valverde obtained the secret of the cave's location from his Indian wife, a descendant of the Incas, and how, dying after a life of luxury, he left a paper for the King of Spain, describing the route to the cave.

Many have tried to follow the route described in the document said to have been written by Valverde. Señor Torres claims to have succeeded.

The find, according to Torres, was made near Alausi and the little village of Nizac, high in the fastnesses of the Andes.

Some Sources

The literature of pirates and buried and sunken treasure is so vast that a bibliography of these closely related subjects, properly and thoroughly done, would fill a book larger than this one. I can do no more here than indicate a handful of the books that have interested and assisted me during years of research.

Always, the first book of reference concerning pirates is:

A General History of the Pirates, by Captain Charles Johnson.

This book has appeared in so many editions and versions that a bibliography devoted to it is quite a sizeable volume. It is:

A Bibliography of the Works of Capt. Charles Johnson, by Philip Gosse. Dulau and Company, Ltd. 34, 35 & 36 Margaret Street, London, W. 1. 1927.

Dr. Gosse's bibliography of Johnson, containing eighty pages, and done in a thorough manner, is still far from complete. I shall not attempt to go into a discussion or a listing of any of the Johnson books here.

Dr. Gosse has a pirate library, exclusively non-fiction, which has now reached 415 items. When his library was much smaller he wrote a bibliography covering it. It is:

My Pirate Library, by Philip Gosse. With an introductory note by Sir Edmund Gosse, C.B. Dulau . . . etc. 1926.

His other notable reference work is:

The Pirates' Who's Who. Giving Particulars of the Lives & Deaths of the Pirates & Buccaneers. By Philip Gosse. Illustrated. Imported by Charles E. Lauriat Company. Boston. 1914.

The standard work of reference on the buccaneers is:

The Buccaneers of America, by John Esquemeling.

As in the case of the Johnson book, this work has appeared in so many editions and in so many versions and adaptations that a mere list of them would make a tome. Esquemeling, a Dutchman, was himself a buccaneer and pirate, and his book has the virtues and faults to be expected in such circumstances.

One of the best trade editions of this work is that issued in London by George Routledge & Sons, and in New York by E. P. Dutton & Co. It is undated, but is one of the Broadway Translations.

Burney is an authority on buccaneers second only in importance to Esquemeling, and I find him easier to read and to believe, in many instances. My own library contains many editions of his book, the best of which is:

History of the Buccaneers of America. By James Burney, F. R. S. Captain in the Royal Navy. London: Printed by Luke Hansard & Sons, near Lincoln's-Inn Fields; For Payne and Foss, Pall-Mall. 1816.

The literature on Captain Kidd is very extensive. Much praise is due to:

The Real Captain Kidd. A Vindication. By Sir Cornelius Neale Dalton, K.C.M.G., C.B., D.C.L. New York, Duffield and Company. 1911.

This book was little noticed, but has been heavily leaned upon by many later writers.

A good novel which contains most of the Dalton information, well handled, is:

The Man They Hanged, by Robert W. Chambers. New York and London. D. Appleton & Company. MCMXXVI.

A good popular, readable life of Drake is:

Sir Francis Drake, by E. F. Benson. New York and London. Harper & Brothers, Publishers. MCMXXVII.

For a scholarly treatment of a phase of Drake's activities:

Sir Francis Drake's Voyage Around the World. Its Aims and Achievements. By Henry R. Wagner. John Howell, San Francisco, California. 1926.

This is a book of 543 pages, painstakingly documented and indexed.

An excellent edition of a very old Drake source book is:

The World Encompassed and Analogous Contemporary Documents Concerning Sir Francis Drake's Circumnavigation of the

World, with an Appreciation of the Achievement by Sir Richard Carnac Temple, Bt.C.B., C.I.B., F.B.A., F.S.A. 1926. The Argonaut Press, London.

A modern summary of several romantic buccaneering careers, published in 1928, is:

Buccaneers of the Pacific, by George Wycherly. The Bobbs-Merrill Company, Indianapolis, Publishers.

William Dampier was a writing pirate. He never achieved great distinction in arms, but as a diarist and press-agent for buccaneers he had few equals at sea. A reliable modern edition of his work:

A New Voyage Round the World, by William Dampier. With an Introduction by Sir Albert Gray, K.C.B., K.C., President of the Hakluyt Society. 1927. The Argonaut Press, London.

A brochure that contains well authenticated material on Blackbeard and Stede Bonnet is:

The Carolina Pirates and Colonial Commerce, 1670-1740. By Shirley Carter Hughson. Baltimore. The Johns Hopkins Press. Published Monthly. May-June-July, 1894.

This is one number of the Johns Hopkins University Studies in Historical and Political Science, Herbert B. Adams, Editor. Hence the May-June-July notation. It consists of the doctorate thesis of Hughson, who is now a monk in a Protestant Episcopal monastery in New York state. It is a rather rare item.

For general and well-authenticated information on pirates who operated in the West Indies, I recommend:

Piracy in the West Indies and Its Suppression. By Francis B. C. Bradlee. The Essex Institute, Salem, Massachusetts. 1893.

A standard work covering New England piratical history is:

The Pirates of the New England Coast, 1630-1730. By George Francis Dow, Curator of the Society for the Preservation of New England Antiquities, and John Henry Edmonds, Massachusetts State Archivist. Introduction by Capt. Ernest H. Pentecost, R.N.R. Marine Research Society, Salem, Massachusetts, 1923.

An entertaining collection of rather imaginative pirate lore is:

Buccaneers and Pirates of Our Coasts. By Frank R. Stockton.

With Illustrations by George Varian and B. West Clinedinst. New York. The Macmillan Company. London: Macmillan & Co. Ltd. 1898.

This book was reissued by the same publisher in 1924.

A book which borrows much from Johnson and has seen many editions is published with varying title pages, but is generally known as *The History of the Most Noted Pirates*. An early edition in my library is:

The Lives and Bloody Exploits of the Most Noted Pirates, Their Trials and Executions, Including Correct Accounts of the Late Piracies, Committed in the West Indies, and the Expedition of Commodore Porter; also Those Committed on the Brig Mexican, Who Were Executed At Boston, in 1835. Embellished with numerous plates from original designs. Hartford, Con.; Published by Ezra Strong. 1836.

An anthology of pirate lore that is well selected and covers briefly many of the characters I have dealt with in "Doubloons" is:

Pirates, Highwaymen and Adventurers. Edited with an Introduction by Eric Partridge. The Scholartis Press: London. 1 B, New Oxford Street, W. C. I. MCMXXVII.

An attractive re-telling of the standard pirate tales, plus some others, is:

Under the Black Flag. Don C. Seitz. Lincoln MacVeagh, The Dial Press. New York. MCMXXV.

Further authentic information on the West Indies pirates may be found in a thin volume titled:

Our Navy and The West Indian Pirates. By Gardner W. Allen. With an Introduction by Rear Admiral Caspar F. Goodrich, United States Navy. Essex Institute, Salem, Mass. 1929.

On the subject of treasure, a good survey of most of the field may be had in:

The Book of Buried Treasure. Being a True History of the Gold, Jewels, and Plate of Pirates, Galleons, etc., Which are Sought For to This Day. By Ralph D. Paine, Author of "The Ships and Sailors of Old Salem," etc. Illustrated. New York. The Macmillan Company. 1922.

A book on the same subject that appeared while "Doubloons" was in process of publication, and which I have not had time to look through carefully, nevertheless deserves a place in this list:

Lost Treasure. True Tales of Hidden Hoards. By A. Hyatt Verrill. Illustrated. D. Appleton and Company. New York, London. MCMXXX.

Richard Hakluyt and the volumes published from year to year and from century to century under the name of Hakluyt are sources of much interesting information about the voyagers, corsairs and pirates antedating the landing of the Pilgrims in Massachusetts. The best modernization and digest of the most important material in Hakluyt, is:

Heroes from Hakluyt. Edited by Charles J. Finger. Woodcut Decorations by Paul Honoré. The Henry Holt Company, New York.

This book was published in 1928.

Much of my data and lore for the story of the O'Driscoll treasure was obtained, as I have indicated, by word of mouth, by collecting legends and fitting them together, and by conversations before peat fires. But these books, among others, furnished invaluable data:

A History of the City and County of Cork. By M. F. Cusack. Kenmare Publications. Dublin: McGlashan and Gill. Cork: Francis Guy, Patrick Street. 1875.

The History of Ireland. By John O'Driscol. In Two Volumes. London: Printed for Longman, Rees, Orme, Brown and Green, Paternoster Row. 1827.

The History of the County and City of Cork. By Rev. C. B. Gibson, M.R.I.A. In Two Volumes. London: Thomas C. Newby, 30 Welbeck Street. 1861.

The County and City of Cork Rembrancer; or Annals of the County and City of Cork. By Francis H. Tuckey. With an Introductory Essay. Cork: Osborne Savage and Son, Patrick Street. MDCCCXXXVII.

The literature of Lafitte is almost as extensive as that touching Captain Kidd. Some good Lafitte legends are modestly published in:

Legends of Texas. Edited by J. Frank Dobie. Published by
the Texas Folk-Lore Society, Austin, Texas, 1924.

In the field of fiction, *Treasure Island* still is, to me and to
millions, the greatest of all tales of pirates and plunder. But some
stories that deserve places in the library of any fancier of pirate
lore have been written in recent years. The greatest of them, I
think, is *Thomas the Lambkin*, by Claude Farrère. It has seen
several editions, but the trade edition in English was published
in 1924 by Dutton. *Porto Bello Gold, by* Arthur D. Howden
Smith, published in 1924 in New York by Brentano's, is a tale
worth any adult's time. *Pieces of Eight*, by Richard Le Gallienne,
published by Collins in London in 1918, is near the top in bloody
pirate fiction.

The above list is merely suggestive. My own pirate library
now contains almost a thousand items; books, pamphlets, proclamations and broadsides.

Three interesting sources of information which I have drawn
upon in the preparation of this book are my collections of old
newspapers and magazines containing accounts of contemporary
piracies and treasure hunts, my collection of pamphlets and book-
lets published for sale at pirate hangings, and a goodly lot of
prospectuses published by treasure-hunting companies, long since
defunct.

Index

313

316 INDEX

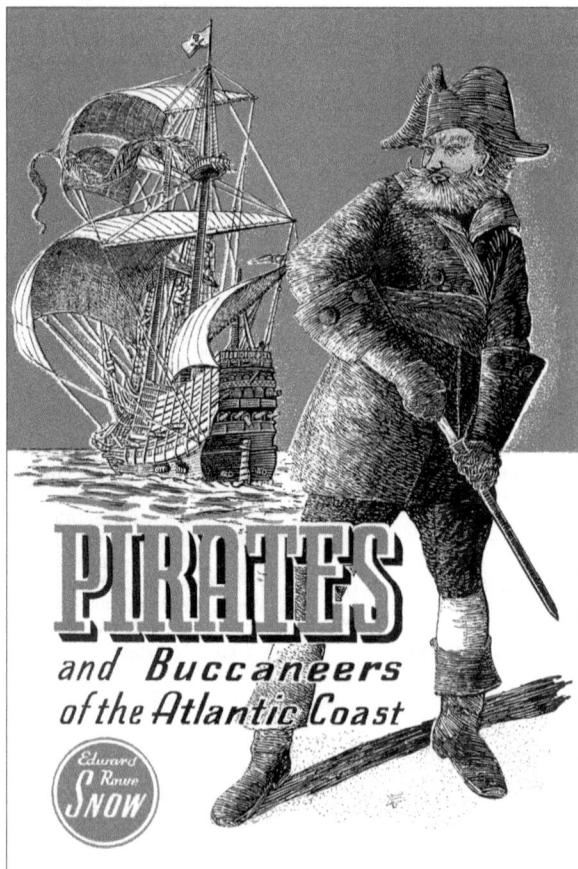

Coachwhip Publications
CoachwhipBooks.com

PIRATE AND
BUCCANEER DOCTORS

Leo Eloesser

Coachwhip Publications
CoachwhipBooks.com

THOMAS PENFIELD

LOST TREASURE TRAILS

Coachwhip Publications

CoachwhipBooks.com

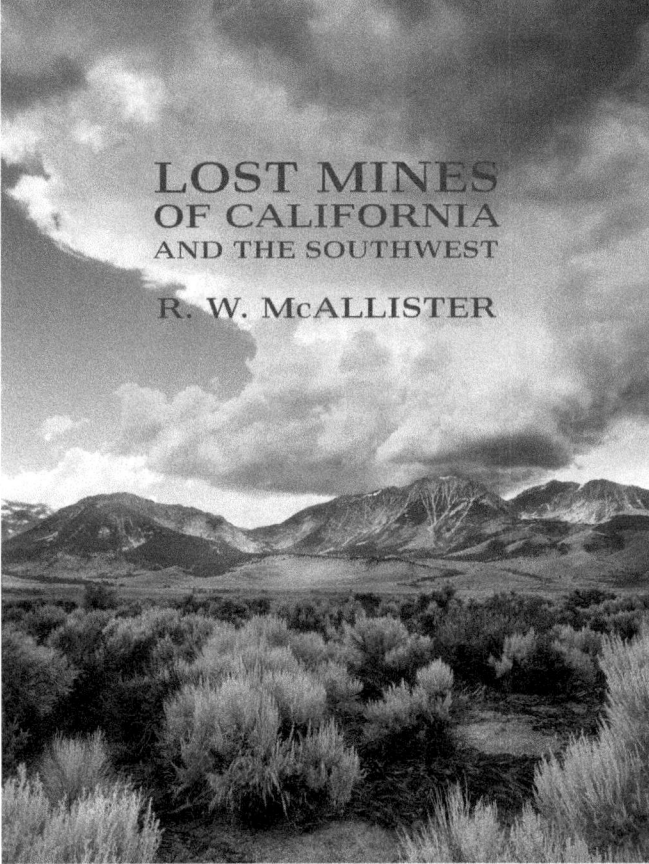

LOST MINES
OF CALIFORNIA
AND THE SOUTHWEST

R. W. McALLISTER

Coachwhip Publications
CoachwhipBooks.com

LOST MINES
OF THE OLD WEST

HOWARD·D·
CLARK

AUTHENTIC STORY OF THE "PEGLEG"
and 21 other stories of FABULOUS LOST MINES.

Coachwhip Publications
CoachwhipBooks.com

THE TOURMALINE

AUGUSTUS CHOATE HAMLIN

THE HISTORY OF MOUNT MICA OF MAINE, U.S.A.

Coachwhip Publications

CoachwhipBooks.com

SUBMARINE!

THE STORY OF UNDERSEA FIGHTERS

By KENDALL BANNING

Author of "THE FLEET TODAY"

Illustrated by Charles Rosner

Coachwhip Publications

CoachwhipBooks.com

THE WAR OF 1812
Henry Adams

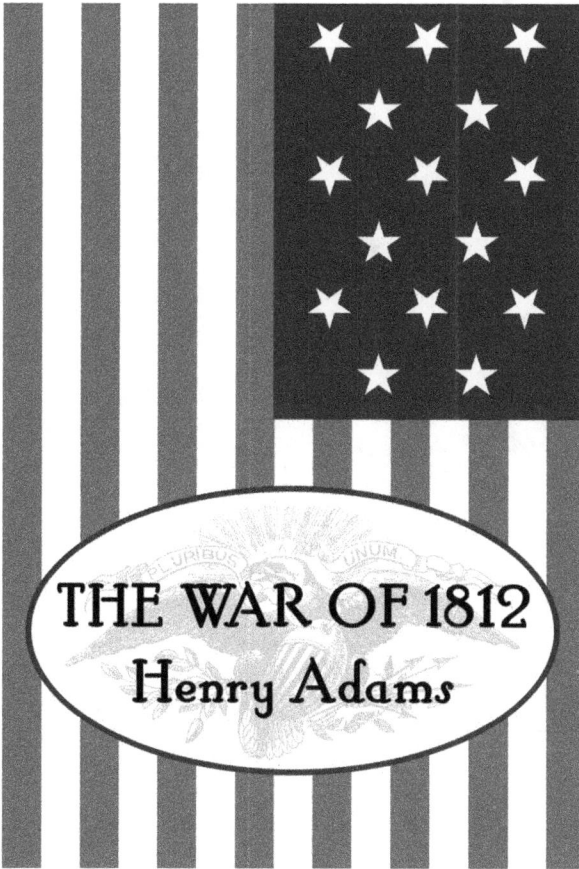

Coachwhip Publications
CoachwhipBooks.com

www.ingramcontent.com/pod-product-compliance
Lightning Source LLC
Chambersburg PA
CBHW060245100426
42742CB00011B/1644